The Global Politics of Sexual and Reproductive Health

Oxford Studies in Gender and International Relations

Series editors: Rahul Rao, University of St Andrews, and Laura Sjoberg, Royal Holloway University of London

Windows of Opportunity: How Women Seize Peace Negotiations for Political Change
Miriam J. Anderson

Women as Foreign Policy Leaders: National Security and Gender Politics in Superpower America
Sylvia Bashevkin

Gendered Citizenship: Understanding Gendered Violence in Democratic India
Natasha Behl

Gender, Religion, Extremism: Finding Women in Anti-Radicalization
Katherine E. Brown

Enlisting Masculinity: The Construction of Gender in U.S. Military Recruiting Advertising during the All-Volunteer Force
Melissa T. Brown

The Politics of Gender Justice at the International Criminal Court: Legacies and Legitimacy
Louise Chappell

The Other #MeToos
Iqra Shagufta Cheema

Cosmopolitan Sex Workers: Women and Migration in a Global City
Christine B. N. Chin

Intelligent Compassion: Feminist Critical Methodology in the Women's International League for Peace and Freedom
Catia Cecilia Confortini

Hidden Wars: Gendered Political Violence in Asia's Civil Conflicts
Sara E. Davies and Jacqui True

Complicit Sisters: Gender and Women's Issues across North-South Divides
Sara de Jong

Gender and Private Security in Global Politics
Maya Eichler

This American Moment: A Feminist Christian Realist Intervention
Caron E. Gentry

Troubling Motherhood: Maternality in Global Politics
Lucy B. Hall, Anna L. Weissman, and Laura J. Shepherd

Breaking the Binaries in Security Studies: A Gendered Analysis of Women in Combat
Ayelet Harel-Shalev and Shir Daphna-Tekoah

Scandalous Economics: Gender and the Politics of Financial Crises
Aida A. Hozić and Jacqui True

Building Peace, Rebuilding Patriarchy: The Failure of Gender Interventions in Timor-Leste
Melissa Johnston

Rewriting the Victim: Dramatization as Research in Thailand's Anti-Trafficking Movement
Erin M. Kamler

Equal Opportunity Peacekeeping: Women, Peace, and Security in Post-Conflict States
Sabrina Karim and Kyle Beardsley

Gender, Sex, and the Postnational Defense: Militarism and Peacekeeping
Annica Kronsell

The Beauty Trade: Youth, Gender, and Fashion Globalization
Angela B. V. McCracken

Global Norms and Local Action: The Campaigns against Gender-Based Violence in Africa
Peace A. Medie

Rape Loot Pillage: The Political Economy of Sexual Violence in Armed Conflict
Sara Meger

Critical Perspectives on Cybersecurity: Feminist and Postcolonial Interventions
Anwar Mhajne and Alexis Henshaw

Support the Troops: Military Obligation, Gender, and the Making of Political Community
Katharine M. Millar

From Global to Grassroots: The European Union, Transnational Advocacy, and Combating Violence against Women
Celeste Montoya

Who Is Worthy of Protection? Gender-Based Asylum and US Immigration Politics
Meghana Nayak

Revisiting Gendered States: Feminist Imaginings of the State in International Relations
Swati Parashar, J. Ann Tickner, and Jacqui True

Out of Time: The Queer Politics of Postcoloniality
Rahul Rao

Gender, UN Peacebuilding, and the Politics of Space: Locating Legitimacy
Laura J. Shepherd

Narrating the Women, Peace and Security Agenda: Logics of Global Governance
Laura J. Shepherd

Capitalism's Sexual History
Nicola J. Smith

The Global Politics of Sexual and Reproductive Health
Maria Tanyag

A Feminist Voyage through International Relations
J. Ann Tickner

The Political Economy of Violence against Women
Jacqui True

Queer International Relations: Sovereignty, Sexuality and the Will to Knowledge
Cynthia Weber

Feminist Global Health Security
Clare Wenham

Bodies of Violence: Theorizing Embodied Subjects in International Relations
Lauren B. Wilcox

The Global Politics of Sexual and Reproductive Health

Maria Tanyag

OXFORD
UNIVERSITY PRESS

Oxford University Press is a department of the University of Oxford. It furthers
the University's objective of excellence in research, scholarship, and education
by publishing worldwide. Oxford is a registered trade mark of Oxford University
Press in the UK and certain other countries.

Published in the United States of America by Oxford University Press
198 Madison Avenue, New York, NY 10016, United States of America.

© Oxford University Press 2024

All rights reserved. No part of this publication may be reproduced, stored in
a retrieval system, or transmitted, in any form or by any means, without the
prior permission in writing of Oxford University Press, or as expressly permitted
by law, by license, or under terms agreed with the appropriate reproduction
rights organization. Inquiries concerning reproduction outside the scope of the
above should be sent to the Rights Department, Oxford University Press, at the
address above.

You must not circulate this work in any other form
and you must impose this same condition on any acquirer.

Library of Congress Cataloging-in-Publication Data
Names: Tanyag, Maria, author.
Title: The global politics of sexual and reproductive health /
Maria Tanyag.
Description: New York, NY : Oxford University Press, [2024] |
Series: Oxford studies in gender and international relations |
Includes bibliographical references and index.
Identifiers: LCCN 2023049378 (print) | LCCN 2023049379 (ebook) |
ISBN 9780197676332 (hardback) | ISBN 9780197676349 (epub) |
ISBN 9780197676363
Subjects: LCSH: Sexual rights. | Reproductive rights. |
Sexual health—Political aspects. | Reproductive health—Political aspects. |
Women—Health and hygiene—Political aspects. |
Women—Social conditions. | Feminist theory.
Classification: LCC HQ65 .T66 2024 (print) | LCC HQ65 (ebook) |
DDC 613/.04244—dc23/eng/20231113
LC record available at https://lccn.loc.gov/2023049378
LC ebook record available at https://lccn.loc.gov/2023049379

DOI: 10.1093/oso/9780197676332.001.0001

Printed by Integrated Books International, United States of America

In honor of my grandmother, *Lola Celing*,

Celestina Macawili Ramilo (1928–2015)

CONTENTS

Acknowledgments xi
Abbreviations xiii

Introduction 1

1. Crisis and the Global Political Economy of Sexual and
   Reproductive Health 15

2. The Household as a Site of Depletion 35

3. Myths of Community Survival 61

4. Patriarchal Bargains and Nation-building in
   the Aftermath of Crisis 87

5. The Global Crisis of Religious Fundamentalisms 118

6. Regeneration and the Politics of Flourishing 150

Conclusion 178

Notes 189
References 199
Index 227

ACKNOWLEDGMENTS

The journey of this book began during my time as a PhD student at Monash University, Melbourne, Australia. I owe a debt of gratitude to Jacqui True, Sara Davies, and Ronli Sifris for their generous mentorship and supervision. I had such a rich start to my academic career because of them. Jacqui's political economy research on violence against women was particularly influential in the development of my research. During this period, the vibrant intellectual community at the Centre for Gender, Peace and Security served as a crucial environment for me to practice my curiosity and to build confidence in the kind of research questions I was interested in. There I benefitted from many exchanges with Samanthi Gunawardana, Swati Parashar, Kate Lee-Koo, Lesley Pruitt, Jenny Hedstrom, Yasmin Chilmeran, Sri Wiyanti Eddyono, Sarah Hewitt, Barbara Trojanowska, Ari Jerrems, and Noor Huda Ismail. The extended feminist networks of the Centre provided me with the incredible opportunity to learn from and be inspired by Ann Tickner, Shirin Rai, Juanita Elias, and Aida Hozic.

I am grateful to all the people who generously supported the research behind this book. From 2015 to 2017, the assistance of the following people was tremendously helpful. I would like to thank Vene Rallonza, Melissa Lao, and members of the Ateneo de Manila University Political Science Department. At the University of the Philippines-Diliman Political Science Department, I am grateful to Maria Ela Atienza, Jan Robert Go, Jean Franco, Dennis Quilala, and Aries Arugay. For research in Tacloban, Leyte, I am indebted to Yvonne Su from York University, Canada, and Ladylyn Mangada from the University of the Philippines Visayas. Ladylyn provided me with the care and guidance that allowed me to gain a contextualized understanding of post-disaster recovery. In Davao, I am thankful to the Ateneo de Davao University Social Research Training and Development Office for access to pioneering survey research studies on reproductive health and crisis settings conducted in Mindanao. I thank all the research participants who shared their time and insights. In several cases, participants extended warm Filipino hospitality and directly ensured my safety and well-being during my trips. They continue to motivate me in thinking of my own ethical commitments in research, and in finding my own way to contribute to wider efforts in promoting gender equality.

This book was completed with the constant support, kindness, and encouragement of my colleagues at the Department of International Relations, Coral Bell School of Asia Pacific Affairs, Australian National University. My colleagues helped sharpen the intellectual contributions of this book through a book manuscript workshop in 2019 and over many conversations regarding our own research projects. Thank you to Bina D'Costa, Mathew Davies, Wes Widmaier, Nico Lemay-Hebert, Eglantine Staunton, George Lawson, Kirsten Ainley, Cecilia Jacob, David Envall, Ben Day, Joseph MacKay, Sarah Logan, and Ben Zala. I am grateful to Cian O'Driscoll and Luke Glanville for feedback on an early draft of Chapter 6. Thank you to Marylou Hickey and Serena Ford for providing valuable assistance with manuscript preparation and cross-checking of references. I acknowledge that the book was written in lands traditionally owned and cared for by Aboriginal and Torres Strait Islander peoples. I pay my respect and gratitude to their elders past and present.

Thank you to the series editors Ann Tickner and Laura Sjoberg and to Angela Chnapko of Oxford University Press for believing in this book. I am profoundly grateful to them for the opportunity to be part of the Gender and International Relations series alongside scholars I greatly admire. I also thank the reviewers of this manuscript for their constructive engagement and support. My thanks to Rhine Bernardino for the book cover which is an image from her *Regla* series. The artwork presents menstrual blood encased in a glass sculpture. I am excited for readers to see how the image visually captures some of the themes discussed in my book.

Finally, this book finds its home in both Canberra, Australia, and Auckland, New Zealand. With it, I thank my parents, Jose and Flordelis, and all the sacrifices they have made to enable me to have the life I enjoy now. I share this achievement with them and our family, Kuya Bj, Kimi, Unica, Theo, Maia, Aj, and Cian. There but for grace go I.

[xii] *Acknowledgments*

ABBREVIATIONS

ARMM	Autonomous Region in Muslim Mindanao
AWID	Association for Women's Rights in Development
BCCs	Basic Christian Communities
BHW	*Barangay* Health Worker
BIWAB	Bangsamoro Islamic Women Auxiliary Brigade
CAB	Comprehensive Agreement on the Bangsamoro
CEDAW	Convention on the Elimination of All Forms of Discrimination against Women
CRC	Convention on the Rights of the Child
CMPL	Code of Muslim Personal Laws
DAWN	Development Alternatives for Women in the New Era
DOH	[Department of Health]
DSWD	Department of Social Welfare and Development
DTB	"doctors to the barrios"
EC	emergency contraceptive
FDI	foreign direct investments
FGD	Focus Group Discussion
FP2020	Family Planning 2020
GCR	Global Climate Risk
GFC	global financial crisis
GGR	Global Gag Rule
GHGs	greenhouse gases
ICPD	International Conference on Population and Development
IDP	internally displaced person
IMF	International Monetary Fund
INGO	international non-government organization
IOM	International Organisation for Migration
IPCC	Intergovernmental Panel on Climate Change
IR	international relations
LGU	local government unit

MILF	Moro Islamic Liberation Front
MISP	Minimum Initial Service Package
MMR	maternal mortality ratio
MNLF	Moro National Liberation Front
NAP	National Action Plan
NDHS	National Demographic and Health Survey
NDRRMP	National Disaster Risk Reduction and Management Plan
NGO	non-governmental organization
OCHA	United Nations Office for the Coordination of Humanitarian Affairs
ODA	official development assistance
OIC	Organization of the Islamic Conference
OFW	overseas Filipino worker
PAMANA program	Payapa at Masaganang Pamayanan, peaceful and prosperous [also resilient] communities
Popcom	Philippine Commission on Population
RH	Reproductive Health Bill/Law
RPRH	Responsible Parenthood and Reproductive Health
SDGs	Sustainable Development Goals
SGBV	sexual and gender-based violence
SIPRI	Stockholm International Peace Research Institute
SRHR	sexual and reproductive health and rights
UCDP	Uppsala Conflict Data Program
UNFPA	United Nations Population Fund
UNHCR	United Nations High Commissioner for Refugees
UNICEF	United Nations Children's Fund
WASH	water, sanitation, and hygiene
WE Act 1325	Women Engaged in Action on 1325
WeNet Philippines	Women in Emergencies Network
WFS	women friendly spaces
WHO	World Health Organization
WPS	Women, Peace and Security

Introduction

Growing up in the Philippines, I often heard the phrase, "*Sa panganganak ang isang paa ay laging nasa hukay.*" When giving birth a woman already has one foot in the grave. My maternal grandmother, who was from a small rural town south of Manila, gave birth to twelve children. As a child, I thought then that she must have had a foot in the grave twelve times, and it struck fear and awe in me. I would ask her, how was it like to give birth to that many children? Did she deliver her babies all by herself? Who helped her and was there a doctor around? Or did she have a *hilot*, the Filipino version of a traditional birth attendant? Because of my grandmother's stories, I became aware of both the strength and fragility of women's bodies at an early age. I grew up attuned to thinking that my grandmother was "lucky" to have survived all her pregnancies, and that it was a sad yet "natural" reality that many Filipino women do not. Maternal death refers to the death of a woman during pregnancy or as a result of childbirth related complications.[1] In the Philippines, maternal deaths have not registered any significant decline since the 1990s, the earliest period when data for this type of mortality became available nationally (WHO 2017).[2] Maternal deaths are largely preventable and have been decreasing globally yet constitute the leading cause of death for girls aged 15–19 years (WHO, UNICEF, UNFPA, World Bank, and UN Population Division 2019). The Philippines has among the highest rate of adolescent pregnancies compared to its regional neighbors in the Asia-Pacific (WHO et al. 2015). One in ten young Filipino women between the ages of 15 and 19 is already a mother or pregnant with her first child (Philippine Statistics Authority 2014). Alarmingly, over the past decade, there has been steady increase in the number of girls aged 10 to 14 years old becoming mothers (Republic of the Philippines Commission on

---

The Global Politics of Sexual and Reproductive Health. Maria Tanyag, Oxford University Press.
© Oxford University Press 2024. DOI: 10.1093/oso/9780197676332.003.0001

Population 2019). Data from the Philippine Commission on Population and Development revealed that for this age group, approximately seven per day or 2,411 girls gave birth in 2019. Left unaddressed, the country will continue to have more and more girls who, though at a pubescent stage in their lives, are already at risk of death because they are pregnant. These deaths are likely to be invisible in many parts of the world because global definitions and standards used for collecting data on maternal mortality still refer to the reproductive age of 15 to 49 years.

Globally, inequalities in mortality disproportionately affect women and girls in low to middle-income countries such as the Philippines and within fragile, humanitarian and emergency contexts (UNFPA 2015). Over half of the world's maternal deaths occur in conflict-affected and fragile states with the highest maternal mortality ratios in the world recorded in countries and communities affected by, or emerging from, war (UN Women 2015; UNFPA 2015). Disasters, which are occurring more frequently and with greater intensity, are becoming the main drivers of protracted displacements globally. Countries and communities that are facing the greatest threat of climate change and disaster hazards are therefore also sites where the risk of women dying due to health complications is amplified (UN General Assembly 2016b). UNFPA (2015) reports that 25% of the more than 100 million people in need of humanitarian assistance are women and girls of reproductive or child-bearing age. They constitute the group at immediate risk of various forms of sexual and gender-based violence (SGBV) including heightened exposure to sexually transmitted diseases (STDs) and HIV/AIDS and unwanted or forced pregnancies. In addition, they are also vulnerable to long-term harms arising from adverse coping mechanisms and adaptation strategies employed by their own families and communities. Crisis-affected populations now spend on average up to 20 years in internal displacement (Askew et al. 2016, 311). Studies have reported an increase in the prevalence of harmful cultural practices such as forced and child marriages because of enduring economic hardship in these crisis settings (UNFPA 2015; Alston et al. 2014). Thus, in these acute cases, the elusiveness of peace is shaping the way women get sick and die.

This book examines everyday inequalities in sexual and reproductive health and rights (SRHR), and the failure to address them in crisis settings from a feminist international relations (IR) perspective. It takes as a starting point investigating why rights of the body to health, sexuality, and pleasure are shaped by fiercely divisive political dynamics and what this distinctively contentious nature means for the routine neglect of women's health and well-being. It also seeks to understand the implications of crisis and post-crisis responses that neglect or exacerbate inequalities in SRHR for inclusive and durable peace globally.

DEFINING BODILY AUTONOMY AND SRHR

SRHR are enshrined within a dynamic and evolving international human rights framework.[3] Several articles in the Convention on the Elimination of All Forms of Discrimination against Women (CEDAW) recognize that extensive forms of discrimination against women and girls on the basis of their sexual and reproductive identities serve as fundamental barriers to human dignity and impede the equal sharing of responsibility between men and women and society as a whole.[4] The 1994 International Conference on Population and Development (ICPD), which was held in Cairo, and the 1995 World Conference on Women held in Beijing were pivotal in placing sexual and reproductive health at the forefront of international human rights and development agendas. The outcome documents of these global conferences set forth the definition and components of SRHR. Under the ICPD Programme of Action, reproductive health is defined as:

> [T]he state of complete physical, mental, and social well-being in all matters relating to the reproductive system and to its functions and processes . . . [It] therefore implies that people are able to have a satisfying and safe sex life and that they have the capability to reproduce and the freedom to decide if, when and how often to do so. Implicit in this last condition are the right of men and women to be informed and to have access to safe, effective, affordable and acceptable methods of family planning of their choice, as well as other methods of their choice for regulation of fertility which are not against the law, and the right of access to appropriate health-care services that will enable women to go safely through pregnancy and childbirth and provide couples with the best chance of having a healthy infant . . . It also includes sexual health, the purpose of which is the enhancement of life and personal relations, and not merely counselling and care related to reproduction and sexually transmitted diseases. (UNFPA 1994/2014, 59)[5]

SRHR have been used interchangeably to encompass the full spectrum of "bodily autonomy." The concept of bodily autonomy is a thematic focus of the 2021 State of the World Population report by the UN Population Fund to highlight how globally and despite variations in cultures and contexts, "[a] woman's power to control her own body·is linked to how much control she has in other spheres of her life" (UNFPA 2021, 7). According to the report, the language of bodily autonomy has evolved over time based on existing human rights frameworks and through vernacular usage by advocates, activists, and human rights experts. While the concept has a wider remit, there are three main dimensions or "indicators" of bodily autonomy that are incorporated in tracking progress of the 2030 Sustainable Development Goals (SDGs) and

INTRODUCTION [3]

specifically Goal 5.6 on universal access to SRHR. An individual has bodily autonomy when he or she is able to make decisions regarding (1) sex; (2) contraception; and (3) health care. In this book, I build on these three main indicators while also employing a richer and more expansive definition based on the "human rights discourse around the body and its needs for security, health and pleasure" (Petchesky 2005: 303). I show that bodily autonomy extends beyond an individual's ability to make decisions regarding sex, contraception, and fertility and to formulate informed choices in accessing health care. It encompasses self-determination in all areas of life and collective struggles to build a better world.

From a human rights perspective, states as duty bearers must not only refrain from restricting the enjoyment of SRHR but also ensure the provision of adequate conditions for their full realization in everyday life and even in times of crisis. For instance, according to the UN Special Rapporteur on the Right to Health:

> An aspect of this [human rights] obligation is that the right to health is progressively realisable. However, due to the destruction or diversion of resources to military or police needs, conflicts often reduce the availability of resources which may, at times, be detrimental to the right to health. Even where resources are available, states may not be able to make use of them due to the insecurity and poor infrastructure in many conflict environments. Nonetheless, progressive realisation is a specific and continuous state obligation. It does not dilute certain immediate obligations of states, including taking concrete steps towards the full realisation of the right to health to all, without discrimination and regardless of the status of persons as combatants or civilians. (UN General Assembly 2013, 5)

A human rights approach is crucial for recognizing that the sexual and reproductive health of all individuals is not a matter of charity, but rather that of accountability (Yamin 2017). In practice, this means an active role among states and the international community in allotting resources for the availability and improvement of comprehensive and emergency health service delivery before, during, and after any crisis. Indeed, tremendous progress has been made to situate SRHR in humanitarian and security agendas (Chynoweth 2015; Onyango and Heidari 2017; Heidari, Onyango, and Chynoweth 2019). For example, UN Security Council Resolution 2122, which is among several resolutions that form the global Women, Peace and Security (WPS) agenda, explicitly recognizes the need for the full accessibility of various sexual and reproductive health services to women affected by armed conflict and in post-conflict situations. The Inter-agency Working Group on Reproductive Health in Crises, formed in 1995, has been in operation for almost three decades. It has been responsible for pioneering important global standards and toolkits such as the

[4]   *Politics of Sexual & Reproductive Health*

Inter-agency Field Manual for Reproductive Health in Humanitarian Settings and the Minimum Initial Service Package (MISP) for Sexual and Reproductive Health. There are also international efforts to expand service delivery from emergency to comprehensive SRHR services especially for contexts marked by protracted crises (Chynoweth 2015).

Though a human rights discourse frames sexual and reproductive health as universal and fundamental to human dignity, unlike other components of health, sexual and reproductive health is fiercely opposed directly or indirectly in policy-making by religious groups and conservative governments (Chappell 2006; AWID 2016). The legal status of SRHR is far from accepted and its progress has been fraught with ideological contestations and reversals despite existing international human rights frameworks. Compounding the effects of economic and legal barriers, SRHR tend to activate doctrinal politics whereby the issues they represent are framed as challenging religious teachings, anti-life, or anti-family (Htun 2003; Htun and Weldon 2018). Moreover, the UN Committee on Economic, Social and Cultural Rights (2016) notes that in all countries, patterns in sexual and reproductive health outcomes continue to reflect intersecting and multiple social inequalities that are reproduced through laws and policies. The denial of sexual and reproductive health information and services continues to be pervasive among specific groups of women and girls who belong to minority ethnic groups or suffer from disabilities (Sifris 2014, 2016; Cook and Cusack 2010).

Financial and political support for SRHR from developed countries remain inadequate in the face of worsening conditions for women and girls in developing countries and fragile settings (UNFPA 2013, 2015, 2019). While there have been commendable improvements, notably in terms of funding increase, this remains insufficient given the scale of needs in displacements and similar crisis settings (UN General Assembly 2016a). For instance, "only about 50 per cent of the UNFPA global humanitarian appeal is achieved each year," which leaves millions of displaced women and girls without adequate access to sexual and reproductive health (UNFPA 2019: 21). Between 2002 and 2013, funding gaps for reproductive health assistance in emergencies were estimated at US$2.689 billion (Tanabe et al. 2015). Furthermore, accessibility of SRHR aid may differ between conflict-affected and non-conflict-affected countries. According to an earlier systematic analysis of official development assistance (ODA) disbursement for reproductive health between 2003 and 2006, non-conflict-affected least-developed countries "received 53.3% more reproductive health ODA per capita than the conflict-affected least-developed countries" (Patel et al. 2009: 6).

Different aspects of sexual and reproductive health are also prioritized differently. For example, during the period 2009–2013, Tanabe et al. (2015) found that maternal newborn health comprised the largest proportion at 56.4% of funding proposals for reproductive health activities submitted to humanitarian health and protection mechanisms. This is followed by reproductive health-related gender-based violence (45.9%) and HIV/sexually transmitted infections (37.5%). According to a study conducted by Patel et al. (2009), HIV/AIDS programs constituted the bulk of "sexual and reproductive health" funding in conflict-affected countries from 2003 to 2006. While ODA distributed for reproductive health increased by 77.9%, two-thirds of this was due to a substantial increase in funding for HIV/AIDS activities. If HIV/AIDS is excluded, funding for reproductive health activities actually fell by 35.9%. A study published in 2015 suggests that ODA funding for HIV/AIDS continues to dominate over funding for other sexual and reproductive health needs in conflict-affected countries (Chynoweth 2015). What this uneven distribution means is that many women and girls are denied the full range of sexual and reproductive health services precisely in situations when they need them the most. Moreover, a human rights approach on its own cannot account for why various socio-cultural, economic, and security-related barriers to SRHR persist and why these barriers are even more pronounced in crisis settings.

WHY THE *GLOBAL* POLITICS OF BODILY AUTONOMY?

Doyal's path-breaking book entitled *What Makes Women Sick?* demonstrated how being a woman is itself a health hazard. Advancing a feminist political economy analysis, Doyal sought to identify and help change "those aspects of women's lives that cause them serious harm" (1995: 3). Understanding women's health, according to her, called for an approach that grasps "commonalities in women's situations" while attending to "the complex social, economic and cultural variety of their lives" (1995: 4). Moreover, answers to women's health problems are not simply bio-medical but rather shaped by gendered ideological and structural factors. Life expectancy and pathways for well-being among women are shaped by the way resources and authority are unevenly distributed within their societies and globally. She argues that much of what makes women sick is defined by their intimate relationships and their status within the household. As she points out, "[I]n the poorest parts of the world it is the physical strains of household labour that have become more visible as women's workload intensifies against the backdrop of social upheaval, economic recession and ecological deterioration" (1995: 29). Doyal's feminist political economy analysis of women's health is instructive of the "daily" wear and tear that women's bodies endure. It underscores the need to critically examine the contexts that drive why women have hazardous lives.

The factors that make women sick are also global. Yet, the significance of bodily autonomy for global peace and security is often hidden or underexamined. The unique contribution of this book is therefore to show that restrictions to sexual and reproductive health can be traced back to macro-level

[6] *Politics of Sexual & Reproductive Health*

processes such as how states and the international community allocate resources during crises and in peacetime. Public health, medical, social science, and legal approaches to the study of sexual and reproductive freedoms reveal the range of political, economic, and socio-cultural determinants of health. These approaches primarily situate causal factors within domestic levels of analysis such as the family, state, and society. For instance, they have shown the adverse impacts of discriminatory laws, poverty, and stigma on women's access to health. These approaches are also important for linking restrictions to bodily autonomy as forms of sexual and gender-based violence exacerbated by conflicts, humanitarian emergencies, and displacements. Like these various perspectives, this book affirms that sexual and reproductive freedoms are never merely private decisions made by individuals or even families. However, it is also vital to understand how these restrictions are in fact consistent with the workings of the global economy and how they are consequences of public values and priorities of societies and a global community in search of peace.

In this increasingly crisis-prone world we live in, the neglect of health and particularly women's health and well-being, seems counter-intuitive. Why are the very sources of care and reproduction of life diminished precisely when the expressed need for care intensifies? Restrictions to SRHR most severely manifesting as maternal deaths represent an anomaly because of the current global emphasis on women's participation and leadership in the everyday and in the context of crises. Inequalities and barriers to SRHR are perplexing because they exist in a wider political context where the importance of gender equality has never been more accepted and women are represented as central to major global agendas. In global development and in the aftermath of the global financial crisis, feminist scholars have highlighted a gender order to economic governance whereby women are valorized as "heroic entrepreneur and selfless altruist[s]" which in turn renders them as the preferred or key agents of growth and post-crisis economic recovery compared to men (Roy 2010: 548; Calkin 2015; Hozic and True 2016). Women can and will always be expected to "rescue" the global economy because they embody "a mode of economic agency that is more responsible, altruistic and therefore conducive to sustainable, post-crisis capitalism" (Calkin 2015: 614; Prügl 2012).

Similarly, in peace and security agendas women are represented as agents of security and, as others argue, even implicitly assumed to be *superheroines* (Shepherd 2011; Cohn et al. 2004). Tremendous expectations and pressures are put upon women as "agents of their own salvation, capable of representing the needs and priorities of others and with the capacity to effect positive transformation in their given environments and in conflict prevention and peace processes" (Shepherd 2011: 511). However, in both cases, the feminization of global agendas compounds, rather than challenges, prevailing disproportionate burdens women bear for daily care and reproduction as part of gendered divisions of labor. They reflect a feminization of responsibility and obligation (Chant 2010) and how particular representations of female altruism are harnessed in the service not just of the state (Molyneux 2007), but also of the global economy and security.

Examining the politics of SRHR reveals important gendered dimensions to IR. What it helps us understand, and hopefully redress, is how the global order operates through a neoliberal logic of depletion. This logic animates the systematic harnessing of female altruism and self-sacrifice in the service of various political projects while simultaneously devaluing the economic contributions of women's social reproductive labor and the costs of sustaining it. Women's labor is harnessed in peacebuilding and post-disaster reconstruction and to support the daily delivery of primary health care. Yet, the rejection of women's bodily autonomy is built into the political economy of crisis responses. Not only does this hinder the sustainable provision of care and domestic labor before, during, and after crisis, it also fundamentally constrains how security is enacted within these spaces. That is, women are hypervisible as the face of global and national agendas, but their bodies and labor are economically kept invisible in the allocation of global resources. These contradictions emerge because in order for the neoliberal logic of depletion to be effective, it requires incorporating edited forms of feminism such as the "bracketing off" of SRHR. Viewed through this logic, restrictions to SRHR are in fact not anomalous. Instead, they are a feature of contemporary global politics.

APPROACH AND STRUCTURE OF THE BOOK

While typically one might think that an analysis of the *global* politics of bodily autonomy entails examining sexual and reproductive health across different country contexts, the approach I take in this book is different. Rather than provide a *survey* of experiences and narratives around the world, I offer a *scalar* analysis that allows me to make visible how bodily autonomy is multilayered, as experienced in the intimate spheres of the everyday and as constitutive of global political and economic processes. I wanted to tell the story of how bodily autonomy for Filipino women, as in many other contexts, is shaped by structural and ideological forces globally. Consequently, the book starts the analysis of the global politics of SRHR from a particular location and begins with women's lives in the household—an approach well-established in feminist scholarship.[6] I weave together different feminist traditions and themes in the study of global political economy and security precisely because bodily autonomy underpins all areas and dimensions of gendered politics. Moreover, I use this "bottom up" approach to highlight that women's experiences do not neatly fit global agendas and narratives, which means that they are generative of alternative insights that can transform existing knowledge. Still, the Philippines does make a markedly perplexing case to start with

[8]   *Politics of Sexual & Reproductive Health*

because it is clearly a country in great need of care, yet is also where the state actively depletes the sources of care including through the continued neglect of inequalities in SRHR. Despite the Philippines being a "model country" for gender-responsive laws and women's participation in peace and security processes, we see different political dynamics operate when it comes to SRHR. I do not think the Philippines is entirely unique in this regard. On the contrary, I find that many of the experiences I discuss in this book resonate across crisis-affected societies. The dynamics are illustrative of the many gendered contradictions that characterize our politics today.

The structure of the book reflects this nested and multi-scalar approach. The chapters are organized to illustrate the continuum of gendered material and ideological factors that drive bodily depletion and their cascading impacts in the everyday, during times of crisis, and in the aftermath. The book presents continuities between physical insecurities and structural and symbolic processes that underpin the accumulation of restrictions to SRHR from the household, community, state, and global levels. Similarly, my analytical approach is reflected by the eclectic range of data and qualitative methods I used. I began by situating Filipino women's sexual and reproductive health in relation to their experiences in internal displacements from two case studies—Mindanao for protracted armed conflicts and Eastern Visayas for a rapid-onset disaster caused by Typhoon Haiyan in 2013. Due to security and ethical concerns for myself and potential participants,[7] I designed the research to exclude conducting interviews directly with internally displaced women and girls. Instead, I analyzed existing survey research conducted among internally displaced peoples (IDPs) in both nested cases. In Mindanao, these surveys were conducted by academics from the Mindanao Working Group based in the Ateneo de Davao University (2006–2010) and by Nisa Ul Haqq Fi Bangsamoro, a local women's non-governmental organization (NGO). The surveys serve as crucial local resources even if they are not widely accessible online. They contained documented evidence of experiences of conflict-affected IDP Moro women and girls, including anonymized reports of SGBV cases and narratives relating to barriers to sexual and reproductive health from survey participants.

For the post-disaster case study, I used survey reports by the Brookings Institution and International Organisation for Migration (IOM) (2015); International Organisation for Migration (IOM), Department of Social Welfare and Development (DSWD), Internal Displacement Monitoring Centre (IDMC), and SAS (2014); and Mangada (2016). These surveys were widely accessible online due in part to the funding and institutions that have supported their publication. In the aftermath of Typhoon Haiyan, the spectacle drew what Gaillard and Gomez (2015) termed as a "gold rush" of researchers interested in disasters. I was aware and critical of my own positionality within this crisis environment and believed that finding available resources was a more

INTRODUCTION [9]

ethical strategy and yielded one of several necessary data points to my analysis. My research was less disruptive and minimized (re)exposing potential participants to unnecessary risks such as interview fatigue or adverse impacts for anyone who would be assisting my research directly or indirectly (e.g., local guides who would facilitate responsible and ethical access to research participants). Drawing from the wealth of first-hand accounts that local researchers and activists have already collected therefore provided me the feminist ethical option of building research solidarity wherein I help amplify and appropriately recognize the frontline work that they do.

I also drew on the experiences and perspectives of those who are tasked by the state and international community to respond to these crises and in the governance of post-crisis transitions. I interviewed key informants in the Philippines over three field trips in January–April 2015, October 2015, and April–May 2016.[8] The field research locations were in Metro Manila, the capital; Davao, Mindanao;[9] and in two provinces in the Eastern Visayas region namely Tacloban, Leyte and Guiuan, Eastern Samar. Desk research identified a diverse collection of actors at different levels who are: (a) directly and indirectly related to the provisioning of sexual and reproductive health care; (b) involved in providing relief assistance and ongoing support for internally displaced populations in crisis settings.[10] Many shared the official perspectives of the organizations they represented, their own personal experiences from working in humanitarian assistance, and stories recounted to them from or by the IDP communities they worked with. A small number of key informants who were from Mindanao and Eastern Visayas also personally experienced being displaced by armed conflicts or by the Typhoon Haiyan disaster. I drew on their insights critically and to help reveal prevailing silences in global discourses and where inequalities are. I contextualized how each informant, because of the positions they held, can resist as well as reproduce gendered barriers to SRHR in everyday life and in times of crisis.

"Studying up," as Nader (1972) argues, is equally important as studying those in the margins of power. To comprehensively understand how power operates, researchers also need to pay attention to those in the middle and upper end of hierarchical structures. Exploring the narratives of those within positions of power or in the intermediaries of where resources and political authority are brokered is crucial because they also allow for reconstructing institutions, identities, and values that define the boundaries of possibility. They provide an important vantage point for interpreting how bodily autonomy, health, and well-being are materially and discursively constructed in internal displacements. Crisis responders—from representatives of state agencies, local and international humanitarian response teams, community health workers to volunteers from charities and faith-based organizations—help illuminate or occlude the daily realities faced by internally displaced populations as well as shape the policies and resources available to them (see also Wilson and Krystalli 2017: 20; Tanyag 2015: 66).

To corroborate and deepen my analysis of IDP surveys and key-informant interviews, I also analyzed official humanitarian crisis monitoring reports and related documents from government, non-government, and international humanitarian organizations such as those regularly conducted by the Philippine Protection Cluster, UN Refugee Agency (UNHCR) and UN Office for the Coordination of Humanitarian Affairs (OCHA). I used national surveys providing statistical information on a range of political, economic, and socio-cultural indicators such as the National Demographic and Health Survey (NDHS) and Philippine Human Development Index reports. This secondary literature provided me with the supporting quantitative data to map out various structural patterns of inequalities in relation to SRHR, thereby revealing variations across national and subnational levels. I used them to highlight that in the Philippines, disparities in SRHR among different groups of Filipino women and girls are systematically overlayed with geographies of access to health care that are already uneven in everyday life, and more so in times of crisis. This approach is consistent with the feminist application of intersectionality that attends to how groups of women and men are differently positioned within overlapping structures of inclusion and exclusion, as well as privilege and disadvantage (see Weldon 2006; Ackerly and True 2010). Secondary analysis of statistical surveys provides another method to reconstruct how society is structurally organized according to variations in the enabling or curtailing conditions to bodily autonomy.

Chapter 1 provides the theoretical background to the book and discusses my synthesis of different feminist perspectives for explaining the global political economy of SRHR in crisis settings. I draw on analysis of women's bodies and social reproduction in the Philippines to unpack the neoliberal logic of depletion and its main elements. Social reproduction, and women's bodies in particular, enables the material conditions for both violence and peace. This chapter lays the conceptual and analytical foundations to the central claim advanced in this book—restrictions to SRHR are not incidental but rather integral to the reproduction of a patriarchal global order.

Chapter 2 examines the first site of bodily depletion: the household. Feminist research in IR has emphasized how gender relations beginning in the household are causal to more global forms of violence and insecurity. Yet, dominant analysis of conflicts and disasters routinely ignore women's household labor as an economic activity that sustains both processes of violence and insecurity as well as post-crisis recovery. In the case of protracted and rapid onset displacements in the Philippines, crisis was embodied by the intensification of women's care and domestic work and their related exposure to forms of sexual and gender-based violence. In Chapter 2, I analyze these interconnected bodily costs in terms of self-sacrificing practices that lead to women's

INTRODUCTION [11]

neglect of their own sexual and reproductive health. However, as much as these practices deplete women's bodies, they may also be instrumentalized by women in asserting their desires for maintaining "normal" lives for themselves and their families despite their displacement.

Chapter 3 examines the community as a site of everyday bodily depletion and where the gendered political economy of crisis interventions plays out. In this chapter, I discuss how restrictions to SRHR are exacerbated under conditions of feminized community survival. As an interconnected arena for household social reproduction, a community's survival depends on feminized forms of labor from the local *barangay* health work to the multi-tasking traditional healer/peacebuilder called the *panday*. These community roles are typically undertaken by women as an extension of their household duties, especially in contexts where social and kinship networks are diffused such as the Philippines. Women therefore comprise the reliable constituents of an underpaid, voluntary, and overworked community workforce because of deeply embedded norms of female altruism, obligation, and self-sacrifice that are reinforced through crisis responses. In the aftermath of crises, a proliferation of survival myths, such as cultural narratives regarding the innate "resilience" and mutual aid among Filipinos, compounds the undervaluing of community work and perpetuates dangerous assumptions that the community is an automatic "safe haven." Crucially, these myths keep hidden how the Philippine state has long relied on and exploited cultural narratives to divest itself of material responsibilities in ensuring the even distribution of community burdens and for adequately resourcing community health and social welfare infrastructures.

Chapter 4 situates restrictions to bodily autonomy in relation to the ongoing project of nation-building in the context of multiple and overlapping crises. Women's bodies biologically and symbolically reproduce the nation and thus access to sexual and reproductive health care and women's status in family laws are highly political. The politics of SRHR in a country is revelatory of ossified outcomes of often-violent negotiations over national boundaries and the terms of identity and belonging. Health inequalities among different group of women and men are indicative of how people are differently positioned vis-à-vis nation—whose bodies are deemed more worthy of protection and whose bodies are excluded or dispensable? Bodily autonomy is at the heart of contestations over authority and resources in a country. National political transitions from crisis such as peace negotiations and post-disaster reconstruction provide opportunities to (re)negotiate or (re)establish gendered political and economic orders. During these periods, contestations over the control of women's bodies can become even more intense and violent. However, drawing on the case of the Bangsamoro peace negotiations and Typhoon Haiyan post-disaster reconstruction in the Philippines, I show that these transitions are also sites of women's patriarchal bargains through

[12]   *Politics of Sexual & Reproductive Health*

which ambivalences in gender equality outcomes emerge. Because women's bodies are their most immediate resource, they employ different embodied strategies—depending on the material and ideological opportunities available to them—to challenge or circumvent existing gendered constraints in society. Chapter 4 presents a different understanding of bodily autonomy in relation to women's crisis-specific patriarchal bargains at the national level and, in doing so, helps explain why some forms of gendered inequalities such those relating to SRHR become more entrenched than others.

Chapter 5 turns to the drivers of bodily depletion at the global level by examining the role of religious fundamentalisms in simultaneously complementing the spread of neoliberal economic ideology and driving the associated fragmentation of feminist activisms as well as piece-meal implementation of feminist agendas. While there remains ongoing debate over terminologies, there is a consensus among activists around the world that the term religious fundamentalisms adequately captures the anti-feminist backlash or countermovement they encounter in their everyday work. Fundamentalist or extremist forces are increasingly present in all major religions and in different geopolitical contexts. Religious fundamentalisms, however, are not new and have been a mainstay of national contestations over the control of women's bodies in the name of nation, tradition, and family. In this chapter, I demonstrate how religious fundamentalisms are not simply reactionary. They have evolved their own global political project and constitute a growing influence in crisis settings. They constitute transnational alliances that are well-resourced, politically adept, and globally coordinated. What brings them together is a fine-tuned resistance to the rights of the body, sexuality, and pleasure—the encapsulation of all that goes against their pro-family, pro-life, and pro-tradition agenda.

Continuing my analysis of patriarchal bargains and embodied strategies that inform the politics of SRHR, this chapter argues that feminist responses to religious fundamentalist opposition that tend to "bracket off" or soften the language on SRHR in order to make incremental gains neither helped in defeating religious fundamentalist forces nor achieved the goals they "sacrificed" comprehensive SRHR for. Instead, such responses have further sown the material and ideological conditions for religious fundamentalisms to thrive. Focusing on Catholic fundamentalism, I show how a tactic of opposing discursive references to SRHR at any global agenda is tied to a broader strategy of sacralizing neoliberalism. Through it, the Catholic Church is positioned as a moral authority—self-styled champion of the poor, of motherhood, and of virtuous women—while maintaining women's subordination in the family, legitimizing the presence of faith-based groups in crisis response, and becoming complicit in unequal global material relations.

Chapter 6 explores alternatives to the prevailing neoliberal logic of depletion by theorizing the concept of regeneration as a (re)imagination of a truly transformative post-crisis reconstruction made possible by ensuring that the well-being of women and the planet are at its core. This chapter extends the arguments of this book by examining how ecological crises are bound up with a global crisis in social reproduction. Analytically, regeneration suggests a fuller spectrum to processes of depletion—from body to ecology. This means that scholars and activists need to examine the linkages between sexual and reproductive freedoms and ecological security and the shared root causes that are driving the interconnected depletion of women's bodies and the environment. Normatively, regeneration potentially serves as an ethical starting point for conceptualizing a transformative approach beyond the prevailing militarized, state-centric, "short-termist," and extractive restoration of societies in the aftermath of crises. Regeneration does away with discourses of post-crisis survival and resilience by orienting frames to the pursuit of interdependent flourishing instead. Politically, the concept of regeneration can inform a rethinking of post-crisis economic priorities to be anchored on care for bodily autonomy, well-being and pleasure, and environmental peacebuilding. It means equally valuing, alongside physical infrastructures, the "slow" and less visible markers of peace. Finally, regeneration potentially informs the existing understanding of justice in the aftermath of crises by emphasizing a deeper and collective interrogation of the interrelatedness of justice and care. Regeneration as justice asks whose bodies are able to pursue what versions of the good life in the face of ecological crisis.

In the conclusion, I reflect on the radical implications for global peace and security when SRHR is recognized not as a collateral issue where patriarchal bargains need to be made in order to advance feminism in global agendas but rather as a cornerstone feminist issue that ties together all sites, forms, and temporalities of gender equality. I chart the future prospects for SRHR in light of the interlinked intensification of anti-feminist resistance and uncertainty due to climate change–related crises. Material and cultural transformations of the current global politics of bodily autonomy can embody feminist futures wherein the pursuit of broadening women's participation and leadership in peace processes, disaster risk reduction, and climate change, is matched by the economic valuing of the contributions of care and domestic work in the household, community, state, and global economy. This is a feminist future where women dying from preventable deaths count as *the* crisis. I conclude that depletion is not inevitable even in dystopic times. Instead, it can and it must be resisted. The enjoyment of sexuality and right to pleasure are integral to the human struggle for dignity even in the face of suffering. I am inspired by how self-care becomes a revolutionary act, especially among people caught in cycles of displacements, for it represents their defiance against invisibility and victimhood and their relentless faith that peace is in bodies that are able to regenerate and flourish. This book is in solidarity with them.

[14]   *Politics of Sexual & Reproductive Health*

CHAPTER 1
Crisis and the Global Political Economy of Sexual and Reproductive Health

INTRODUCTION

Inequalities in health and restrictions to people's well-being, especially among women, are fundamentally rooted in a much deeper, profound yet "normalized" multi-scalar crisis of social reproduction. The right to bodily autonomy, which includes not just the absence of violence but also the freedom to pursue sexuality and pleasure, is materially connected to the reproduction of political, economic, and ecological life. The giving and receiving of care are basic to human survival and intimately tied to people's ability to freely decide who they want to love, whether they want to have a family, and when, and importantly, whether and how they can love and care for their own bodies. However, the most glaring contradiction we are seeing today is how, globally, a heightened feminization of survival is being matched by the further extraction or "hollowing out" of resources for directly replenishing the health and well-being of women and girls particularly in crisis settings. In the name of championing women's rights and through the strategic cultural and religious valorization of female altruism and self-sacrifice, women are made hypervisible as the face of global agendas, yet their bodies and labor are economically kept invisible in the allocation of global, national, community, and household resources.

This book situates the contemporary global politics of sexual and reproductive health and rights (SRHR) in relation to how the depletion of women's bodies is not *incidental* to the current neoliberal global economy and security but rather *integral* to their very reproduction. In this chapter, I provide my theoretical approach, which synthesizes multiple feminist traditions and approaches in international relations in order to reveal the relationships between *bodily* or *physical* harms manifested at the basic level of SRHR outcomes

The Global Politics of Sexual and Reproductive Health. Maria Tanyag, Oxford University Press.
© Oxford University Press 2024. DOI: 10.1093/oso/9780197676332.003.0002

and the gendered *structures* and *ideologies* that govern crisis and the everyday on a global scale. It seeks to bridge feminist peace, security, and political economy by theorizing the neoliberal logic of depletion and its implications for bodily autonomy. Extending existing theoretical definitions of depletion, I conceptualize it not merely as an *outcome* of neoliberal global economic and security approaches but also as their very *ordering* principle. That is, depletion is the prevailing logic to how global authority and resources are allocated in "crisis" and the everyday. This logic of depletion functions by incorporating edited forms of feminism, such as the harnessing of women's labor and participation in crisis responses from peacebuilding and post-disaster reconstruction to the daily delivery of primary health care, while "bracketing off" critical inflows that nourish and sustain women's bodies. In this manner, the ongoing survival of societies and the global economy are made possible under conditions of social reproductive contradictions for as long as many people, women and girls in particular, are denied their bodily autonomy.

This chapter is divided into three parts. The first section discusses feminist perspectives that challenge binary accounts of "crisis" and the "everyday." Feminist scholarship contributes to making visible how a *crisis* is in fact not exceptional but rather rooted in less visible, "less serious," but relentless, gendered *crises*. Crisis is endogenous to the neoliberal global order and persists precisely because of ongoing depletion of social reproduction and SRHR specifically. With this as a starting point, I show how the "normalized" crisis of social reproduction serves as a permanent background to the more "visible" crisis posed by events like recessions, conflicts, and disasters. The second section defines the neoliberal logic of depletion. Depletion as a feminist concept originates from research on political economy and development. I explain the importance of extending its meaning so that it not only refers to the *cost* or *outcome* of neglecting social reproduction—which is how it is currently understood—but also to a pervasive *ordering principle* for how the global economy interlinks with militarism and global security. The third section discusses the two elements of depletion namely, the feminization of survival and care debt spirals. I illustrate how these two elements set the stage for restrictions to SRHR especially in crisis settings.

THE "PERMANENT" CRISIS OF SOCIAL REPRODUCTION

Increasingly, everyday life is marked by a variety of "crises" from wars, terrorism, violent extremisms (or heightened threats thereof), natural disasters and ecological crises, financial crises, health pandemics, refugee crises and internal displacements, political crises reflected in polarization, authoritarianism, and populism, to the harsh confluence of all these on a global scale. These crises demonstrate with piercing clarity how much people's lives and

[16] *Politics of Sexual & Reproductive Health*

sense of security are interconnected, yet also that the burdens and costs of survival are profoundly unequal. There is a danger that contemporary securitization and crisis narratives will become more effective in dissociating harms and violence experienced by people as "crisis-specific" or "exceptional" rather than rooted in structural inequalities and symbolic discrimination that disproportionately impact marginalized peoples in everyday life. Through a feminist lens, crises are structurally connected to the banality of violence, discrimination and marginalization that occur in times of "peace" or stability. However, prevailing representations and approaches to these crises continue to ignore the importance of economically resourcing women's health, care labor, and social reproduction more broadly.

Feminist and critical scholars have argued that what gets left out and what gets included in discursive representations and historical accounts of "crises" are issues of power (Sjoberg et al. 2015; Tickner 2015). Crisis, as a discourse, makes visible particular configurations to the global order and hides others. Crises are also material in that they are indicative of gendered relations of production and reproduction, and of structures that allocate who is in charge, which solutions are deemed appropriate, and how decisions are made. Feminists interrogate how power operates before, during, and after a crisis in direct and indirect ways by paying attention to gender relations as present "in every site of human interaction from the household to the international arena" and embodied by "how women's and men's bodies are nourished, trained, and deployed, how vulnerable they are to attack, what mobility they have" (Cockburn 2004: 28). We see gendered material and discursive power operate by obscuring the full character and range of causes to any crisis.

"Continuums" of violence, for example, emerge when we pay attention to gender relations and interrogate crisis from the standpoint of women's lives. Drawing on international women's and peace activisms, Cockburn (2010) pointed out how they are able to map the systemic and interlinked nature of violence through their different geopolitical locations. These activist networks perceive "'war' not just as spasms of war-fighting, but as part of a continuum leading from militarism (as a persisting mindset, expressed in philosophy, newspaper editorials, political think tanks), through militarization (processes in economy and society that signify preparation for war)" (2010: 148). Violence is not only about individual perpetrators and victims but also cuts across political, economic, and socio-cultural dimensions; and occurs across different sites—in battlefields, displacement camps, within families and kinship or ethnic networks, at the level of the state and globally (Cockburn 2004, 2010). The concept of continuum of violence is core to feminist international relations (IR) scholarship on security and peace. It analytically reveals violence as multidimensional across different forms, layers, sites, and temporalities (True and Tanyag 2019; Marchand and Runyan 2010; Tickner 1992). It informs feminist approaches that link crisis-related violence against women

CRISIS AND SEXUAL AND REPRODUCTIVE HEALTH [17]

with insecurities emerging from everyday political economy processes that are increasingly globalized (True 2012; Meger 2016). Relatedly, seeing violence as a continuum underscores the importance of marginalized sites for rethinking security beyond "states of exception" to account for incremental, less dramatic but relentless insecurities that occur in the everyday (Robinson 2016).

Are crisis exceptions or rather by design? On the one hand, crises are most commonly seen as atypical—relating to or embodying ruptures to the way things are. A crisis generally refers to a time of uncertainty, unease, and insecurity. It pertains to a turning point, critical juncture, or "shock" to the status quo. On the other hand, crises can be viewed more critically as cumulative and predictable outcomes of pre-existing or historical configurations of ideas and institutions. Indeed, feminist scholars and activists working on crisis in relation to the global political economy and development argue the latter (Fraser 2013; Federici 2012; Elson 2010; 2012). For instance, Sen and Grown (1987), writing for the organization Development Alternatives for Women in the New Era (DAWN), explained the genesis of crises they were observing in the 1980s in terms of the failures of "short-sighted" policies and crisis response. According to them, "[w]hen a structure or system reaches a stage when it must either undergo major changes or break down, it is in a state of crisis. Temporary solutions may mitigate some of its effects, but so long as its main structural causes remain untouched, the crisis persists, demanding resolution, and things cannot go back to 'business as usual'" (1987: 50). Sen and Grown distinguish between more visible and observed crisis in the economic system and its underlying or less visible, interrelated crisis in terms of how people especially the poor survive on a daily basis. In their words, "[a] crisis in state spending under economic and/or political pressures can create a crisis of basic reproduction" (1987: 51).

The critique raised by DAWN in the 1980s framed "reproduction failures" or "crisis of basic reproduction" as outcomes of global political economy. Fraser's (2017) analysis of the "crisis of social reproduction" makes a subtle distinction by interpreting it as internal or inherent contradiction to neoliberal capitalism. According to her, "[O]n the one hand, social reproduction is a condition of possibility for sustained capital accumulation; on the other hand, capitalism's orientation to unlimited accumulation tends to destabilise the very processes of social reproduction on which it relies" (2017: 22). Fraser observes that the global crisis of social reproduction intersects and exacerbates other strands of a more generalized crisis encompassing economic, ecological, and political dimensions (2017: 21). Similarly, Gill and Bakker (2011) argue that the crisis of social reproduction needs to be conceptualized as part of a "global organic crisis" defining the world today. This organic crisis is driven by the "intensified power of capital through neoliberal political and constitutional reforms and on the other hand, a weakening of the conditions for stable and sustainable social reproduction" (Gill and Bakker 2011: 221; Bakker and Gill

[18]   *Politics of Sexual & Reproductive Health*

2003). Yet governmental responses to the morbid symptoms of this neoliberal crisis are intersecting "with deepening and long-term threats to our social and ecological reproduction" (Gill and Bakker 2011: 329; Bakker and Gill 2003).

Crises are systemic, protracted, and cyclical because they are generated by deeply embedded material and ideological factors that devalue the importance of social reproduction. Feminist scholars, for instance, argue that social reproduction is taken for granted in light of its very ubiquity (Robinson 2011, 2016; Harman 2016; Elson 2012; Folbre 2014). Care economies constitute material relations of paid and unpaid care work that are typically undertaken by women in the household and community (Razavi 2007). Care work is not counted as "productive" economic activity because of prevailing masculinist biases, assumptions, and policies that only see the "formal" and market economy. Yet, the "private" and intimate sphere of the family or household is not separate from but rather has always been connected to the "public" sphere of political and economic agendas. Consequently, care economies especially at the household and community levels are an integral aspect of national and global economies but are often underestimated and made invisible in macroeconomic accounting and policymaking (Folbre 2014; Razavi 2007). Moreover, the costs of care and social reproduction are taken for granted because they are also culturally "normalized" as acts of maternal "love" or "duty" in the household. Across many societies, care provisioning is primarily women's "bottomless" obligation (Brickell and Chant 2010).

Social reproduction is also made ever-present by gendered and racialized divisions of labor globally. This is highlighted by professions that are feminized and racialized not simply because they are associated with women's work in the household, but also because these occupations are represented as not requiring skills or "technical" knowledge and tend to be populated primarily by "Third World" or Global South women (Safri and Graham 2010; Chin 1998; Mitter 1986). Hence women, particularly those employed as domestic workers, garment factory workers in export-processing zones, nurses and caregivers, have been most vulnerable to depletion and their working conditions are treated as a hidden and acceptable cost to reproducing the global economy (Elias 2004; 2010; Parreñas 2001; Yeates 2009). For example, domestic and care workers routinely experience violence because of the nature of their work but this does not count as "crisis" except in a number of cases where national economic interest and bilateral or regional state relations were threatened (Chin 1998; Elias and Gunawardana 2013; Elias 2010). Even then, state responses have prioritized restoring economic relations rather than transforming how care economies are valued in the global economy.

While there is a consensus among scholars that the crisis of social reproduction is expansive and affects all areas of human life, much of the theoretical and practical discussions have focused on the global economy as the object or arena where transformations ought to occur. Yet, I argue that labor associated with reproducing life remains unpaid, underpaid, or uncounted not only because of economic devaluing but also because of how such devaluing complements masculinized interpretations of security. Feminist scholarship on human security and on reconceptualizing global security more broadly illustrates this point. For example, Robinson's (2011) work on the importance of "care ethics" has demonstrated how care practices and responsibilities are ever present across different types of crises and in everyday life. According to Robinson, feminist ethics of care re-orients narrow understandings of security, which privileges states and militarism to "recognise the importance of care as a fundamental aspect of human flourishing, as well as the need to preserve and facilitate good caring relations, while refusing to valorise or idealise care" (2011: 61). Feminist care ethics provides an alternative lens and moral orientation to what ought to be taken seriously and hence, given priority in crisis settings. It seeks to critically examine security contexts and securitization by placing value on "the centrality of adequate relations and institutions of care for the continuity and security of people's everyday lives" (Robinson 2016: 122). Moreover, it "compels us to attend to the insecurities of 'the everyday'" (2016: 119). In unraveling everyday insecurities for a more human-centered security, feminist care ethics traces the devaluing of care across different levels or scales of care relations in the household, community, and state as connected to the global political economy of militarism (Robinson 2016). It helps lay bare the prevailing values, norms, and assumptions pertaining to care and their role in shaping the material distribution of societal responsibilities and collective capacities before, during, and after crises.

Harman's (2016) research on the Ebola crisis also demonstrates how the cost of care and social reproduction becomes even more conspicuously invisible and "normalized" during health crises because global health strategies routinely take the feminized health workforce for granted. She points out the complete absence of discussions on social reproduction and the care economy and lack of gender analysis at every stage in the international response. Harman argues that without accounting for how health systems rely on the paid and unpaid care work largely performed by women, unequal gender relations were left unquestioned within the emergency response. The invisibility of women and gender were further compounded within the intersections of global health governance, Ebola crisis response, and legacies of gendered exclusions in post-conflict reconstruction in West Africa. In this example, we see a continuum in the inbuilt training to not pay attention to gender relations in emergencies and modes of reproducing "gender norms in masculinised spaces of decision making and implementation" that continue in long-term or post-crisis settings (Harman 2016: 534). Consequently, this research suggests that the need to put care at the center of rebuilding health systems in the aftermath of pandemics and disease outbreaks was incompatible with pandemic responses that reinforce masculinized and militarized security.

[20] *Politics of Sexual & Reproductive Health*

By contrast, valuing care and social reproduction would have made significant improvements for women's lives and directly contributed to strengthening health systems precisely because of women's distinct reliance on and direct participation in care economies. We can expect similar, or worse, outcomes in other forms of crisis when women's labor and care economies are also simultaneously relied upon for survival but economically invisible in the accounting of costs and distribution of rewards in a crisis aftermath.

Feminist engagements on theorizing the crisis of social reproduction need to account for a multiplicity of contexts that are underexamined and thus contribute to why economic and security challenges remain intractable. As Kunz (2010) cautions us, research on the crisis of social reproduction tends to be universalizing and does "not adequately or fully represent transformations occurring in countries where social reproduction has always been a predominantly 'private' matter for the majority of the population" (2010: 914). Moreover, there is a need to account for the types of labor and economic activities that are rendered invisible as part of the interlinking of neoliberal political economy with security. Examining the logics driving the "permanent" crisis of social reproduction can raise important insights into how a large part of crisis response and post-crisis recovery are subsidized by and enacted through the control of women's bodies. It can show how the invisibility of care and social reproduction in existing models of post-crisis recovery can heighten the concurrent reliance on and erasure of women's bodies through neoliberal policies of austerity, which, among others, involve cutting back on social welfare provisions and conditioning greater volunteer work to the disproportionate detriment of women and girls in current and future crisis settings (Elson 2010; UN Women 2014).

These issues are most consequential for women and girls belonging to indigenous, minority, and internally displaced groups who have historically and in contemporary ways been denied bodily autonomy. Displaced women and girls continue to disproportionately represent global cases for high maternal mortality. They are more vulnerable to unmet needs for family planning, complications following unsafe abortion and heightened risks for HIV and STDs (UNFPA 2015). Compounded by higher prevalence of risk for sexual and gender-based violence, women and girls experience bodily harms that typically form the "hidden crisis" that accompanies any conflict, disaster or emergency.[1] SRHR remains misunderstood, devalued, and misrepresented in crisis situations. There is still an immense need for "better analysis and understanding of the ways in which sexuality and sexual violence, pregnancy, childbirth, HIV and AIDS, and racialised and gendered power relations take on whole new meanings—and help give meaning to—situations of armed conflict and disaster" (Petchesky 2008: 5). Examining the global politics of sexual and reproductive health is as much about how "[C]rises expose extant weaknesses in health systems, impacting differentially on sub-populations, especially women, children and adolescents" (Askew et al. 2016: 311), as it is revelatory of what is deemed "trivial" and "normal" under prevailing definitions and practices of security.

In the next section, I explain my feminist analysis of the neoliberal logic of depletion, which brings together different feminist perspectives on peace and security to generate a fuller picture of how securitized "crises"—such as armed conflicts, disasters, and climate change among others—are systemically connected with the "non-crisis" of ensuring the sustainability of care and social reproduction. While a crisis of social reproduction has long been underway, its embodiments intensify in situations and periods of crisis. Moreover, examining settings where the occurrence of multiple crises is the norm and social reproductive conditions have historically very low baselines provides crucial insights to the complex challenges to (re)imagining ways to resource social reproduction amid competing security demands and prioritization.

DEPLETION AS A NEOLIBERAL LOGIC OF CRISIS AND THE EVERYDAY

Recurrent crises are occurring not by accident but precisely because the global order is driven like clockwork by a particular neoliberal logic—that of depletion. Depletion is a concept that has distinctly emerged in feminist analysis in economics, development, and global political economy (Elson 2012; Rai, Hoskyns, and Thomas 2014). It has been articulated, largely in the context of economic crises, to describe the cost and associated harmful consequences of the economic neglect and devaluing of social reproduction in the sustainability of life itself. Depletion through Social Reproduction, according to Rai, Hoskyns, and Thomas, occurs when there is "a critical gap between the outflows—domestic, affective and reproductive—and the inflows that sustain [the] health and well-being" of those engaged in social reproduction (2014: 86). The concept does not refer to the "'natural' wear and tear" associated with undertaking social reproduction but rather to the threshold with which it becomes harmful (2014: 91). Indeed, depletion highlights the "structural aspects of social reproduction that undermine the sustainability of the everyday lives of women and men in a given social context" (2014: 89–90). Hoskyns and Rai observe that "a widespread and growing depletion of the capacities and resources for social reproduction—that is, the glue that keeps households and societies together and active" has been ongoing yet continues to be "noticed" only in ad hoc ways. Consequently, the lack of serious engagement with the costs of social reproduction has far-reaching and potentially long-term consequences because "[W]ithout unpaid services and their depletion being measured and valued, predictions are likely to be faulty, models inaccurate and development policies flawed" (2007: 297).

[22] *Politics of Sexual & Reproductive Health*

Depletion has originally been expressed by Rai, Hoskyns, and Thomas (2014) as "harms." First, according to Rai, Hoskyns, and Thomas, depletion as a harm "occurs when there is a measurable deterioration in the health and well-being of individuals and the sustainability of households and communities" (2014: 91). There are four types of harms in relation to depletion: discursive, emotional, bodily, and citizenship entitlements. Based on this definition, depletion constitutes a measurable effect that indicates interrelated gendered power, hierarchies, regimes, and structures. Though depletion has not originally been used directly to explain forms of gendered violence, there are clear overlaps in terms of how harms can constitute as violence (Rai, True, and Tanyag 2019). Harms are not just physical injuries, in the same way that violence does not refer only to those harms directly inflicted on an individual body. Both concepts imply a continuum between individual health and well-being and broader structures that significantly impact life chances by relegating unequal status and levels of access to resources and decision-making, as well as in the symbolic representations that justify and render these inequalities as "natural" (see Harding 1986; Haraway 1988; True 2012; Dominguez and Menjivar 2014; Rai, Hoskyns, and Thomas 2014).

I build on these existing definitions and use bodily harms to holistically refer to sexual and gender-based violence, restrictions to sexual and reproductive health, deterioration of emotional, mental, and psychosocial well-being, and the interlinkages of all these. I use structural and symbolic forms of violence because they capture dimensions that might be missed by the language of discursive harms and harms to citizenship entitlements. For instance, symbolic violence speaks to the complicity of women in neglecting their own health in pursuit of fulfilling culturally idealized femininities; while structural violence refers to much more than the boundaries that define who counts as a citizen but rather whose humanity and pursuit of the good life is recognized or deliberately denied. In bringing together the language of harms and gendered violence, my aim is to provide a holistic conceptualization of the different dimensions, processes, and agents to depletion.

At a time of multiple and intersecting crises, depletion can no longer be analytically confined to economic crises especially when many of the consequences of prior crises can accumulate and (re)define the starting point for the next and future crises. Indeed, the costs of economically neglecting care and social reproduction in times of crisis have gained attention in connection to conflicts and post-war reconstruction (Rai, True, and Tanyag 2019; Hedstrom 2017; Bergeron, Cohn, and Duncanson 2017; Cohn and Duncanson 2020); disasters (Bradshaw 2014), and health crises (Harman 2016; Folbre 2014). Important work needs to be done to examine the extent and nature of depletion that occurs during and in the aftermath of crises, as well as the implications of depletion for peace and post-crisis outcomes. Depletion routinely occurs in daily life, but as Elias and Rai point out "in times of crises, economic downturn, war, and social conflict, there can be an intensification of this harm" (2015: 428). By now, it is also insufficient to conceive of depletion simply as cost or after-effect. Depletion manifests as an overarching logic when it enables the reinforcement of narrow definitions of security through processes of militarism and the pursuit of state sovereignty. Militarized and state-centric security obscures how everyday practices of care, especially within families and communities, are the bedrock of peacebuilding (Vaittinen and Confortini 2019). The logic of depletion is evident in the prioritization of formal political and economic systems in crisis response despite these systems' direct reliance on care work and social reproduction more generally. It describes the ways in which contemporary security and economic policies structure everyday life and how gradual and holistic peace involving material and ideological transformations necessary to replenish social reproduction are traded off in crisis responses based on "urgency" and in the privileging of auditable "technical" fixes.

Feminist scholars have long raised the need to account for resourcing care or caring regimes in development and economic decision-making for countering depletion (Elson 2012; Chopra and Sweetman 2014; Razavi 2007). To make care central to all types of policy and decision-making is to be guided by asking (1) who cares? (2) who pays? and (3) where is care provided? (Razavi 2007: 20). While it may be clear from a feminist lens that care must be a continuing priority during and after crises, there are still immense challenges in making care visible to policymakers and crisis responders. There have been a variety of proposed approaches on reforming care provisioning. A radical solution proposed by Federici (2012), which stems from her analysis of and personal involvement in an international campaign, is to demand "wages for housework" as a way of revolutionizing the material relations that define women's lives. Razavi (2007) has recommended the strengthening of what she calls the "care diamond" or the architecture to care provisioning, which comprises families or households, not-for-profit actors, markets, and the state. Care provisioning can be supported through cash benefits and tax allowances; employment-related measures such as paid carer's leave and flexible work arrangements; and state-funded childcare services. Other efforts focused at making care work visible have emphasized time-use surveys and developing methods to account for the distribution of care within households. For their part, Rai, Hoskyns, and Thomas (2014) propose an equation for measuring depletion based on the rates and thresholds at which it takes place. Measurement, according to them, is necessary for demonstrating the extent of depletion and can thereby inform ways for alleviating social reproduction.

Discussions of resourcing care and social reproduction, however, are "seldom combined with a larger analysis of financial flows or fully integrated into the larger discourse of economic development theory or policy" (Folbre 2014: i129) and much less in terms of security policies and in the context of emergency response. Care solutions and measures have been implemented or proposed overwhelmingly in relation to "peacetime" contexts. These solutions, while crucial and viable in times of stability, do not lend themselves easily to the distinct governance challenges—from data collection and adequate protection measures to access to health care—in wartime or complex emergencies where violence is normalized. Yet, as Elson (2012) argues, crises can deepen pre-existing insecurities when there is a failure to recognize, reduce, and redistribute unpaid care work. How then do care and social reproduction get replenished with a continuum of violence in mind? How do we know or measure long-lasting depletion resulting from successive failures in crisis response to take care work seriously? There are no straightforward answers to these questions. This book seeks to demonstrate that we learn a lot about care, social reproduction, and violence by examining how women's and men's sexual and reproductive health and well-being are differently replenished and cared for. The relationship between women's health and crisis of social reproduction remains under-examined. Indeed, depletion is framed in reference to the reproduction and sustainability of life but thus far has not been articulated directly in relation to the politics of sexual and reproductive health, despite obvious overlaps and interrelations. I argue that this is because feminist analyses of care and social reproduction are still largely disconnected from the rich literature, for instance, on the transnational influence of religious fundamentalists in restricting access to health. Except for a number of studies that have shown how the global economic environment and particularly economic crises have had gendered health impacts, further research is required to understand how macroeconomic trends and processes undermine women's health at the crossroads of other crisis environments such as conflicts and disasters (see Mohindra, Labonté, Spitzer 2011; Fonn and Ravindran 2011; Bakker and Gill 2011; Gill and Bakker 2011).

Employing a feminist political economy analysis of depletion in crisis interventions is an urgent task for highlighting social reproduction and particularly women's health and well-being as central to feminist peace. Such a critique implies significant redistribution of resources away from militaries or the "security sector" toward resourcing caring institutions and activities, which includes sexual and reproductive health, as part of long-term crisis response. Elias (2016) provides an important starting point by asking "whose crisis" and "whose recovery"? According to her, feminist analysis of care and social reproduction reveals how the very guaranteed presence of social reproductive labor "enables the kinds of risky financial behaviours that trigger crises in the first place" (Elias 2016: 120). These insights have broader relevance for expanding feminist critiques of different crises based on how social reproduction and, specifically, women's bodies enable the material conditions for both violence and peace. As I argue throughout this book, depletion is about the control of women's bodies, which has been at the heart of authoritative struggles over claims on how society and the roles and relationships within it ought to be (Yuval-Davis and Anthias 1989; Yuval-Davis 1997). These authoritative struggles are increasingly globalized and demonstrate where the intersections of international political economy, war, securitization, and crises are and how they are gendered (Bedford and Rai 2010; Sjoberg et al. 2015; Elias and Rai 2015).

ELEMENTS OF THE NEOLIBERAL LOGIC OF DEPLETION
A Global Feminization of Survival

In 2000, Sassen observed what was then an emerging trend of illicit or "shadow" cross-border circuits, largely populated by migrant and immigrant women, as systemically connected with governments' revenue enhancement and profiteering. These circuits form part of a broader "feminization of survival," which according to Sassen, embodies how it is "increasingly on the backs of women that these forms of making a living, earning a profit and securing government revenue are realised . . . that households and whole communities are increasingly dependent on women for their survival" (2000: 506). Sassen originally conceptualized "feminization of survival" in relation to hidden economic activities and processes that serve as counter-geographies of globalization. She points out that global economic processes, often represented as gender neutral, have had in fact enormous and gendered costs particularly in terms of how national governments meet the burden of debt servicing, marketization, and post–economic crisis austerity—all of which have made daily life more difficult and precarious, especially for people in the developing world. Consequently, these economic processes have necessitated alternative global circuits that have incorporated increasing numbers of women, such as in the form of the global sex industry and in the generation of migrant remittances for national economic survival. Sassen draws on a number of developing countries but particularly the Philippines, where labor migration of a largely female workforce engaged in care and domestic work as well as in entertainment and hospitality has become not just a short-term strategy for addressing economic shocks: rather, it has made viable an export-oriented, remittances-driven national economy. The feminization of survival is not simply a shadow or hidden activity in the Philippine economy. Instead, it is highly bureaucratized and culturally valorized as necessary for household and national economic survival.

The first element of depletion I examine builds on the material and ideological continuities between Sassen's (2000) original conceptualization of feminization of survival as a "hidden" feature of global political economy and the "hypervisibility" of women and gender in global governance particularly in peace and security agendas, which are the modus operandi in

[26] *Politics of Sexual & Reproductive Health*

"neoliberalism with a feminist face" (Prügl 2017, 2015; Calkin 2015; Roberts 2015). In global development agendas, gender equality and particularly the altruism of mothers is fashioned as key to a country's development success (Roy 2010; Molyneux 2007). For example, Roy argues that the then Millennium Development Agenda (2000–2015) no longer represented the "Third World Woman" as a victim but rather as a heroic entrepreneur and selfless altruist (2010: 548). Feminists have critiqued how through the language of "smart economics," women and girls, especially in developing countries, are instrumentalized for boosting economic growth as well as rescuing economies in the aftermath of the global financial crisis (Roy 2010; Griffin 2015; Calkin 2015). Yet, as Griffin (2016) argues, representations of the global economic crisis served to embed unequal gender relations by framing "women as potentially corrective bodies in the global financial system [which] has been profoundly and problematically, essentialist, seeking to exploit women's 'innate' and 'feminine' gifts for responsibility, domesticity, and circumspection" (2016: 182). Popular imagery and visual representation of the economic crisis re-affirmed rather than transformed representations of the global financial system as immersed in masculinity and "symbolic of white, masculine corporate power" (Griffin 2016: 190). Women's contributions to the economy may be instrumentally represented or valued narrowly to affirm biologically essentialist or maternalist assumptions (Roy 2010; Calkin 2015). Consequently, this very recognition risks reinforcing stereotypical, caregiving roles for women and girls and perpetuating the norms that underpin unequal gendered division of labor.

Women's inclusion on the basis of culturally valued maternalism repurposes free or "voluntary" labor as duty or sacrifice. Female altruism also partly informs why social reproductive labor is treated as a "special" form of labor, one that cannot readily be given a monetary value (Doyal 1995; Molyneux 2007). As shown for example in, Molyneux's (2007) analysis of state anti-poverty programs in Latin America, female altruism and self-sacrifice are strong cultural constructions of femininity in Latin America that have been harnessed in the service of the state. Women were targeted as agents or participants based on the assumption that their time and labor in these social programs were elastic. The costs of their labor are "absorbed" as simply a continuation of their "mothering role" (2007: 36). Therefore, there is a risk with the hypervisibility of feminism in global agendas, especially in post-crisis response and recovery, that the same dynamics are occurring wherein women and girls do not necessarily share in the rewards or benefits brought about by their labor; and that is expected of them. Like two sides of the same coin, feminization of survival is driving the corresponding "feminisation of responsibility and/or obligation" such that "women are working harder in and outside the home . . . however, in most cases, [they] appear to see no justification to expect or demand more as a result of giving more" (Chant 2010: 114).

These two variants of feminized survival go hand in hand under a logic of depletion. The hypervisibility of women as self-sacrificing and feminism as "smart economics" in neoliberal governance allows for the heightened yet economically hidden reliance on women's labor and social reproduction. Analyzing depletion processes requires examining how both these visible and invisible modes of feminized survival are simultaneously compounding the demand for social reproduction while also negating its sustainable supply. However, from the logic of depletion, the inclusion and valorization of women in state programs and global agendas are mechanisms fraught with feminist dilemmas. On the one hand, it alerts us to how "states are indeed abdicating their responsibilities and 'dumping' them on women" through cultural valorization of maternal virtues (Molyneux 2007: 42), and on the other, to the pragmatic limitations of demanding more from the state when the state is structurally weak in addition to being male-dominated and informed by masculinized security.

Worryingly, the implications of neoliberal feminization of survival in crisis settings to women's bodily autonomy have been under-examined. Critical feminist analysis is needed to illustrate the costs and connections between the broadening acceptance of women as key agents of peace and security and the exacerbation of the responsibilities they bear especially in crisis settings (Chant 2010; Brickell and Chant 2010). There is a need to bridge existing analyses of feminization of survival in the context of anti-poverty and global development programs (Chant 2010; Brickell and Chant 2010) with those of crisis settings and in their aftermath as part of a far-reaching and intensified logic of depletion. To what extent can we see continuities in how women and girls are being valorized as individual agents of the global economy as well as peace and security in ways that either do not alter or exacerbate the unequal gendered allocation of obligation and rewards? How are crisis-specific processes driving the depletion of their bodies and labor at critical junctures for transforming gender order? For example, the global Women, Peace and Security (WPS) agenda has been regarded as a ground-breaking security framework, for it has profoundly opened spaces for preventing sexual and gender-based violence, promoting women's participation in peace processes, and recognizing the necessity for gender perspectives in conflict analysis, peacebuilding, and post-conflict reconstruction (UN Women 2015). Shepherd's (2011) analysis of the WPS agenda, however, raises caution over how gendered discourses reproduced through the agenda can translate to mounting expectations and pressures on women to embody *superheroines*—as agents of their own salvation and everybody else's. Such a tremendous burden results from, and compounds, survival costs, given unequal distribution of responsibilities between different groups of women and men (see Cohn, Kinsella, and Gibbings 2004).

The WPS agenda is part of a wider global normative meshwork on women's rights and gender perspectives across a range of other crisis settings

[28] *Politics of Sexual & Reproductive Health*

such as post-disaster risk management and rehabilitation (Bradshaw 2014; Economist Intelligence Unit 2014) and climate change (MacGregor 2017; Arora-Jonsson 2011, 2014). Yet, the same discursive or symbolic valuing of women's victimhood, altruism, and superheroism persists across peacebuilding, post-crisis reconstruction, and climate change. In global peace and security agendas, women tend to be simultaneously—or "schizophrenically" to borrow Shepherd's (2011) term—represented as either vulnerable victims of conflict, economic crises, disasters, and climate change; or as virtuous women who are capable of saving their families, communities, country, and the world. The feminist analysis developed throughout this book sheds light on how feminization of survival compounds the demands on women's bodies and on social reproductive labor in everyday life and during crises. Moreover, it is through this intensification of bodily costs that the abstract concept of global security is made flesh in crises and their aftermaths. Ultimately as Enloe puts it, "to operate in the international arena, governments depend on ideas of masculinized dignity and feminized sacrifice to sustain their sovereignty" (1989/2000: 197). These ideas also have material consequences particularly in terms of how and whose contributions are rewarded to the detriment of women's health and well-being and the long-term erosion of the conditions for human life.

Feminization of the "Care Debt Spiral"

The second element of depletion that I examine is the intensification in the hollowing out of health care and social reproduction more generally. I use the term "care debt spiral" to highlight how globally, governments and communities have been running on unsustainable care deficits through the serial withdrawal of resources that can promote sustainable reproduction of human life. The logic of depletion drives these care debt spirals whereby governments more intensely rely on women's social reproductive labor and the care economy as "shock absorbers" for surviving routine crises and emergencies. Yet, they do not repay this heightened reliance with inflows to restore "borrowed" resources in social reproduction particularly in sexual and reproductive health services and support. This care debt accumulates as the template crisis response is to further extract and "hollow out" women's bodies and the care economy. Spiraling care debts mean that we will continue to witness demands on social reproductive labor increase, while inflows to health and well-being decrease.

Critical scholars of global health and the international political economy have pointed out the disastrous impacts of neoliberalism on health. These adverse consequences have accumulated over decades of structural adjustment programs, unequal trade relations, post-crisis austerity, and security prioritization (Sell and Williams 2020; Bakker and Gill 2011; Gill and Bakker 2011; Mohindra, Labonté, and Spitzer 2011; Harman 2016; Nunes 2014). Indeed, Mohindra, Labonté, and Spitzer (2011) observe that there is a growing disconnect between neoliberal interventions purporting to advance gender equality and the pervading lack of access to primary health care and sexual and reproductive health for women and girls. At a time when women and girls are symbolically and physically made responsible for the survival of whole nations and economies, the expectation that they can continue to "pour from an empty cup" is also intensifying. What this suggests is that governments assume they will never default on their care debts because norms of female altruism and self-sacrifice are made to be in constant supply.

The hollowing out of social reproduction via health care is linked with the feminization of survival. Women are expected to "step in" to deliver health care services, including in crisis response, while states increasingly divest these responsibilities into the private sphere (Davies et al. 2019). They are often described as the "backbone" of health care by predominantly occupying the often "informal" or unpaid frontlines of service delivery. Household and community care provisioning rendered disproportionately by women and girls directly and indirectly "fills in the gaps" of poor health infrastructures. Global health governance and local health systems reproduce and exacerbate the invisibility of feminization of survival because gender equality in global health leadership remains elusive (Davies et al. 2019; Shannon et al. 2019). In crisis contexts where sexual and gender-based violence are rife, access to health is crucial for ensuring effective protection mechanisms and access to justice for victims. Women and girls face gender-specific barriers to health—from accessing services to being represented in leadership and decision-making—yet are also made indispensable to the functioning of health systems. These profound gendered health inequalities are intelligible from a logic of depletion, as are their structural and symbolic connections with the feminization of survival in global politics today.

The Philippines, as a major global exporter of care and health professionals (Barber 2011; Ball 2004), illustrates how a country can function despite and because of spiraling care debts globally. The strategic positioning of the Philippines as a care work exporting country starkly reveals the logic of a global economy increasingly dependent on immediate or short-term feminized survival at the cost of the long-term depletion of women's bodies. According to WHO (2016), there is a global shortage of the human resources for health and more than half of this shortage is for nurses and midwives. The lack of nurses and midwives is most severe in two regions: Southeast Asia where the Philippines is located, and Africa. Shortage in these regions is structurally linked with the Global North's dependence on foreign health workers. Data from 86 countries show that in high-income countries, 15.2% of health professionals are foreign-born or trained (WHO 2020: 48). The global trade

[30]   *Politics of Sexual & Reproductive Health*

in nurses is such that 1 out of 8 or 13% of nurses worldwide are practicing in a country other than where they were born or trained (WHO 2020). For example, Filipinos represent the third biggest nationality group for National Health Service Staff in England (UK Parliament 2020).

Care deficits, though global, can also be geographically concentrated. While producing a highly feminized labor export to meet global care demands, the Philippines experiences a "permanent" health crisis, especially in rural and crisis-prone areas. For example, attendance at births by skilled health personnel is a crucial determinant for preventing maternal deaths. This is due to the greater accessibility of emergency assistance in case pregnancy or birth-related complications arise (WHO 2015). The most conflict-affected areas in the Philippines are in the Bangsamoro region of Mindanao where ethnic and religious minority groups, the Moros and Lumads, reside. It is also the region in the Philippines most severely below the WHO's minimum threshold of medical or health personnel. The case of Mindanao underscores that those faced with the greatest need for addressing diseases and health emergencies are also those with the least access to health personnel and resources (see WHO 2017). There have been attempts by previous governments beginning in the 1990s to address these shortages especially within rural areas and at the *barangay* or *barrio* levels. Initiatives such as the "doctors to the barrios" (DTB) program were developed to encourage volunteers to temporarily relocate in these provinces at great personal costs including lower salaries and standard of living (Philippines Department of Health n.d.). DTB reflects measures chiefly reliant on mobilizing altruism and sacrifice among urban doctors which, on their own, are inadequate in the face of significant structural inequalities (Cabato 2016). Unsurprisingly, the DTB has not been a sustained initiative and care deficits continue to accumulate in the Philippines nationally and particularly in remote, rural, and crisis-affected areas.

Chronic shortages in care and health workers in the Philippines are occurring in tandem with worsening conditions for sexual and reproductive health because these processes share the same gendered structural and symbolic root causes. Female altruism and feminized sacrifice in the context of Philippine labor migration align with the interest of local Catholic religious fundamentalists in entrenching the cultural ideal of the "non-complaining and silenced Filipina" (Roces 2009: 272). The same discourses of female altruism are used by local Catholic religious actors to legitimize restrictions on women's bodily autonomy. Being compliant and subservient makes Filipino women not only ideal care workers overseas but also valued mothers, wives, and daughters in Philippine society. For a country that is regularly entangled in global and local care crises, the need to replenish basic access to health care, especially for women and girls, and ensure the sustainability of care economies seems obvious. Yet, it took more than 14 years for national legislation, the Responsible

CRISIS AND SEXUAL AND REPRODUCTIVE HEALTH [31]

Parenthood and Reproductive Health Act of 2012 (more popularly known as RH or RPRH Law), to be enacted.

The RH Law was passed as a result of several enabling political conditions notably that then President Benigno Aquino III considered it a legislative priority (see Chapter 4). However, the law still remains ineffective, as the state recognition of reproductive health has not been matched by actual allocation of state resources (Commission on Human Rights Philippines 2016). Local Catholic Church leaders and "pro-life" groups significantly continue to challenge SRHR reforms in the country on the basis that doing so runs counter to the "Filipino culture of life"—one that valorizes motherhood in society. It is this same valorization of maternal virtues and identities that enables the Philippines to keep its economic advantage and maintain the flow of remittances. The national economy is able to function on decades of care deficits because it has also been successful in reproducing and maintaining norms that render women at the service of the Philippine state and the global economy. This servicing, however, comes at the cost of their bodily autonomy. As a Filipino senator argued during the intense public debates over the RH Law in 2012, "our [Filipinos'] biggest export is OFWs [overseas Filipino workers]. That is export. That's why I'm against RH. What will improve our economy is the excess population that is used to accepting jobs that others don't want to handle" (as quoted in Macaraig 2012).

Globally, we can examine similar care debt spirals at different scales in relation to militarism. In times of crises, resources may be moved farther away from bridging health inequalities, which is an important part of peacebuilding. For example, health problems still continue to be intelligible as political concerns primarily when they directly threaten or endanger national and international stability such as through the spread of infectious diseases and bioterrorism (McInnes and Lee 2006; Nunes 2014). Egregious health inequalities that fundamentally impede individual self-determination remain politically and economically neglected (Nunes 2014: 957). Foreign aid allocations and public health expenditures have not increased to match rising health needs among vulnerable populations such as internally displaced peoples (IDPs). The World Health Organization notes that while for many countries there is a need to mobilize and effectively use domestic resources, "only an increased and predictable flow of donor funding will allow them to meet basic health needs in the short to medium term" (WHO 2012). The problem is not simply that we do not have the resources to address health needs, rather, it is about how resources are distributed and ideas of security that govern these decisions. As Petchesky argues, "in the reality of a world governed by neo-liberal capitalist regimes, sexual and reproductive health and rights and the right to the highest attainable standard of health care are entirely subject to resource availability and held hostage to inequitable patterns of resource distribution that belie the myths of scarcity" (2005: 303).

[32] *Politics of Sexual & Reproductive Health*

According to the military expenditure database compiled by the Stockholm International Peace Research Institute (SIPRI), countries worldwide spent a total of US$1,981 billion on militaries in 2020 (SIPRI 2021), the highest military spending since the Global Financial Crisis. Crucially, SIPRI also notes that military spending is growing at a faster rate than the world population (SIPRI 2020). In the crisis-prone region of Asia Pacific where protracted conflicts and severe environmental disasters routinely intersect, military spending across the region accounted for 27% of the global total for military expenditure at US$523 billion. The Asia Pacific has by far the largest growth in military spending compared to other regions in the world, with a 51% increase from 2010 to 2019. It remains the only region where military spending has continued uninterrupted and accelerated since 1989, or after the Cold War (SIPRI 2020).

The prioritization reflected by global resource allocation reinforces the already pervasive idea that security is chiefly dependent on militaries and that this security is *for* the state. Effective financing to build peace is still lacking such that "aid to fragile contexts is often for 'firefighting' rather than for long-term structural change" (OECD 2016: 26). The same pattern holds in response to economic crises wherein the default is to double down on the very ideas and institutions that have generated crisis in the first place. As Sell and Williams (2020: 12) point out, "deeply embedded beliefs in the primacy of economic growth over health and development persist and gain even more purchase in times of economic crises." Health and especially *women's* health become further invisible from the economic accounting of the conditions necessary for recovering states and the global economy. The primacy of so-called market fundamentalism manifests in the unfailing belief in "neoliberal conceptions of health" which effectively "colonizes and delimits ideological alternatives" (Sell and Williams 2020: 12). It is crucial therefore to analyze how global peace and security is being progressively "locked in" by a logic of depletion at each and every crisis. States can and have been able to operate on care deficits in the name of feminism, while harnessing women's bodies in the service of post-crisis recovery to their own bodily depletion.

CONCLUSION

Restrictions to sexual and reproductive health are at the heart of a global crisis of social reproduction. This crisis serves as a permanent background to wars, catastrophes, and upheavals. It also defines the terms of everyday life, especially for women and girls. Building on feminist scholarship that traces the internal logics of contemporary capitalism, I demonstrate how a particular neoliberal logic of depletion is manifested in bodily ways by the twin feminization of survival and sacrifice and the spiraling of care debts. While depletion, care crisis, and crisis of social reproduction have been analyzed primarily in relation to development and economic crises, and less so in wars and conflicts, I have shown in this chapter analytical tools employed in this book for examining their overlaps and continuities. If these crises are symptomatic of a broader logic that defines the global order today, then it is imperative that we draw on multiple feminist perspectives and traditions across global political economy and security. Indeed, feminist scholars working across different forms of crisis and insecurities have been concerned with how to overcome and transform the material and ideological root causes that render crises recurrent. They have long emphasized holistic models of peace and security, which continue to underpin this rich and continuously growing body of work even as transformative change remains elusive. Multi-perspectival feminist analysis has enabled me to show connections between the politics of women's health and well-being and the sustainability of social reproduction, as well as the material and ideological drivers that predispose societies and the world to gendered crises.

In the next chapters of this book, I trace the workings of depletion by examining women's health and well-being in relation to crises in the household, community, state, and global levels. I draw on the Philippine case to illustrate the sharp contradictions and pathologies emerging when national security is strongly tethered to valorizing female altruism and self-sacrifice while obscuring the bodily costs this security entails. At a time when multiple crises are occurring, stemming the feminization of survival and the corresponding intensified restrictions to women's bodily autonomy in the Philippines and globally will constitute a core feminist political and analytical project. My focus on the global politics of bodily autonomy is not so that health and well-being can be instrumentalized as a "renewable" resource for unfettered global economic growth and accelerated concentration of power and resources in crises. Studying it matters because it reveals to us how the global order operates, and by understanding this, we might have a chance at transforming it.

CHAPTER 2
The Household as a Site of Depletion

INTRODUCTION

To begin the analysis of sexual and reproductive health and rights (SRHR) in the household is unsurprising. After all, sexual and reproductive health is commonly understood in terms of *family planning*. Despite referring to a more expansive definition of bodily autonomy, SRHR is still prevalently interpreted to narrowly mean maternal and child health and responsible parenthood. Because the home has been the "natural" starting point for learning about rights of the body, it has also been much harder to reframe SRHR as *political* and not just private. Meanwhile, home life—and particularly the gendered distribution of social reproductive labor—continue to be routinely taken for granted in mainstream analyses of global peace and security. For instance, it remains far less common that the household, as a site of economic activity, is examined as enabling the conditions for violence as well as survival during and after crises. This invisibility of household social reproduction in security frameworks and approaches to address conflict situations, disasters, and humanitarian emergencies explains how and why macro-processes and structures that deny bodily autonomy are left unquestioned.

This chapter aims to show that SRHR issues are in fact deeply political by making visible how households materially shape and are shaped by processes of violence and peace. Moreover, in order to fully understand sexual and reproductive decision-making especially in crisis settings, we need to ground our analysis in the social reproduction crises of conflicts, disasters, and other emergencies. I show how this can be done by theorizing the household as a fundamental site of depletion for both social reproduction and the very bodies that ensure its continuation. First, the chapter examines how the household, as a unit of analysis, has been examined in feminist political economy and security studies literature. Synthesizing insights from these two main

---

The Global Politics of Sexual and Reproductive Health. Maria Tanyag, Oxford University Press.
© Oxford University Press 2024. DOI: 10.1093/oso/9780197676332.003.0003

bodies of feminist scholarship, I argue that women's social reproductive roles performed through and within the household not only serve an economic function but are also integral to conflict and disaster dynamics as well as to everyday experiences of peace. Second, drawing on empirical evidence in internally displaced and crisis-affected households in the Philippines, I examine how crises lead to intensified provisioning of unpaid care and domestic labor and why this intensification consequently entails bodily costs in the form of restrictions to sexual and reproductive health and other interrelated forms of gender-based violence. I argue that these costs are exacerbated during periods of crisis, because assumptions regarding the family as a safe haven and its various resources as constituting bottomless safety nets also intensify. Taken together, the intensification of bodily costs and harmful gendered assumptions regarding the home mutually reinforce material gaps in crisis response and recovery such that the daily survival of family units in times of crises disproportionately depletes women's health. Third, the chapter turns to examining how social reproductive labor can be resignified toward the replenishment of women's bodies. While the political economy of crisis-affected households enables processes of depletion, the household is also a foundational site for everyday peace and resistance.

WHY THE HOUSEHOLD? THEORIZING CRISES AND BODILY AUTONOMY IN INTERNATIONAL RELATIONS

Feminists have long theorized and empirically drawn the links showing how the domestic, private, daily, and intimate sphere of the family matters for global politics (Safri and Graham 2010; Mountz and Hyndman 2006; Marchand and Runyan 2010). In the discipline of International Relations, feminist scholarship has made a distinctive contribution by revealing the household as a unit of analysis for conceptualizing and exposing the many embodied yet overlooked dimensions of the global economy and security. It is analytically relevant for exposing how, what, and where global political and economic processes are fundamentally enabled and sustained by gender relations (Chin 1998; Safri and Graham 2010; Hoskyns and Rai 2007). Women's everyday lives constitute the very fabric of globalization and consequently distinctly bear its multiple and compounded costs.

The Global Household as Economic Shock Absorber

Feminist political economy analyses have shown that the household is a site of economic activity generating contributions that support macroeconomic processes. The impacts of economic crises are therefore always and immediately

[36] *Politics of Sexual & Reproductive Health*

felt at home. The global financial crisis (GFC) and the Asian financial crisis illustrate how economic crises are differently experienced by men and women especially in terms of intergenerational and long-term harms including in the area of gender-based violence, health care, trauma, and poverty (Elias 2016). Rather than serve as critical junctures for overhauling systemic failures in the global financial architecture, these crises were matched by economic policies of austerity and state retrenchment on social welfare services (Bello 1999; Elias 2016) thus, further hollowing out inflows to social reproduction at the household. And yet, women's bodies ultimately absorb macroeconomic shocks in performing daily care labor and in other coping mechanisms such as when this labor is outsourced or "passed on" to other female members of the family or women belonging to a lower socio-economic rank. Feminist scholars have argued that mapping the consequences of undervaluing unpaid household social reproduction is an important corrective to dominant representations of what counts as the cost of global economic transformations (Safri and Graham 2010; Ehrenreich and Hochschild 2003; Kunz 2010; Parreñas 2003; Elias and Roberts 2016). From a feminist perspective, the household functions as a "safety net" and is seen as a bottomless source of care and domestic labor during periods of global crisis and disruptions from the "everyday." However, the impacts of economic crises on social reproduction in the home may be rendered even more invisible or tacitly accepted because the home is assumed to naturally and sufficiently mitigate care demands despite the absence of state inflows to sustain care provisioning (Elson 2010, 2012, 2013).

It certainly may appear to be the case that the range of resources within the household are elastic in the case of "global households." Global households refer to the phenomena of transnational families whereby increasingly multiple and intergenerational migrant workers economically sustain geographically dispersed but intimately connected families and kinship networks (Safri and Graham 2010). For a remittance-driven country like the Philippines, overseas Filipino workers (OFWs) who are breadwinners to global households generate financial inflows which have remained broadly stable and typically account for around 9%–10% of national gross domestic product (Tuaño-Amador et al. 2022). Globally and in the Philippines, remittances have outranked foreign direct investments (FDI) and official development assistance (ODA), especially in fragile contexts (OECD 2016; Bayangos 2012; Nicolas 2012). OFW remittances, however, are not "crisis-proof" because Filipino migrant workers are highly vulnerable to repatriation and job loss when there are economic shocks. This vulnerability is shaped by the global economy where their labor tends to be considered "cheap" or representations of their being foreign make them dispensable and devalued.

Indeed, Spitzer and Piper (2014) observed that the 1997 Asian financial crisis resulted in the repatriation of OFWs and predominantly women migrant workers, but reintegration programs from the Philippine government were neither uniformly nor widely available. Assistance remained primarily stop-gap, and the economic emphasis on national labor export was unabated. With these shortfalls, repatriated migrants had to rely on family and extended kin for support. Differential access to state resources and varying levels of capacities to mobilize income and livelihood through familial lifelines led to unequal household recovery and intensified social reproductive demands. There is a mutually reinforcing cycle between repatriated OFWs who were subsequently unable to re-deploy and households that end up trapped in debt and poverty. It is necessary to have capital to invest in securing new overseas contract work within a highly bureaucratized process, which is difficult when household resources were low even before the crisis or if have been severely depleted in its aftermath. This demonstrates that economic hardships for many OFW families predated and lasted long after the immediate impacts of the Asian financial crisis. When the GFC occurred in 2008, many Filipino households, which were still in recovery a decade after the Asian financial crisis, had to then recalibrate household social reproduction in light of the new economic turmoil. Indeed, "[F]or many migrant workers and their families, these most recent shifts are among the other groundswells of economic and social crises that have made their lives more precarious in recent decades and which many feel will not abate in the near future" (Spitzer and Piper 2014: 1012).

Elias's (2016) analysis shows how economies—from crisis to stasis and back—are sustained by the interplay of material and cultural conditions (see also Elson 2010). For instance, material pressures on household social reproduction are complemented by a cultural and symbolic valorization of women's sacrifices in maintaining home life amid crises and of families coming together in mutual aid and entrepreneurship. Elias (2016) argues that discourses of "resilience" and "risks" deployed by state and international actors to describe the Asian financial crisis rested on gendered expectations that women, more than men, were socially responsible and possessed better understanding and prioritization of household needs. Representations of women's post-crisis economic resilience are not new but rather a continuation of national, regional, and global maneuvers to fashion women as drivers of economic growth enabled by a neoliberal shift from feminist emancipatory to a "business-case" model of gender equality (Calkin 2015; Elias 2016; Roberts 2015; Prügl and True 2014). In the case of the Asian financial crisis, it was also interpreted as an *Asian* crisis. This had the effect of overemphasizing the cultural role of crony capitalism despite the structural extent to which "it had emerged as a crisis within contemporary capitalism—'essentially a product of the globalisation of financial markets' (Bello 1998)" (Elias 2016: 111). The framing of the crisis as culturally rooted effectively directed attention away from the need to re-imagine global economic governance, while simultaneously fueling the heightened exploitation of social reproduction especially at the household level.

[38] *Politics of Sexual & Reproductive Health*

Global households continue to be a revelatory site of contradictory gendered outcomes driven by global economic policies. Women's status within global households offers a counterview of "globalization from below," challenging neoliberal economic logics that privilege economic growth and unfettered extraction despite economic upheavals, or even more so then (Marchand and Runyan 2010). While women are mobilized as a global labor force, this is insofar as a gendered and racialized division of labor is reproduced: women from the Global South face lower wages and segregated work in caring, service, hospitality, and "flexible" or temporary-contract sectors, in addition to typically receiving limited or no access to health care, especially for sexual and reproductive health. In turn, globalization has intensified a "feminization of survival," where the responsibilities and obligations women face are compounded by and through multiple shifts in undertaking caring labor, beginning at home and cascading on a global scale (Sassen 2000; Brickell and Chant 2010). The problem is structural, given how the simultaneous outsourcing of care services in the Global North is deepening care crises in labor-exporting countries in the Global South such as the Philippines.

A continued lack of accountability and economic reform at national and global levels is a cost of neglecting the household as an important site where political and economic authority is reproduced. By contrast, feminist analyses of economic crises "point to an alternative feminist understanding of 'risk' that places the social reproductive economy at its centre, demonstrating the way in which the existence of the socially reproductive economy *enables* the kinds of risky financial behaviours that trigger crises in the first place" (Elias 2016: 120). A template of crisis rhetoric and response recurs from different crises in that we continue to witness the "off-loading" of responsibilities at the household level disproportionately on women (Elson 2013: 193; Elias 2016). Moreover, gender inequalities in the finance sector foster a male-dominated and hypermasculine sphere of decision-making, which in turn underpins the privileging in macroeconomic policies of the idea that resumption of the formal and paid economy is *the* marker of post-crisis recovery. This idea has been taken as canon in part because of continued denial of the interdependence of production and reproduction, which a feminist political economy analysis of the household reveals.

The Home as a Conflict Front

The home features in feminist conflict and post-conflict analysis. Within this body of scholarship, the household is examined as an integral part of tracing the structural connections of gender relations with war, militarism, and political turmoil. It is where multiple forms of violence and insecurities occur in a continuum—from domestic violence to war and from global politics to the "everyday" (Cockburn 2004; Brickell 2012; True 2013). For example, crises related to war and militarism embody similar patterns of rhetoric and response to household-level social reproduction. The home is where geopolitics play out, particularly through the organization and instrumentalization of human life for the purposes of state-building, political transition, and anticolonial resistance (Chilmeran and Pratt 2019; Brickell 2012; Cockburn 2010; Yuval-Davis 1997). Macro-processes of security and their linkages with household dynamics reveal different ways that masculinities and femininities are harnessed in the service of state militarism and war-making (Enloe 1989/2000; Cockburn 2010).

As feminists have long pointed out, wars are gendered in that they draw on feminized duty or sacrifice such that part of being dutiful mothers, wives, and daughters is to ensure that the home is in support of the war front (Enloe 1989/2000; see also Elshtain 1987). The household, and especially the continued performance and imaginaries of home-making, have played a role in legitimizing wars and the ways in which national identity is built through the home (Elshtain 1987; Yuval-Davis 1997). The obvious connection to sexual and reproductive health is in the biological reproduction of soldiers. Filipina poet Grace Monte de Ramos (2003) sums it up in this excerpt:

> I cannot cry, though I am told
> It is better to cry and let go. Where is my son's body for me to bury?
> I only wear my grief in the lines
> Of my face, my sunken cheeks. Silent, I mourn a woman's
> Bitter lot: to give birth to men
> Who kill and are killed.

Literature on women's participation in violence, terrorism, resistance, and rebellion document how agency is framed in troubling tropes of "mothers, monsters and whores" (Sjoberg and Gentry 2007, 2015; Hilsdon 1995). Sjoberg and Gentry (2007) draw on a diverse range of cases to demonstrate how maternalism—whether its fulfillment, dysfunction, or deviance—is a crucial theme in linking gender and global violence (see also Sjoberg and Gentry 2015). Women participate in perpetrating violence as nurturers and enablers of the violence perpetrated by men in their families. Representations of women's agency are often tied to motherhood or underpinned by essentialist notions of "maternal instincts." That is, their motivations for violence are "limited to decisions about their femininity and maternity—taking care of or avenging their men." In effect, violence is virtuous because it is for "avenging lost love and/or a destroyed happy home" (Sjoberg and Gentry 2015: 72). Such narrow representations evoke how the household is part of defining the extent of violence and limits to caring practices. The disposable *others* are those who do not and cannot belong to one's household and as such, are undeserving of care.

[40] *Politics of Sexual & Reproductive Health*

Women's participation in violence, in other cases, is viewed as a perversion of femininity (Sjoberg and Gentry 2007, 2015). As *monsters* and *whores*, violent women are cast as *outside* of or an aberration of cultural and religious ideals of the household and family. Within such frames, cultural and religious ideology have historically informed definitions of sexual virtue—from chastity to sex for procreation only and not pleasure—with the fulfillment of women's place within the household. Ultimately, the yoking of some women's violence with sexual depravity serves to undermine *all* women's bodily autonomy and well-being because it forecloses sexuality as part of healthy, dignified, and fulfilling lives. While feminist analysis has shown how the "whore" archetype has been used to narrowly characterize why women commit acts of violence, the analysis has yet to be explicitly connected with the very same material and ideological factors that are also complicit in denying bodily autonomy globally.

The household—and particularly women through the gendered division of labor—is part of the *material* reproduction of violence and militarism (Enloe 2000; Hedstrom 2017; Basham and Catignani 2018). Care, domestic, and emotional labor largely performed by women enables the labor of soldiers. "'[H]ome and hearth' is, therefore, a significant site *from* where war materialises" (Basham and Catignani 2018: 155). Yet, outside feminist scholarship, the costs of daily provisioning social reproductive labor in conflict settings and how these are disproportionately borne by women continues to be unaccounted for, thus severing the household from broader and prevailing political economy analysis of armed conflicts and/or military power. This results in an underestimation of the analytical and material relevance of the household in understanding contemporary global political economy and security—especially in making visible how economic processes interconnect with processes of violence and insecurity. Additionally, thus far, feminist scholarship in peace and security has examined conflicts and disasters separately and much less as *social reproduction crises* that compound the depletion of women's health and bodily autonomy.

Social reproduction conceptually bridges global issues of economy, security, and health. For example, Marchand and Runyan (2010: 248) draw out connections more explicitly, stating that "this [global] financial crisis is in some sense, like the 'war on terror,' unending to the degree that it further affirms financial authority with greater levels of impunity for financial harms." Robinson (2011: 59) makes a similar argument noting that care labor serves as the "permanent background to the 'heavyweight' moral and political issues related to globalization of human rights and human security." As a permanent background, the cost of doing social reproduction has been analytically taken for granted or even undermined in the study of global security; and yet "[t]he widely recognized aspects of human security . . . cannot be realized in the absence of robust, equitable, well-resourced relations and networks of care at the household, community, state, and transnational levels." Viewed in this way, it is from the healthy provisioning of social reproductive labor within the household that peace materializes in the day to day. This book seeks to re-dress these forms of oversight, beginning with this chapter, by demonstrating how the depletion of social reproduction at the household level is mutually constitutive of and integral to reproducing the global economy and its sys-temic crises. Furthermore, the material and cultural or ideological drivers that shape gendered outcomes and processes, and especially sexual and reproduc-tive health within crisis-affected households, are also increasingly driving the sources of macroeconomic and political insecurities globally.

CRISIS-AFFECTED HOUSEHOLDS IN INTERNAL DISPLACEMENTS

Globally, internal displacements are defining the conditions and constraints on household social reproduction for millions of people. In the Philippines, millions of Filipinos are routinely internally displaced by cyclical, intermit-tent, and protracted conflicts. Frequently, people who have been displaced by conflicts are simultaneously or consecutively exposed to environmental disasters such as typhoons, flooding, and drought. Displacement in two main regions of this research—Mindanao and Visayas—is experienced more in-tensely because any plans or gains toward resettlement, return, and recovery are thwarted by the multiple crises that have long characterized the human security landscape in the Philippines. I use the term crisis-affected house-holds to refer to households that span across and beyond internal displace-ment sites and consist of both immediate family and relatives impacted by displacements and extended transnational kinship networks including over-seas migrant workers. Crisis-affected households bring together internal displacements in the Philippines and labor migration to reveal the broader global processes of expulsions and their relationship with household-level de-pletion (Sassen 2014). Drawing on these case studies, I show how crises (re) configure the form and function of the household and how such reconfigura-tions are profoundly embodied whereby daily household survival is at the cost of depleting women's health and well-being.

Armed conflicts in Mindanao have disproportionately affected households and communities belonging to Moro minority ethnic groups for more than 40 years since the Moro separatist insurgency began in the 1970s. According to the Uppsala Conflict Data Program (UCDP) database, the Philippines has several ongoing conflicts involving intra-state, non-state, and one-sided vi-olence, the majority of which have occurred and are occurring in Mindanao.[1] In the Bangsamoro region of Mindanao, clan feuds and community-related violence called *rido* are prone to morph into different forms of non-state and intra-state conflicts (International Alert 2014: 28; see also Torres 2014).[2] The concept of "conflict strings" has been used to describe this process and draw

[42] *Politics of Sexual & Reproductive Health*

attention to how armed conflicts in the region are multi-causal and involve multiple warring parties. Conflicts can be triggered simultaneously by disputes over land, political rivalry, and/or competition over economic resources. They may constitute violence perpetrated by state forces, separatist rebels, or private armies. However, these different conflicts largely involve and/or emanate from clan dynamics in the region (International Alert 2014). Conflict strings highlight how insecurity in Mindanao can be intractable because of the way different types of conflict can simultaneously occur, interact, and exacerbate one another.

Families directly located in areas where conflict strings occur are faced with the prospect of either being forcibly and permanently displaced from their homes or remaining in place and risking exposure to further violence. Displaced families may seek refuge with host relatives or extended kin offering shelter away from the conflict, where they may eventually resettle (Kok 2015). Those who do not have such ties are displaced in camps and/or transitional sites as "internally displaced persons" (IDP) (see Figure 2.1). In some cases, families no longer have homes to return to, as these have been burned down by the military or rebel groups (IDMC 2015b; CEDAW 2004). When families cannot easily return home, they are likely to be trapped in a prolonged state of displacement, directly undermining their well-being and limiting their long-term prospects for peace. It is through prolonged displacement in camps with

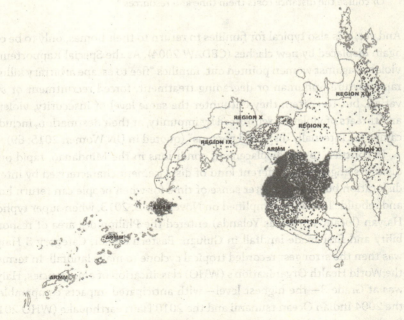

Figure 2.1. Geographic distribution of IDPs in Mindanao
Source: UNHCR and Mindanao Protection Cluster (2015: 2)

THE HOUSEHOLD AS A SITE OF DEPLETION [43]

poor health, water, and sanitation facilities that IDPs are exposed to abuse, exploitation, disease, and death (Kok 2015). Families indefinitely contend with, among other issues, inadequate shelter or overcrowding in camps, food shortages, lack of access to clean water, sanitation, and hygiene facilities, and a range of protection issues including sexual and gender-based violence (SGBV) perpetrated by armed groups against IDP families, or violence among IDPs themselves (IDMC 2009). For instance, as part of the Philippines protection cluster, the United Nations Office for the Coordination of Humanitarian Affairs (OCHA) documented hundreds of infants and children that have become ill and/or eventually died due to the harsh living conditions in the camps (see OCHA 2014, 2015b).

Due to similar or worse threats to life in the IDP camps and transitional sites, some families make the difficult decision to return to their original home. Indeed, in a survey conducted among IDPs in Zamboanga, 92% of the 699 respondents overwhelmingly expressed a preference to return home compared to relocating to other places or remaining longer in the camps (Nisa Ul Haqq Fi Bangsamoro 2014). As one informant who has worked with IDPs in Zamboanga reported:

> Now they are being made to relocate to transitory sites. The women do not want this because it will be further away from their homes. It will be difficult for kids to go to school and they usually just walk so this brings greater danger for them. Of course the distance costs them time and resources.[3]

And yet, it is also typical for families to return to their homes, only to be once again displaced by new clashes (CEDAW 2004). As the Special Rapporteur on violence against women pointed out, families "flee to escape arbitrary killings, rape, torture, inhuman or degrading treatment, forced recruitment or starvation, but too often, they encounter the same level of insecurity, violence, and threats of violence, reinforced by impunity, at their destination, including camps for internally displaced persons" (quoted in UN Women 2015: 69).

In contrast to the displacement conditions in the Mindanao, rapid onset disasters engender a different kind of displacement characterized by intense dislocation but with a clearer sense of time for when people can return home and rebuild. This was exemplified on November 8, 2013, when super typhoon Haiyan (locally known as Yolanda) entered the Philippines area of responsibility and first made landfall in Guiuan, Eastern Samar. Category 5 Haiyan was then the strongest recorded tropical cyclone to make landfall. In terms of the World Health Organization's (WHO) classification of emergencies, Haiyan was at Grade 3—the highest level—with anticipated impacts comparable to the 2004 Indian Ocean tsunami and the 2010 Haiti earthquake (WHO 2013). By the next day, Haiyan devastated the entire Visayas region of the Philippines

[44] *Politics of Sexual & Reproductive Health*

and directly affected 14 million people, or more than 10% of the country's population. The disaster resulted in approximately 6,300 reported deaths, 1,785 missing bodies, and at least 4 million IDPs (Novales 2014; OPARR 2014; Oxfam 2015).

Among the provinces severely affected were Cebu, Leyte, Southern Leyte, Western Samar, and Eastern Samar. In these localities, up to 90% of housing and infrastructure were damaged while the whole coast of Leyte was wiped out (OCHA 2013; Novales 2014). Tacloban, a city within Leyte, was among the most severely impacted by the calamity and served as one of the main hubs from where the disaster response was coordinated. It was reported that a significant population of IDPs were able to stay with either host families or extended kin outside Leyte and Samar. Others promptly returned to their original lands even in the absence of safe shelter, risks to physical security, and vulnerability to future weather hazards (Sherwood et al. 2015; IOM et al. 2014). Among Typhoon Haiyan survivors, there was a strong preference to be in familiar and *familial* sites of displacement rather than remain in evacuation camps where people felt more insecure due to locally known protection issues in bunkhouses and "tent cities" at the time (IOM et al. 2014: 14).

Rapid onset disaster-induced displacements can be distinguished from those due to armed conflicts. By and large, disasters like Typhoon Haiyan are seen as having relatively clearer beginnings and an end (at least until the next disaster happens). People could at least see when a storm is brewing which they are less able to do when conflicts will erupt. As one informant pointed out:

> One cannot simply return home when home has already been rendered unlive-able. Conflict is more heartless, with calamities you can still bounce back and return to homes. This is because the early warning system is more effective in disaster.[4]

In general, a greater proportion of households impacted by disaster-induced displacements were able to resume normality, however slow the process was, compared to those affected by conflicts in Mindanao, many of whom still live in constant fear of being displaced because the region remains politically fragile and violent conflicts continue to intermittently occur. This dynamic is perhaps best captured by how humanitarian responders have referred to conflict displacements in Zamboanga as a "forgotten crisis" after Haiyan occurred (OCHA 2014, 2015a).

Crisis competition is increasingly the structural context within which displaced households are (re)configuring everyday life in the Philippines. Different types of displacements routinely occur and compete for resources and political attention in the country. Consequently, understanding these differences is important to developing a nuanced account of the relationship between SRHR and household depletion especially in times of crisis. As the UN Special Rapporteur Chaloka Beyani (2015) concluded after visiting displacement camps in both Mindanao and Visayas:

> Indeed it was evident to me that the Government's response to conflict-induced displacement in locations such as Zamboanga and Cotabato differs significantly to its commendable response to disaster and climate change induced displacement elsewhere as evident in the condition of some of the transitional and permanent shelter options provided to IDPs.

This high-level statement alerts us to the impacts of crisis competition in generating variegated social reproduction outcomes across different displacement sites such that one episodic disaster resulting in a massive death toll can rally national and global attention compared to low-intensity, protracted conflicts where casualties are spread out thinly but over an extended period of time (see Davies, True, and Tanyag 2016: 465). Moreover, seasonal conflicts and violent disasters are enmeshed in other social reproduction crises in the Philippines. State capacity to address local conflicts and disasters, from the lens of social reproduction and bodily autonomy, are in a continuum with state capacity and responses to regional and global economic shocks. Policies of further state retrenchment on social welfare provisioning and heightened militarism at every crisis will lead to intensified reliance on social reproduction among households already struggling with their own safety nets.

INTENSIFIED SOCIAL REPRODUCTIVE LABOR IN CONFLICT AND DISASTER SETTINGS

Crises are embodied in gendered ways, and this is most visible in the gendered labor that ensures the continuity of daily household functions. The maintenance of social reproduction is what makes a home amid displacements and devastations from conflicts and disasters. Gendered divisions of labor mean that the responsibility of making life as normal as possible falls heavily on women. In Mindanao, while men represent a greater proportion of battle-related deaths, women distinctly experience the long-term harm of conflicts in addition to immediate impacts such as death and displacement. These long-term harms emanate from their daily care of and domestic work routines for the family, while also often taking on more conflict-related responsibilities and facing pressures from cultural expectations of self-sacrifice. Moro women have reported that care and domestic work is made more onerous as a result of displacement. As one female informant reported, the basic act of food provisioning, such as preparing and cooking meals, is made more difficult in evacuation camps where everything is makeshift.[5] In response to crisis situations,

[46] *Politics of Sexual & Reproductive Health*

household responsibilities may be reallocated but without necessarily altering underlying expectations. For example, evidence from the Philippines indicates that any changes in the household allocation of responsibilities, such as men doing childcare or cooking, tend to be short-lived and that "normality" manifests in re-establishing, if not further entrenching, care and domestic labor as women's jobs.

Surveys on Moro women in displacement indicate that "women overwhelmingly tended to view their economic contributions during conflict less as examples of empowerment and more as an exhausting strain" (Dwyer and Cagoco-Guiam 2012: 13). For example, based on a survey conducted by the Mindanao Working Group for Reproductive Health, Gender, and Sexuality (Cabaraban 2006), women reported that men as husbands, whether before or during conflict, were expected to and did most of the productive labor for the family such as "earning a living" and "obtaining food." Meanwhile, women as wives were found to be in charge of reproductive tasks such as cooking and doing the laundry (Cabaraban 2006: 101). However, certain types of conflict such as clan feuds lead to restricted mobility for men because they are targeted in revenge killings or, in the case of insurgencies, they are more likely to be suspected as combatants and subjected to forced recruitment (Dwyer and Cagoco-Guiam 2012: 10). In such circumstances, men are unable to earn income because they are forced into hiding. When men cannot fulfill their household duties as the provider or breadwinner of the family, women step in and undertake both productive and reproductive labor under precarious conditions. Moro women engage in different informal economic activities to ensure that their families survive displacement. They typically borrow money from various sources including relatives, loan sharks, and the government. In addition, they are more likely the ones who solicit and/or queue for food and relief assistance (Cabaraban 2006; Dwyer and Cagoco-Guiam 2012). Women have to routinely deal with and "improvise" sub-standard living conditions as they attempt to continue with their familial duties. That is, "care work responsibilities increase in times of conflict . . . *Babae ang dumi-diskarte* [it is the women who find ways]."[6]

Moro women provide care and domestic work for armed men for both Moro rebel groups and the military (IBON Foundation 2006). Many women, especially in areas where the military transits, were reported to have been routinely underpaid for goods they sold and forced to cook meals for soldiers (IBON Foundation 2006; Cabaraban 2006). Military presence contributes to heightened insecurity, particularly for women and girls, and in some cases the insecurity is linked with an exacerbation of their social reproductive labor burdens. Women's acquiescence to rendering services for the military is a way in which they prevent further violence and insecurity being inflicted on their families and community. Through the Bangsamoro Islamic Women Auxiliary Brigade (BIWAB), women support male Moro rebels and the rebellion more broadly by providing care and domestic work including medical assistance. Officially, BIWAB members "bear no firearms but they have been trained to use them in case the situation calls for it" (Sarmiento 2012).

BIWAB women support rebels, who are very likely related to them by blood or kinship networks, in addition to performing expected household duties for their own families. Supporting the rebellion in this regard keeps them in a subordinate status, separate from the "real" soldiers, because their involvement is but an extension of their duties as mothers, wives, sisters, and daughters. When women directly take part in armed conflicts as combatants, this may be regarded as undermining the masculine identities of Moro men as protectors (see Chapter 4 for further discussion). For instance, the "reversal" of gender roles within the household as a consequence of conflict is still dismissed by some Moro men as "like water going upstream" (Institute of Bangsamoro Studies and the Centre for Humanitarian Dialogue 2011: 26). As the metaphor suggests, the gendered division in the household obeys a natural order that remains unperturbed even in conflict situations because such order is understood as stemming from biological differences between men and women.

In the case of disaster-induced displacements, the unpaid care work disproportionately performed by women and girls also served as the backbone for survival at the household level. Studies reported that men suffered higher mortality rates during Typhoon Haiyan as they were more likely to have stayed behind in order to guard their homes or to protect family possessions (Novales 2014; Ching et al. 2015). Post-Haiyan, boys were more likely to have stopped schooling to help fathers in farming or fishing, although this was noted to have been fairly common among impoverished families even prior to the disaster (Novales 2014: 36). Based on qualitative interviews conducted by Mangada (2016: 97) among 15 women survivors from Tacloban City, "[I]n Tacloban City, like any other locale in the country, women do not think solely of their needs. . . Prior to Haiyan, the informants juggled household duties and the occasional job to earn and contribute to their family income and welfare. Super Typhoon Haiyan did not alter these responsibilities—instead, it exacerbated and accentuated their pre-existing vulnerabilities." Women also contributed through religious work to help facilitate spiritual healing and psychosocial recovery of their communities (see Figure 2.2).

Men and boys were primarily confined to performing productive labor and any reconfiguration of the division of labor at the household level proved only temporary or short-term (Novales 2014: 31; Mangada 2016: 97). Another survey found that "11.4% of households were identified as female singleheaded households, and that 36% of households included one or several persons with specific needs (pregnant or lactating women, persons living with a physical disability; members who were seriously ill or with special needs; persons living with a chronic illness; and separated children)" (IOM et al. 2014: 19). In addition, of the estimated 4 million people displaced by Typhoon

[48] *Politics of Sexual & Reproductive Health*

Figure 2.2. Women on a religious procession in the aftermath of Typhoon Haiyan
Source: Photo by Philippe Lopez, Agence France-Presse

Haiyan, 1.7 million were children (IOM et al. 2014: 11). This means that for women who are primary caregivers in a context of extreme disaster, not only were their care obligations distinct due to living in makeshift and insecure shelters, but the demands on them were compounded by multiple specific care needs of the elderly, the young, and infirm, all while having to contend with their own personal trauma.

Female-Headed Households in Conflicts and Disasters

Conflicts and disasters place in sharper focus the intensification of social reproductive labor within female-headed households, which are prevalent in conflict-affected areas of Mindanao where the majority of IDPs are women and children (IDMC 2015b). In the two case studies in the Philippines, deaths in times of conflicts and disasters mirrored the cost of the gendered division of labor: men were more likely to die in battle-related deaths or in protecting land and property from floods, activities that conform to masculine ideals of patriarch protector and breadwinner. However, these ideals persist long after the death of men in crisis-affected households with the burden of living up to them merely being displaced onto women. Even in the presence of pre-existing strong kinship networks, protracted conflicts and routine large-scale disasters in the Philippines mean that these usual safety nets of aid from extended and transnational families may not always be available or are eventually depleted.

This occurs either because other relatives contend with the same pressures to survive or whole clans and communities have suffered the loss of male breadwinners.

Families hosting displaced kin in their own homes experience secondary impacts even if they do not experience conflict or disaster directly. For instance, host families have to deal with food shortages and the sudden lack of privacy within their own homes. As pointed out by an informant, the relatives of IDPs in a way end up being displaced within their own homes too:

> Displacement goes beyond the evacuation centers. Many actually prefer to move in to their relatives instead of staying in camps because it is at least safer to stay at relatives' houses. Sure for a short period of time, the relatives might share their resources to accommodate displaced kin. But what if they are also very poor and live in a small house as is the usual case?[7]

Because displacement to host relatives is harder to identify and remains poorly monitored, such households are effectively excluded from conflict or disaster relief assistance by state and international humanitarian organizations (see IDMC 2015b). Hence, female-headed households do not have a bottomless pit of familial ties upon which to draw. For Moros with a high-regard for clan pride, the failure of host relatives to adequately take care of displaced kin, because of their own poverty, leads to the emotional strain of "losing face" (see also Busran-Lao 2005: 38). These conditions intensify self-sacrificing practices, particularly among Moro women, even in households not directly impacted by conflicts. Commonly, as Moro women reported, "we're used to this. If food is lacking, we don't mind being hungry as long as the children can eat" (focus group discussion (FGD) participants, quoted in Magcalen-Fernandez 2006: 29). These socio-cultural and economic dynamics influence the limits of help-seeking behavior among women who suddenly find themselves both sole caregiver and sole provider for their families.

Post-Haiyan reports also indicated the heightened vulnerability of women to intensified reproductive burdens. As corroborated by one informant, "after the storm, there was an increase of widows. Female-headed households suffer most in the bunk houses and in the disaster context more broadly. They have multiple burdens for care work and survival."[8] The absence of a "male protector" severely constrains women's mobility in accessing relief and economic opportunities for post-disaster rehabilitation, thus compounding an already intensified mode of social reproduction (Novales 2014; Mangada 2016). Economic desperation pushes women and girls as mothers, wives, and daughters to undertake negative coping mechanisms through "selling" their bodies in exchange for relief goods or money to buy those goods on the black market. This practice, allegedly fairly common, is locally known as *palit bigas* which literally translates to "in exchange for rice."[9] The trade of sex in conflict areas such as Zamboanga and

[50]   *Politics of Sexual & Reproductive Health*

Cotabato IDP camps reportedly thrived within weeks of communities being displaced there due to scarcity and the inequitable distribution of local and foreign humanitarian relief assistance. Many women, girls, and boys as young as ten years old were reported to have engaged in prostitution.[10]

Female-headed households are also faced with heightened and multiple risks to their physical security while in IDP camps. In the absence of a male protector or provider, women and girls belonging to such households are disproportionately vulnerable to being targeted by various armed as well as unarmed men in the IDP camps. As a United Nations Population Fund (UNFPA) program coordinator pointed out, "the economic consequences of losing the family breadwinner are compounded by the fear of vendetta and 'rido' or 'clan war,' whose victims include women and children" (*New Humanitarian* 2008). Indeed, a majority of the informants confirmed the prevalence of intimidation and heightened risk for sexual violence in IDP camps, especially when women have to travel to obtain food and water and when they are accessing toilet facilities. Furthermore, as the country representative of an international organization argued, "[E]ven in food distribution . . . women especially in female-headed households are at a disadvantage because in order to queue for relief someone else must be with the children."[11] The children left behind by a mother who travels to collect food rations are vulnerable to being targeted for SGBV. The same vulnerabilities were observed in disaster-induced displacements. According to an informant:

> Among the usual complaints of women in bunkhouses is that they are violated by voyeurs [mamboboso] or *nabobosohan* because the common toilet and shower areas are made of weak material that a cigarette can easily burn a hole through. So either they take a bath with husbands guarding them, or for single women and girls they shower quickly.[12]

Examples of everyday forms of insecurity in displacement sites are often framed as *infrastructural* problems and addressed as such. However, they are indicative as well of *structural* or pre-existing gendered hierarchies that normalize women and girls as available targets for such sexual violence. That is, when women and girls are expected to face sexual violence in toilet and bathing facilities, this reinforces an unwritten rule that they need to have their husbands or "male protectors" guarding them in the first place, which female-headed households may not necessarily have. They are targeted precisely because it is accepted that women and young girls are obedient—they will not disturb the "peace" and will uphold family honor. For example, even when women experience violence in evacuation camps, "in the case of married women, they would rather keep the incident to themselves than tell their husbands to manage stressors in the family or to lessen or avoid conflict in the community."[13]

Men's use of physical violence was linked with their inability to fulfill their breadwinner roles at a time of financial loss. According to a male informant from an international development non-governmental organization (NGO), "the rise in VAW [violence against women] after the [Haiyan] disaster is caused by the economic strain many families are experiencing."[14] A female informant affirmed that "domestic violence is usually triggered by marital rape, verbal abuse, financial problems."[15] At the same time, as one informant observed:

> [D]omestic violence has also been triggered by the sudden availability and fre-
> quency of gender programs which involve organizing women into attending
> seminars. The usual story goes that because the wife has been out all day attend-
> ing different "gender seminars," she did not have enough time to still do the
> household duties her husband expected she would do. The husband has been
> tired all day earning cash for work in the cleaning up of debris only to come
> home to find the wife has not cooked rice! So the husband gets mad, the wife
> fights back and the beating ensues.[16]

Domestic violence by men arises when women and girls fail to meet their care and domestic work obligations. In such cases, violence is deliberately used to exert control over women's domesticity, thus reinforcing the same gendered household ideals that men themselves were unable to fulfill due to the crisis.

Paying attention to these invisible costs to social reproduction in times of crisis is crucial for ensuring recognition of, and redress for, the gendered strategies women and girls deploy in order to keep a very fragile peace in their homes. This peace, although tentative, has been a necessary condition for constituting a normal home life amid so much disruption, even as such strategies also expose them to further violence.

FEMALE ALTRUISM AS A CULTURAL BASIS OF HOUSEHOLD DEPLETION

Among displacement sites in the Philippines, conflicts and disasters have exacerbated and multiplied women's household and caring responsibilities, and yet, these were matched by restrictions on sexual and reproductive health. In both conflict and disaster case studies, women and girls reportedly did not feel entitled to care for their own sexual and reproductive health. Neglecting one's health and other self-sacrificing practices were justified in relation to prevailing cultural and religious beliefs around female altruism and were exacerbated by pre-existing barriers to accessing sexual and reproductive health information, services, and supplies among IDPs. Local norms of self-sacrifice, while typically expected among Filipino women, were regarded as even more

[52] *Politics of Sexual & Reproductive Health*

appropriate because of intensified domestic responsibilities in displacement sites. That is, the greater the sacrifice, the more virtuous the woman.

At its most basic, self-sacrifice for women and girls occurs in the context of personal hygiene and self-care. Various Moro women reported that beauty through maintaining physical appearance is a luxury they as IDPs can no longer afford (Magcalen-Fernandez 2006). Even in "normal" circumstances, when a woman takes time to take care of herself, she risks being deemed a "bad woman" because self-care may be interpreted as putting her needs first before and above her family, thus representing time away from her primary obligation as a care*giver*. Especially in displacement sites, these expectations intensify for women and girls such that even maintaining one's physical appearance is regarded as inappropriate, irrelevant, or even capricious. Moreover, basic hygiene, which supposedly makes a woman's beauty more apparent, can also expose her to a range of SGBV such as rape and bride abduction. In Basilan, Sulu, and Tawi-Tawi, a Moro woman leader reported that women and girls vicariously fear for their appearance in the context of bride abduction by armed men (also in Magcalen-Fernandez 2006). And yet, for many Moro families routinely displaced by strings of armed conflicts, there is little time to recover and even less time for women to attend to their own health and well-being.

Prohibitive cultural norms and beliefs about self-care among IDP women and girls are exacerbated by the material conditions in camps and transitional sites that render them disproportionately prone to sexual and reproductive health complications. For example, in the case of Mindanao, one of the most commonly cited health problems is urinary tract infections (Cabaraban 2006; Daguino and Gomez 2010). The rise in these infections among IDP women and girls is attributed to their inability to urinate properly and in clean and sanitary conditions. In some cases, women reported that they end up with such intensified care and domestic work in IDP camps that they "forget" to urinate. Fear of conflict suddenly breaking out, and/or the threat of sexual violence as they travel to camp toilet facilities, resulted in women and girls restricting the frequency of their urination (Amoyen and Diaz 2010; Daguino and Gomez 2010). One Moro woman recounted, "I had to hold my bladder because I was afraid to go out of our tent in evacuation area, especially at night time just to urinate" (42-year-old, female IDP, quoted in Daguino and Gomez 2010: 38). The absence of clean and sanitary conditions specifically in the camp toilet facilities means that IDPs end up washing themselves in contaminated water or not at all.

In many parts of the world and not just in Mindanao, women's restricted access to sexual and reproductive health treatment in times of crisis is compounded by pre-existing sexual myths, including the idea that having any form of health "problem" in a woman's vaginal area means she is or has been "unclean" and promiscuous. A woman from Basilan narrated her experience in displacement:

THE HOUSEHOLD AS A SITE OF DEPLETION [53]

> I am embarrassed to tell you this, *Indah*, but . . . "mine" was itching terribly and it was already sore from my scratching. What I did was to pour [disinfectant] alcohol on it but it was so painful! Maybe it's because during those days, I wasn't able to wash well because there is very little water and we were on the run. As Muslim women, we have to wash our private part.
>
> Asked why she did not go to the doctor for consultation, the woman exclaimed, Ay, it's so embarrassing! The doctor might think that I am a bad woman. (Female FGD participant, quoted in Magcalen-Fernandez 2006: 25)

This woman's experience highlights how reproductive health was undermined both by the lack of clean water and the fear that seeking medical attention might bring shame to herself or her family and clan (Magcalen-Fernandez 2006). Moro IDPs were often faced with choosing between not practicing religious ablutions or using unclean water and compounding the health costs of displacement. Women and girls therefore face both religious and cultural pressures that push them to sacrifice their sexual and reproductive health.

While the health of both men and women are affected in internal displacements, women experience harm distinctly due to their reproductive needs during menstruation and pregnancy. Indeed, high rates of pregnancy-related complications among Moro women are directly attributed to armed conflicts in Mindanao. In March 2015, there were an estimated 695 pregnant and 595 lactating women in evacuation centers and transitional sites in Zamboanga (OCHA 2015c). Women were reported to have given birth or experienced miscarriages while fleeing from violence. Frequent eruption of conflicts, especially in acute areas of the Bangsamoro region, may also lead to decreased mobility among populations for fear of being caught in the crossfire. This adversely constrains women's access to antenatal and postnatal care, which requires regular and timely access to health care, if available (see also Bosmans et al. 2008). In addition, the emotional, physical, and psychological stressors in IDP camps contribute to and exacerbate pregnant women's suffering of stillbirths, premature births, and miscarriages. Finally, childbirth in the IDP camps can have a traumatizing effect on women. What would normally be a joyous and beautiful family moment can turn into something fearful and degrading. For example, one woman reported that, "It was difficult to give birth inside the tent. It was very cold. Many people were looking at me and I felt helpless and ashamed but could not do anything but suffer in silence" (28-year-old, female IDP, quoted in Daguino and Gomez 2010: 28).

In the post-disaster case, the distinctly gendered consequence of calamities is such that "pregnancies don't wait for debris to be cleared and for livelihoods to be restored" (UNFPA Executive Director, quoted in Novales 2014: 25). According to UNFPA (2015: 43), "250,000 women were pregnant when Typhoon Haiyan hit in November 2013 and approximately 70,000 were due in the first quarter of 2014." Many women—estimated at 900 per day—gave birth in evacuation camps and transitional sites without privacy and skilled birth attendants, thus compounding their maternal mortality risk as well as contributing to trauma (Valerio 2014). Kristine Valerio (2014: 151), who served as a gender-based violence coordinator in Tacloban and was part of the team deployed in Haiyan-affected areas, pointed out that "while these women survived Haiyan, it was a challenge for them to survive the difficulties caused by pregnancy-related complications and trouble in lactation." Women's reproductive or biological needs and their distinct positioning in society blur the artificial distinctions between emergency and rehabilitation phases of disasters.

Another example is the pronounced increase in adolescent pregnancies in Haiyan-affected areas, which has led to a so-called "post-disaster baby boom" (WHO 2014b). Various sources corroborate this drastic increase in adolescent pregnancies in Eastern Visayas and especially in Tacloban after the super typhoon (Gabieta 2015; Rivera 2015). For example, it was reported that "at the Eastern Visayas Regional Medical Center, the region's biggest government-owned facility, the number of childbirths has almost doubled from an average of ten a day. Almost half of the mothers are young women, according to a hospital staff member, and the youngest is 14 years old" (Gabieta 2015). The "baby boom" is associated with several disaster-related factors that underscore the importance of recognizing adolescent sexual and reproductive health before, during, and after a crisis. According to a female city population officer:

> For every calamity there is always a "baby boom" afterwards. The overall mindset for the many actors and the affected communities is that survival came in first. The safety of youth was the least priority especially when you look at the bunk houses. Seeking comfort through physical or sexual activity ensued.[17]

A male representative for an international NGO stated that:

> After the storm, we have seen a high increase in teenage pregnancy for the whole region. Even before the storm, teenage pregnancy and marrying young as a consequence of teenage pregnancy are common. This helps situate how there are a lot of female headed households in the bunk houses which are below 18 years old.[18]

The Haiyan disaster exacerbated the existing high rates of adolescent pregnancies in Eastern Visayas as well as in the Philippines—among the highest prevalence compared to regional neighbors in Southeast Asia (Rivera 2015; Demographic Research and Development Foundation 2014; *New Humanitarian* 2012). Another informant pointed out that a lack of access to SRHR during emergencies breeds interrelated long-term harms such that, "after the storm, the risk and incidence of HIV/AIDS and STDs (sexually transmitted diseases) are on the rise. Teenage pregnancy is also on the rise."[19] This example clearly illustrates how care and health needs can exponentially increase when access to sexual and reproductive health care is severely curtailed.

Finally, that this post-disaster "baby boom" in Eastern Visayas occurred in the face of heightened risk and reported cases of SGBV, highlights failures and gaps in human protection for those in internal displacement. One informant expressed concern at the time regarding "the prevalence of adolescent pregnancies in the region in the aftermath . . . we are not really sure if most of these were consensual or coerced."[20] It was reported that among Haiyan-affected households, "many children [were] physically abused and [were] subjected to forced labour. Many have stopped going to schools to work instead."[21] The surge in adolescent pregnancies post-Haiyan is thus situated within the utmost devastation of health infrastructures and the lack of humanitarian and development assistance targeted at addressing sexual health. At the same time, heightened vulnerability to SGBV constrained whatever limited opportunities existed for accessing relief assistance and post-disaster livelihood, as well as SGBV crime reporting and protection.

Depletion through social reproduction is thus strongly evident among households headed by adolescents who are themselves still *children*—mentally, physically, and emotionally—and yet are experiencing parenthood at a young age. Ensuring survival for such families means tremendous burdens that push women and girls in particular to commit acts of self-sacrifice. When children are left without access to education and exposed to early pregnancies, in some cases as a result of rape, the whole family suffers an intergenerational and cyclical vulnerability to the harsh consequences of future disasters and unresolved armed conflicts. Their experiences form part of and cascade to social reproduction crises at the national level.

THE HOUSEHOLD AS A SITE OF PEACE AND RESISTANCE

Extended periods of displacement means that women, as part of the affective and sexual labor they are expected to provide, have been and continue to become pregnant despite and/or because of the deplorable conditions in IDP camps. Marital and extramarital sexual relations eventually resume as families continue with their lives in camps and "transitional" sites. Household social reproduction also signifies resistance in the sense that families strive for normality in their home life amid the chaos that surrounds them. Committing to social reproduction expressed in love and intimacy is how peace materializes in the everyday.

Beyond Violent Sex

Sex and intimacy play an important role for household social reproduction before, during, and after crisis. Sexual experiences in crisis settings that are neither entirely nor necessarily violent in nature are invisible when emergency and crisis assistance stems from a narrow focus on "bad" or "violent" sex. Feminist scholars have critiqued the "fetishization" of sexual violence in the humanitarian and international development sectors such that sexual relations become intelligible only as violent phenomena or manifest as negative and oppressive experiences especially for women and girls (Petchesky 1997; Lind 2009; Jolly 2010; Mertens and Pardy 2017). In Mindanao, there were reports of how crisis response included ensuring that married couples were able to resume sexual relations. For example, according to a public health officer:

> Our providers follow where our patients evacuate to—day and night. We always offer quality services even there . . . We are sensitive to evacuees' needs. One time, we had to put up a make shift "motel" room in the evacuation centre to accommodate couples' sexual needs. (Quoted in Lee 2008: 69)

Upon conclusion of the 2016 Philippine Commission on Human Rights national inquiry on Reproductive Health, it was recommended that "'*Kubo-kubo*' houses (huts) should be made available whenever displacement occurs for couples to 'exercise sexual rights' while recovering from calamities" (Commission on Human Rights Philippines 2016: 21). Such a positive recognition of sexual rights in crisis settings is not widespread. In general, conditions for IDPs, including the lack of privacy and inaccessibility of contraception, fail to recognize and address the reality that sex and intimacy do not cease even in times of conflicts or disasters. Without access to birth control and abortion, sexual activity in the camps accrues more risks to women who will have to bear an unwanted pregnancy and/or the possibility of giving birth while in the camps, which heightens maternal mortality risks (UNFPA 2015). Indeed, according to Daguino and Gomez (2010: 31), "the primary concern of women while at the evacuation centre was the lack of privacy. Privacy was necessary for them to satisfy their sexual needs and to maintain their personal hygiene."

Sex becomes a way by which women as wives provide affective labor to their husbands while at the same time mitigating stressors within their households. For instance, as one woman stated:

> Although we were at the evacuation centre, my husband would like to have sex with me . . . there were divisions in the sleeping quarters within the EC [evacuation camp] so it was all right. If I didn't give in to the advances of my husband, he would surely be bad-tempered. (28-year-old, female IDP, quoted in Daguino and Gomez 2010: 43)

Women may gain fulfillment by being able to provide intimacy to their partners, in effect alleviating their own personal suffering by building harmony in their home life. Some women reported a desire to continue with their pregnancies, despite the higher risks associated with giving birth while in the camps, because sexual relations and procreation were necessary for maintaining bonds. Crucially, acts of love are and can be replenishing. In the words of one woman:

> I got pregnant during the conflict but we didn't mind. My husband was happy especially when I gave birth to a boy since my two elder children are all girls and also he was very grateful to God that someone will bring the family name in the next generation to come. (Female FGD participant, quoted in Magcalen-Fernandez 2006: 25)

Sex and intimacy allow men and women to attain a sense of normality in their daily lives and to resist disruptions due to being internally displaced. This view of sexuality differs from what is implied by an overwhelming focus in protection interventions, which regard sexual experiences in IDP camps in negative terms thereby privileging narratives and experiences of women's victimhood. In the field and practice of international development, gendered assumptions of sex and sexuality remain unquestioned. Moving beyond the limiting representation of "violent sex" in the household opens space for alternative forms of masculinities too. Practices of love and care in internal displacements provide a rich counterpoint and resistance to dominant narratives of men as perpetrators of violence in their families and communities. It shines a light on men's vulnerability and equal need for care and affection, which must be nourished in order to replenish social reproduction in times of crisis. In the disaster aftermath, it was pointed out that "[m]any women and young girls chose: cohabitation, early marriage, sex work. Sex is a coping strategy in all these contexts because it is used as a way to ensure survival, not simply the survival of the women concerned but of their dependents and their family."[22] An informant stressed the importance of acknowledging the blurred lines and spaces for agency in relation to sex, desire, and intimacy in the aftermath of the disaster to more richly understand people's needs and experiences. This entails generating a more nuanced understanding of how bodies—both sexual and affective labor—become the immediate and only available resource to promote individual and family welfare in times of crisis.

Last, in Mindanao there is also an example of how sex among couples has been used to facilitate not just household peace but also the cessation of community-level violence. The case of "sex strikes" in Dado, Maguindanao, is illustrative of how sex serves as an "empowering" tool for women to negotiate power relations at the household level. Dado women, as a form of resistance, collectively decided to withhold sex from their husbands, many of whom belong to Moro rebel groups and were engaged in both *rido* and intra-state conflict with the military. Consequently, one of the sex strike leaders' husbands rallied other men to promote peace because "continued fighting would damage the

[58] *Politics of Sexual & Reproductive Health*

[local] economy as well as his marriage" (Global Nonviolent Action Database 2011). Within weeks, communal violence stopped, which then facilitated the setting up of UNHCR's small-scale sewing cooperative in Dado. Dubbed as a modern-day *Lysistrata*, these sex strikes gained international recognition including endorsement from the UNHCR as an example of "unconventional" but "effective" modes of peacebuilding (see Global Nonviolent Action Database 2011; Houseman 2013). "Sex strikes" and the leveraging of household politics to prevent local conflicts have been documented historically and in various countries as diverse as Colombia and Kenya (Smith 2011).

From this example we see that armed conflict provided an opportunity to reconfigure the balance of power within the household, albeit temporarily. In the long run, such a strategy does not problematize women's traditional and heteronormative role of servicing the sexual needs of their husbands. That is, while these sex strikes can be celebrated for facilitating peace through a cessation of armed conflict, they run the risk of re-embedding the gendered division of labor in the household because sex is not seen as a mutually shared need. More to the point, women are implicitly regarded as providers of sex rather than equal receivers. While some women can effectively use sex to bargain within the patriarchal structures of the household, data on IDP women suggest that many suffer from SGBV perpetrated by their spouses or intimate partners. The survey report by Nisa Ul Haqq Fi Bangsamoro (2014) corroborates this in that various forms of domestic violence such as verbal abuse and marital rape were reportedly endured by wives from their husbands while in IDP camps. Moreover, women attempt to reconcile with these forms of violent behavior as "conflict-specific" or as a way their husbands deal with the stresses of conflict (Nisa Ul Haqq Fi Bangsamoro 2014). Stemming women's bodily depletion in times of crisis therefore requires transforming femininities to eliminate pre-existing norms that censure women from caring for their own bodily needs and as a relational component, taking seriously men's sexuality and sexual health.

CONCLUSION

The household is indispensable to understanding how crises are embodied and why the deterioration of women's health and bodily autonomy are the embodiments of crisis. In times of conflict and disaster, we see the simultaneous and cumulative harnessing of women's social reproductive labor and the hollowing out of health inflows that can sustain and renew this labor. While household social reproduction is fundamental to human life and survival, its continuity is made to rest upon the extraction and depletion of women's bodily autonomy and well-being. This is most evident when we map the interconnections of the intensification of care and domestic labor and the deepening of restrictions to sexual and reproductive health in internal displacements. The home or household is where social reproductive contradictions collide and cascade.

In this chapter, I examined depletion to show that it occurs in the absence of self-care among women to sustain their bodies, which are at the forefront of mitigating immediate and long-term consequences of crisis situations. Meeting overlapping and compounded social reproductive obligations serves as the backbone for the survival of families in times of conflict. However, this survival often comes at great cost to women's health and well-being. When women do more to "fill in" these household gaps, which are particularly acute in protracted displacement, the male provider ideal is not necessarily challenged. Instead, armed conflict or disasters serve to "excuse" men's inability to provide for the family, thereby leaving the male provider ideal relatively intact. That is, once the conflict ends or once debris has been cleared, men are seen as able to resume their gendered positions in the household where women are expected to be the primary caregivers. Although crises may generate frustration on the part of men who are unable to fulfill the breadwinner role, it is precisely through the adaptability and persistence of female altruism that we see how the costs to, and responsibilities for, recovery are profoundly unequal.

The discussions in this chapter demonstrate the potential for deepening our understanding of the dynamics and drivers of conflict or disaster-related risks and hazards when we view gendered violence and insecurities in displacements as part of a broader, ongoing crisis of social reproduction in the household. This knowledge can better inform interventions that mitigate rather than exacerbate the linkages between intensified social reproductive labor, SRHR, and SGBV. As a crucial starting point for understanding the global politics of sexual and reproductive health, I argue that we need to pay attention to the collision of cultural-religious constraints to bodily autonomy with the gendered material conditions that structure everyday social reproductive labor as the twin drivers that make women and girls insecure in crisis situations. Inadequate interventions to promote SRHR among women and girls in crisis situations indicate that the cost of servicing households is extremely manifested in women's bodies when they suffer violence and poor health outcomes. That is, women attend to the needs of everyone else while intensely less able to attend to their own. Consequently, this means that health and well-being among women may serve as an indicator of how different households are able to cope in contexts of protracted displacement. When women are able to allot time, access health resources, and feel "entitled" to care for their own needs, then collective well-being can improve in a more equitable and sustainable way.

[60]   *Politics of Sexual & Reproductive Health*

CHAPTER 3
Myths of Community Survival

We neighbours help each other. If they have water and we have none, they give us some. That's what we also do, sharing.

Basilan female FGD participants, quoted in Magcalen-Fernandez 2006: 29

Women are targeted for aid and development programs but these heavily rely on women's volunteer work. We insist in our projects that we make sure to cover the transport costs of women at least. They really lose out on productive and reproductive work when participating in gender seminars or trainings.[1]

INTRODUCTION

The decisions that make for healthy sexual and reproductive lives are never entirely private; neither are they made by individuals alone. This is even more acute in the context of conflicts and disasters wherein many families and communities are increasingly dislocated, and when material and cultural pressures for survival intensify. Social reproduction—particularly who does the paid and unpaid care work and how—is foundational to understanding how individuals are able to relate to one another and with their community. A person's health is clearly a precondition for and outcome of inclusive community life. Yet, both care work and the bodily costs it entails are typically undervalued or underexamined in analysis of conflicts, disasters, and related emergencies. For instance, despite the "local turn" in international relations (IR) and for peacebuilding and international development specifically, there remains a gap in understanding how social reproductive labor, which is necessary for sustaining healthy communities, constitutes a form of civic and political engagement. Additionally, this

The Global Politics of Sexual and Reproductive Health. Maria Tanyag, Oxford University Press.
© Oxford University Press 2024. DOI: 10.1093/oso/9780197676332.003.0004

leads to an underappreciation of how sexual and reproductive health and rights (SRHR) serve as a vital litmus test in assessing the quality of post-conflict and post-disaster recovery among communities.

This chapter examines bodily autonomy within the political economy of care and control in communities especially during crises by drawing on experiences of internally displaced populations in the Philippines. Crisis-specific restrictions to SRHR emerge and are reproduced in the context of gendered material and ideological conditions that deplete community social reproduction. I show how community-level depletion manifests in terms of how women perform different types of community labor as an extension of the caring they do for their households within a wider context of restrictions to bodily autonomy. When SRHR is not addressed as a symptom and root cause of community depletion, both state and non-state crisis responders risk reproducing gendered inequalities and generating new sources of tensions in a crisis aftermath. There is a compounding of harms involved when we fail to account for both the bodily costs that accumulate and cascade across the household and community and the increasingly global myths that keep these hidden.

THE COMMUNITY AND THE CRISIS OF SOCIAL REPRODUCTION IN THE EVERYDAY

The community is an interrelated and interdependent site for how societies organize social reproduction at household, national, and global levels. It pertains to groups of people characterized by common practices, resources, and networks of exchange. The community is also an imagined construct upon which shared identities, ways of life, and collective meanings of care are built. Rai, Hoskyns, and Thomas (2014) identify the community as a site of depletion, which can exacerbate or mitigate depletion at individual and household levels. They stipulate that:

> In measuring DSR [depletion through social reproduction] in communities, we would need to assess: the "thickness" of social networks, the incentives and disincentives that people have to join these networks, the extent to which they are seen as strategies to mitigate individual and household DSR, their sustainability and the interface of informal networks of formal institutionalized state structures with the private sector. The nature and levels of voluntary work also need to be measured. (2014: 97)

While the community has been a core analytical category in the social sciences generally, and in areas such as anthropology and development studies particularly, the "community turn" in IR and across security and development agendas is more recent. This shift has three main implications for understanding the politics of SRHR.

[62] *Politics of Sexual & Reproductive Health*

First, within IR scholarship, the emerging attention to community ties and practices coincides with an emphasis on the equal importance of analyzing the "local" and everyday politics as causal to the "global," and not simply the other way around (Bjorkdahl, Hall, and Svensson 2019). Traditionally, the focus of IR has been on the macro-level of processes, phenomena, and actors. Questions of structure and agency, while occasionally raised in relation to individuals, institutions, or identities, nevertheless remain confined within "high stakes" issues in international politics. Rarely were the mundane, ubiquitous, and intimate taken seriously as driving forces of the global. Now, however, there is broader scholarly interest in unveiling the mutual constitution of the community and global order in ways that showcase the multiplicity and multi-scalar workings of power. Yet, this has been exactly what feminist IR scholarship has been doing for a long time (Bjorkdahl, Hall, and Svensson 2019; Enloe 2013), even as there has been little acknowledgement of this contribution within the discipline and despite how feminist concepts are too frequently omitted. The growth of "everyday IR" research provides an opportunity to (re)interrogate how global processes are gendered and reproduced in bodily ways. As Enloe (2011: 447) reminds us, while the everyday often appears "pre-political," it has always mattered in feminist research for revealing "the causes of patriarchal social systems' remarkable sustainability"—importantly, to expose "that power [is] deeply at work where it [is] least apparent." The "community turn" in IR is thus enriched by continuously ensuring gender is a permanent fixture in the analytical toolbox of the everyday. This entails, as feminist scholars' have argued, drawing attention to "how the everyday is reconstituted through a widening and deepening of capitalist market relations into all spheres of social life" (Elias and Roberts 2016: 788; also Bakker 2007; Fraser 2013; Elias and Gunawardana 2013). It also involves understanding the everyday as it is contrasted with the temporal and spatial relations of crisis such as those evoked by a politics of spectacle and in the tyranny of urgency (see Enloe 2013; Sjoberg, Hudson, and Weber 2015; Tickner 2015; and Hozic and True 2016).

The community is another site for examining what is global about the crisis of everyday social reproduction as it serves as a basic, "grassroots" unit in increasingly internationalized crisis responses. We discover how crises are made "everyday" from the standpoint of those whose bodies and labor bear the brunt of survival. The everyday itself is in crisis due to depletion of social reproduction manifested by the deterioration of bodily autonomy and well-being. At the same time, prevailing understandings of the "everyday" take as a given unequal gendered divisions of labor as "normal." For instance, feminist research has shown that care and domestic work are ever present in households and communities even in the face of disruptions caused by health pandemics (Folbre 2014; Harman 2015), economic crises (Elson 2009, 2010; Kunz 2010), and armed conflicts. Yet, there remains a lack of systematic analysis of how global peace and security are increasingly dependent on practices of care and domestic work within communities during and after crises. Particularly in the context of conflicts and disasters, to what extent are community forms of labor gendered, and how have such gendered divisions of community labor serviced post-conflict and post-disaster recovery? By examining the community and micro-level interactions that constitute it, I argue that we are able to trace a richer and more comprehensive way to show how power operates not just across multiple scales of socio-political economic relations beyond individuals and households, but also the bodily costs of crisis rhetoric and time zones as enacted through myths of community.

Second, beginning in the 1990s and as a specific response to externally driven and top-down development, there has been a global shift toward the community as a site of "empowerment" where processes of redistribution and inclusion, especially in decision-making for marginalized peoples, can begin.[2] In the context of conflicts and disasters, for example, the shift toward community-based governance, programs, and assistance have been notable. In peacebuilding, conflict prevention, disaster response, and risk reduction, the community has gained significance as a unit of intervention for transforming societies (Smyth and Sweetman 2015). Consequently, promoting community participation began to be conditionally tied to donor funding and through the proliferation of participatory and community-based research methods. There is widespread acceptance of the indispensability of participatory processes for sustainable development, crisis response, and post-crisis recovery, to the extent that critical scholars have warned against the "tyranny of participation" (Cooke and Kothari 2001; Guijt and Shah 1998). As a result, the community is materially and culturally reproduced through "bottom-up" and participatory approaches in ways that are not necessarily beneficial to already marginalized members. Participation taken as an unquestionable hallmark of "good" governance enforces a simplified (mis)representation of the "community" as a homogeneous entity devoid of intra-group tensions, which means also without gender. As Guijt and Shah (1998: 1) argue, "the language and practice of 'participation' often obscures women's worlds, needs and contributions to development, making equitable participatory development an elusive goal." Moreover, "[i]nequalities, oppressive social hierarchies and discrimination are often overlooked, and instead enthusiasm is generated for the cooperative and harmonious ideal promised by the imagery of 'community'" (Guijt and Shah 1998: 7–8).

Participatory approaches become vehicles through which accounts of the community and especially of the poor or crisis-affected can become "sanitized," abstracted, and detached from global politics of their everyday realities. This relates to what Su, Mangada, and Turalba (2018) observed as "happy-washing" in the aftermath of Typhoon Haiyan in the Philippines wherein stereotypes of Filipinos as innately happy people who are able to bounce back easily from one crisis to another are discursively exploited. The risk is that an

[64] *Politics of Sexual & Reproductive Health*

overemphasis on uplifting community morale can be used "in the erasure of where things went wrong, the foreclosure of productive discussions of what can be done better, and importantly, mechanisms for communities to make governments and international organisations responsible for protection" (Su and Tanyag 2019: 19). Indeed, as Kothari (2001: 151) points out, the "tyranny of participation" may come at the expense of accounting for "the capacity of individuals and groups to resist inclusion, resist projections about their lives, retain information, knowledge and values, and act out a performance and in so doing present themselves in a variety of ways." Despite established feminist critiques of "gender-lite"[3] participatory mechanisms, there remains a tendency to mythologize "the community" which, as this chapter demonstrates, further heightens in crisis situations because it occurs in tandem with the paradoxically simultaneous reliance on, and devaluing of, care and domestic labor in the household and feminized community work. This also manifests perniciously when women are brought in to participate but subsequently lack control over the decision-making process and do not have equal ownership of the decision outcomes.

Crisis-prone sites in the Philippines are illustrative of the way "[g]rand narratives shape the design of humanitarian responses and subsequent mobilisation of national and global resources for rebuilding" to the effect that "accounts of mutual aid, resourcefulness or local ingenuity, and self-reliance are mythologised and eventually ossified as 'truths'" (Su and Tanyag 2019: 8). However, representations and stories of community survival and their everyday "self-reliance" become even more alluring in times of crisis when there is a supposed natural inclination to uplift the morale of both affected communities and crisis responders. Myths of community need to be scrutinized precisely in contexts where they are overly deployed, such as in a crisis aftermath, to lay bare the vested interests they serve to camouflage in the distribution of resources and authority over how societies recover, and at what costs. For example, De La Rocha (2007: 45) identifies "a powerful myth that has spread throughout international development agencies: that poor households are able to survive in spite of macroeconomic policies that foster unemployment, increase poverty and decrease the amount of resources in the hands of the poor." This myth is underpinned by assumptions that the poor survive through social capital and community safety nets that are limitless and readily harnessed without regard for the range of costs their maintenance entails especially for women and girls (Elson 2010). And yet, an increasing reliance and pressure on social reproduction through care within kinship ties and community support in the absence of state contributions to replenish social support systems, especially during times of crises, inevitably leads to the very erosion of mutual help, solidarity, and social exchange among communities (De La Rocha 2007: 47). The broadening of efforts to make visible community-based crisis response may be harnessed in the service of crisis social welfare austerity. Paradoxically, as Elson (2010: 208) points out, "[c]ommunities may respond to the crisis through an increase in organised volunteer work, for both self-help, and to help those hardest hit [but] The crisis may reduce the provision of such support, at a time when the demand for support is growing."

Third, the importance of gender in humanitarian practice, international development, and security policy-making is never more widely accepted than before, yet mainstreaming efforts have not translated to transformations in the social, political, and economic relations of women, especially at local levels of villages and communities and in crisis situations marked by conflicts, disasters, and climate change. Instead, feminist scholars observe the currency and adaptability of binary narratives of women as victims or survivors and vulnerable or virtuous that counteract substantive gender equality reforms (Arora-Jonsson 2011; see also Sjoberg and Gentry 2007; Bradshaw 2014; Smyth and Sweetman 2015; Hall and Shepherd 2013). The reproduction of these binary gendered narratives in the context of community survival forms an integral part of myth-making in crisis response and recovery. As crisis responses increasingly become more globalized and banal, there is a tendency for myths of survival and binary narratives to become even more naturalized (Su and Tanyag 2019). Such discourses mystify and hinder in the material analysis of the co-constitution of crises and gender relations particularly as these intersect with other social, political, and economic hierarchies beginning with the household and communities.

In the Philippines, among the most dominant of discourses used in crisis settings is "resilience." Resilience, as a development and humanitarian buzzword, has constituted an amorphous discourse that is vulnerable to appropriation and use in the legitimizing of virtually any political or economic agenda at the national or global level. In the broader humanitarian and development discourse, resilience has been used as a "mobilising metaphor" to underscore the strengthening of capacities in the face of future threats (Smyth and Sweetman 2015: 406). It has been used to denote reconstruction and recovery in ways that "build back better." Central to enacting resilience is strengthening local capacities and resources among communities, which is a global sustainable development goal (Goal 11) and increasingly a globally accepted metric for the efficacy of post-crisis reconstruction and in response to climate change (see Chapter 4). Resilience, therefore, is situated within the long continuum of normative visions to empower communities via participatory modes of governance. However, resilience risks becoming like other forms of survival myths when it functions as a discursive tool for harnessing gendered norms such as female altruism at household and community levels, while responsibilities and accountability in post-crisis recovery and reconstruction are increasingly divested away from the state. This divestment may reinforce the gendered allocation of care burdens, which also informs whose contributions are rewarded and how in crisis transitions. Importantly, research participants in the Philippines emphasized that poor communities besieged by constant threats of disasters or conflicts are limited to immediate survival. A constant refrain I heard from informants was, "how can they think of preventing future disasters when they still face food insecurity on a daily basis?"[4]

Raising questions of social reproduction provides a different lens through which to understand crisis in the everyday, and one which opens up analysis of the significance of bodily health and well-being for enabling or constraining community forms of labor. Crisis responses built on a romanticized view of the community obscure, rather than account for, crisis-intensified depletion through social reproduction and its relationship with restrictions to bodily autonomy. In the next section, I examine how community social reproduction intensifies in the aftermath of conflicts and disasters and how this intensification carries disproportionate costs for a largely feminized community workforce.

BARANGAY WORKERS AND THE CRISIS OF COMMUNITY SOCIAL REPRODUCTION

The *barangay* refers to the local community, *barrio*, or village in the Philippines. Under Article X, the 1987 Philippine Constitution designates the *barangay* as the primary administrative unit in local governance. Beginning in the 1990s and with the enactment of the Local Government Code of 1991 (Republic Act 7160), governance in the country was significantly transformed, with many of the functions previously held by the national government devolved to local government units including *barangays*. The Code stipulates that local government units shall "enjoy genuine and meaningful local autonomy to enable them to attain their fullest development as self-reliant communities and make them more effective partners in the attainment of national goals" (Section 2). It enshrines self-sufficiency as a pre-requisite for "accelerating economic development and upgrading the quality of life for the people in the community" (Section 5). The responsibility for the delivery of basic services and facilities was divested away from the central or national government to local communities. The responsibilities devolved to the *barangay* units "include, but are not limited to":

(i) Agricultural support services, which include planting materials distribution system and operation of farm produce collection and buying stations;

(ii) Health and social welfare services, which include maintenance of barangay health centers and day-care centers;

(iii) Services and facilities related to general hygiene and sanitation, beautification, and solid waste collection;

(iv) Maintenance of katarungang pambarangay [*barangay* justice system];

(v) Maintenance of barangay roads and bridges and water supply systems;

(vi) Infrastructure facilities such as multi-purpose halls and pavements, plazas, sports centers, and other similar facilities;

(vii) Information and reading centers; and

(viii) Satellite or public markets, where viable. (Section 17, b(1))

Since decentralization began, *barangays* have had an ever-growing list of responsibilities, especially in crisis situations, when they are positioned as "frontlines" in emergency response and relief distribution, conflict management and prevention, disaster risk reduction, and resilience. Yet, the burgeoning of burdens devolved at local levels has not been matched by social reproductive inflows that support the sustainability of *barangays* in the daily provisioning of community life.

Decentralization in the Philippines was part of a global shift in governance away from centralized state authority and toward increasing the responsibilities of communities, especially in the health sector (Atienza 2004, 2006; see also Nunes 2020 for a comparison of Brazil). This global shift aligned with changes in foreign aid toward promoting national "self-sufficiency" especially in health care delivery. For example, USAID's provisioning of health care supplies was scaled down and gradually phased out in the Philippines and other developing countries (see Chapter 5). Atienza (2004) argues that decentralization in the Philippines was among the most radical in the 1990s, not just in comparison to the country's own history of decentralization but also compared to neighboring countries in Southeast Asia and other developing countries at the time. She points out that, first, these reforms coincided with democratization in the country in the aftermath of Ferdinand Marcos's dictatorship, during which centralized authority failed to deliver basic services. Consequently, promoting local autonomy was "meant to be the centerpiece of a government that came into power by overthrowing a dictator" (Atienza 2004: 28). Second, compared to decentralization across the developing world, "Philippine health reform gives the widest range of choice or decision space over many functions that were devolved to LGUs [local government units]" (Atienza 2004: 51).

In an archipelagic country such as the Philippines, proponents believed that by devolving specific national functions to local governments, remote and rural communities were set to benefit the most in ensuring that participation translated to more responsive solutions to community problems. However, despite the much-celebrated experiment and optimism surrounding decentralization in the country, there is strong evidence from both scholarly research and government data sources that "devolution by itself does not guarantee improved health service delivery . . . the Code itself provides only a framework . . . it did not solve fiscal, personnel and supply difficulties" (Atienza

2004: 50). Crucially, the weakness of decentralization in the Philippines is that it has proven to detrimentally impact comprehensive service delivery and access to justice along gendered lines. This is most evident in areas of sexual and reproductive health services, in protection and prevention of violence against women, and in effective social welfare delivery before, during, and after crises.

In principle, devolution allows local governments to craft health policies that are more responsive and accountable to the particular needs and circumstances of their constituency. The national government, through the Department of Health, is still responsible for setting a general health care framework, while the financing and delivery of services fall within the ambit of LGUs. However, in practice, local politics and vested interests have undermined the inclusivity and efficacy of health service delivery which were originally intended as part of decentralization (Lakshminarayanan 2003; Atienza 2004; Lee, Nacionalies, and Pedroso 2009; Commission on Human Rights Philippines 2016). Pre-existing patron-client relations, strong religious influence over family laws, and opposition to gender and sexuality issues resulted in distinct gendered impacts of decentralization. In tandem with the rolling back of the state, conservative and religious fundamentalist forces leveraged this opening in strengthening their policy influence. For example, based on the Philippine Commission on Human Rights (2016: 15) national inquiry in 2016, it was found that decentralization has contributed to the uneven implementation and support for the Reproductive Health (RH) Law. The Commission noted the existence of "policies passed by local government units which show disregard for and disrespect of women's choice of family planning methods and commodities despite availability of resources." Not only was access to health distributed on the basis of patronage, more locally known through the *palakasan* system,[5] which meant the selective provision of goods and services based on kinship, friendship, and/or political affiliation. Decentralization also allowed conservative politicians to use "local autonomy" as a means to govern based on their religious beliefs and enabled them to curry favor with local Catholic religious leaders. Indeed, as Lakshminarayan (2003: 99) points out, "if a local government unit decided for political reasons (e.g. due to local Catholic Church pressure) not to provide contraceptive services, women in that locale were effectively denied access to methods."

In some cases, local authorities have issued executive orders that declare their cities and towns to be "pro-life," which then justified banning access to contraceptives. These edicts ranged from refusal to locally fund contraceptives to outright prohibition within their locality (see Chapter 5; Tanyag 2015; Lee, Nacionalies, and Pedroso 2009; Ruiz Austria 2004). Local governments, especially at the *barangay* level, are also differently resourced, which has resulted in varied strategies to mitigate budgetary gaps and shortages. For instance, the Commission reported a prevalence among certain municipalities and *barangays* to require "donations" or voluntary fees before patients can avail of sexual and reproductive health supplies and services, which under the law are free (Commission on Human Rights Philippines 2016). Fragmented health service delivery has made it difficult to monitor human rights violations for denial of care, discrimination, and harassment perpetrated by local health personnel against sexual minorities, adolescents, people with disabilities, those with HIV/AIDS, sex workers, indigenous and ethnic minorities, and women seeking treatment for abortion-related complications.

While the devolution of authority and function at local levels is shaping the material conditions for community social reproduction, discursive or cultural and religious norms on community labor also play a complementary role. For example, *Barangay* Health Workers (BHWs) constitute the most basic unit of community health care and social service delivery, which includes maternal, newborn, and child health care (Rodriguez 2014; Commission on Human Rights Philippines 2016: 5). As a frontline service, they are tasked with referrals to other bigger health facilities, organizing and coordinating medical missions, assisting birth deliveries, and serving as family planning counsellors, among others (Commission on Human Rights Philippines 2016). BHWs bridge massive gaps in health care especially for rural and remote areas. For example, in 2015 there were only 74 doctors in the former Autonomous Region in Muslim Mindanao (ARMM) for a population of 3.3 million (OCHA 2015d). That is approximately 1 doctor per 44,595 people, which is significantly below World Health Organization standards. Additionally, the day-to-day provision of health assistance is heavily borne by BHWs. Figure 3.1 shows a sample chart kept in an urban locality in Eastern Visayas. It serves to record and monitor the ratio of BHWs per person across three *barangays* wherein one BHW is allocated to assist approximately 20 to 60 people.

From a feminist political economy lens, BHWs, along with other forms of community work, are devalued precisely because they are feminized and seen as an extension of women's housework. BHWs in the Philippines were initially meant to serve as voluntary auxiliary forces, and they continue to be considered so even as the tasks delegated to them have gradually increased (Commission on Human Rights Philippines 2016). Community health care work has historically targeted women who were either unmarried or mothers familiar with their *barangays* or local community; hence, its voluntary nature. The creation of BHWs operates on gendered assumptions such that "stay-at-home" women are naturally altruistic, that their "free time" can easily be harnessed in the service of their community, and that community work is not "professionalized" work. Thus, "despite the wide-ranging services expected of them [BHWs], their work is considered 'voluntary' and therefore, not regularly compensated" (Magcalen-Fernandez 2006: 15). Moreover, the occasional provision of honoraria legitimizes adding more and more administrative responsibilities onto them, which in turn serves as proof of the "cost effective" benefits of decentralization for the state.

		Sto. Niño	Sta. Cruz	Paco	
Fully Immunized Children	Sto. Niño	●	●	●	●
	Sta. Cruz	●	●	●	●
	Paco	●	●	●	●
Access to Safe Water	Sto. Niño	●	●	●	●
	Sta. Cruz	●	●	●	●
	Paco	●	●	●	●
With Sanitary Toilets	Sto. Niño	●	●	●	●
	Sta. Cruz	●	●	●	●
	Paco	●	●	●	●
BHW Ratio	Sto. Niño	1:60	1:63	1:67	1:40
	Sta. Cruz	1:44	1:47	1:49	1:25
	Paco	1:25	1:23	1:20	1:20
BHW Honorarium (Amount)	Sto. Niño	500 / BHW	550 / BHW	600 / BHW	600 / BHW
	Sta. Cruz	300 / BHW	350 / BHW	400 / BHW	400 / BHW
	Paco	140 / BHW	140 / BHW	140 / BHW	140 / BHW
Brgy. Health Budget %	Sto. Niño	29.000	32.000	35.000	35.000
	Sta. Cruz	16.920	16.920	14.400	14.400
	Paco	9.932	9.932	9.932	9.932
Brgy. Health Plan	Sto. Niño	NO	NO	YES	YES
	Sta. Cruz	NO	NO	YES	YES
	Paco	NO	NO	YES	YES

Figure 3.1. *Barangay* health profile sample chart
Source: Author, Eastern Visayas

The Republic Act 7883 or the Barangay Health Workers' Benefit and Incentives Act (BHW Act) of 1995 stipulates that a BHW is one who voluntarily renders primary health care services in the community. But these provisions are exactly just that—privileges or "perks" to the job that can and may be given when available. They are typically "one-off" and discretionary. For example, BHWs by law are entitled to a hazard and subsistence allowance, but the amount is to be determined by the local government based on its prevailing circumstances (BHW Act, Section 6(a) and (b)). Similarly, the Magna Carta of Public Health Workers of 1992 stipulates several incentives and benefits afforded by the state to public health workers, but these exclude BHWs, because as volunteers they are not employed per se. As examined in Chapter 1, national initiatives such as the "doctors to the barrios" assume that health provisioning, especially at the community level, can be sustainable through relying chiefly on mobilizing cultural values of altruism, sacrifice, and patriotic duty among Filipinos (Philippines Department of Health n.d.). BHWs, who already face limited financial support from the state and very few opportunities for professional growth, bear such cultural pressures more heavily.

BHWs servicing crisis-affected communities are at an even more precarious and depletive condition, because in addition to a lack of pay, they face violence and displacement. In crisis-prone communities, all types of health workers are expected to sacrifice salary and accept a standard of living that includes risks to their physical security. For example, a rural health nurse from Basilan, Mindanao, stated, "worse, our salaries are always delayed. We are not given bonus and 13th month pay; our [government insurance] premiums are not paid" (quoted in Magcalen-Fernandez 2006: 16). Magcalen-Fernandez (2016: 16) explains, "[T]his story told by a Rural Health Nurse, illustrates the neglect and indifference plaguing the local health sector. It is not surprising that she will soon be leaving for Saudi Arabia to work as a nurse, joining the exodus of health professionals which further exacerbates the critical situation." Moreover, "[I]n the absence of doctors and nurses, BHWs bravely try to fill the void but their services are not given fair recompense."

Indeed, a Moro woman informant recalled how in her village in Bangsamoro, the local community once pooled resources to send women for health training, but they opted not to return and instead worked overseas.[6] Another Moro woman explained that, the "JICA [Japan International Cooperation Agency] donated a health center, just the building itself some time ago. But it is now wasting away due to a lack of personnel and good management."[7] This was corroborated by another informant who expressed a similar view:

> [Y]ou may have the infrastructures for health care centers but then where will you get the people to work there? At the community level, social work is not a valued job because it remains unremunerated and not a "career" profession. So the most crucial health services are difficult to sustain because it is both lacking in government funding and personnel.[8]

As a result, Barangay Health Stations may be available, but they are not regularly staffed by health workers. Community health facilities, especially those in crisis-prone areas, are often dilapidated or makeshift and are poorly resourced, which means compounded labor and amplified health risks for health workers themselves.

The experiences of BHWs show that community social reproduction is depleted not only because labor is left unreplenished but also because it is continuously exploited and repurposed. In smaller, more remote, and poorer communities, the same groups of women who work in providing *barangay* health assistance are also tapped for disaster relief coordination, *barangay* violence against women patrols, and/or to provide and disseminate public information on a range of policies and ordinances. It is also common for many community workers to draw on their personal savings to augment available community resources and to continue performing basic duties. A City Population Officer from Tacloban I interviewed argued that "[T]ransformative programs require so many resources and funding . . . and yet many social services are on a voluntary basis. If we get paid, we still shell out our own private time and money."[9] This attests to the extent in which many workers are personally invested in the wellbeing of the community they serve and belong to (Rodriguez 2014).

[72] *Politics of Sexual & Reproductive Health*

Another woman in charge of a women's and children's community shelter in Tacloban shared a similar experience. In the aftermath of Typhoon Haiyan, she experienced greater difficulty in stretching the shelter's budget, and she had to draw from her own money. She received less from the government because of the disaster, despite an increased demand for shelters from rising cases of rape and sexual violence. Yet she felt it was incumbent on her to use her own resources, otherwise the women and children in her shelter would suffer even more. Frontline community workers such as her have already been filling in the gaps created by state cutbacks or shortages on social welfare for a long time, but the burdens definitely intensify in crisis situations. In her words:

> They tell us there is not enough money available. That amount in my many years working as the city social welfare officer since 2010, that was the lowest budget we were given [after Haiyan]. How can that amount be enough for the whole year? We provide food and basic amenities here, pay utilities too. To survive, I would normally use my personal money just so we could all eat here. Come to think of it, that is really normal for government employees at low levels like us, we end up covering so many things with our own money.[10]

Consistent with the logic of depletion, those who are harnessed by the state to provide social protection are also those sorely lacking in protection and "safety nets" themselves. Furthermore, it is prevalent among BHWs to not know their entitlements and rights. There is no standardization of the workload distribution and honoraria given across each *barangay* (see Figure 3.1). The appointment of BHWs, whether to provide them an allowance, and how much, are subject to patronage and so have been highly politicized, and the distribution of benefits is grossly uneven (Commission on Human Rights Philippines 2016). Consequently, this arrangement can make BHWs feel beholden, "grateful," or "indebted" and therefore less likely to make demands for improved work conditions in case they risk losing what little remuneration they are receiving. Patronage and decentralization thus combine to enforce servitude among BHWs and community workers more generally.

The expectation of sacrifice is most evident and intense for community work in the context of armed conflicts in Mindanao. Community social service jobs are routinely inadequately protected from escalating security risks associated with providing vital health services and supplies in fragile settings. A notable example was the 2001 Abu Sayyaf siege of Lamitan, Basilan, wherein the terrorist group specifically targeted a local hospital. Among the violent atrocities perpetrated by the group was the killing of the only doctor in Lamitan and the brutal raping of a nurse. As a result, Lamitan had a "doctorless hospital" for several years (Magcalen-Fernandez 2006). Since then, health infrastructures are believed to be high-risk for terrorist activity. Globally, similar tactics by armed groups in conflict is reportedly undertaken to destabilize communities and create vulnerability (see also Lee 2008; Urdal and Che 2013: 492; UN Women 2015: 75). Without adequate protections in place and long-term prospects for establishing peace in the region, both paid and voluntary community health workers service conflict-affected communities at great personal risk, including tremendous physical and psychological strain.

The experiences of BHWs and community workers in the Philippines demonstrate how norms of feminized sacrifice and volunteerism operate effectively to extract ever increasing demands on women's bodies in the name of community building. The ongoing devaluing of community social reproduction by the state has allowed it to reap savings on the back of a largely feminized voluntary labor force in the absence of material inflows to build and strengthen public health systems. Additionally, this depletion generates cascading harms that impact community workers and their families as the crisis of community social reproduction both constitutes and reproduces household depletion. Community workers and especially BHWs are integral to socially reproducing their own families as well as others in their communities. A deterioration in their individual well-being can translate into negative health care experiences for others too. For example, among the findings in the Commission on Human Rights Philippines national inquiry was that many people, especially indigenous women, young adolescents, and sexual minorities, experience poor health care service, discrimination, and abuse at the community level. There were reports of maltreatment by, and prejudice among, community health workers, so much so that marginalized and minority groups are dissuaded from seeking health care regularly. The consequences of this are exacerbated for SRHR in light of deep cultural and religious barriers such as shame and stigma in accessing health care. An inclusive and comprehensive social welfare service cannot be sustainably built on altruism because not everyone will behave altruistically. "Bottomless" care from community workers cannot be expected when they themselves are already overburdened, lacking in care, and sometimes incurring debt and financial hardship in order to do their jobs (Rodriguez 2014). The Commission thus concluded:

> As volunteers, BHWs cater to the entire community receiving minimal and sometimes no allowance at all. BHW allowances are dependent on the LGU, and their appointment are [sic] often politicized. They are however very significant in the delivery of health services in the community level. Overburdened and underpaid, BHWs continue to partner with the LGU and the DOH [Department of Health] in delivering services to the community, a task that should be duly recognized and compensated (Commission on Human Rights Philippines 2016: 5).

[74]   *Politics of Sexual & Reproductive Health*

DEPLETING COMMUNITIES OF CARE

Social reproduction and particularly care and domestic work makes community civic and political participation possible. There can be no community well-being in the absence of the everyday labor that goes toward building belongingness, delivery of services, maintenance of common or shared public spaces, and the collective reproduction of local values, practices, and beliefs among others. At the same time, for many women, care and domestic work for the community is done as an extension of the expected care labor for the family and kinship networks. In crisis-affected and fragile settings of internally displaced communities in the Philippines, women were actively embedded within multiple community roles, from conflict prevention and peacebuilding to disaster response and climate action. Yet they and the communities they belong to face restrictions to bodily autonomy and well-being on a daily basis.

Increasingly at global and national levels as evidenced by the global Women, Peace and Security (WPS) agenda and relevant Philippine legislations and action plans, there has been a growing recognition and indeed celebration of women's catalytic roles in community peacebuilding, resilience, and recovery in the context of post-conflict and post-disaster. Crises are also revealing the existence of "communities of care" that operate through relationships of mutual aid, commoning, and reciprocity which in turn not only ensure societies recover in the aftermath but also serve as safety nets from future risks and shocks. However, paying attention to the material and ideological conditions that support or deplete the daily provisioning of care at household and community levels, especially in times of crisis, exposes who disproportionately bears the burdens of community survival and at what cost.

Caring Communities and Women's Labor

Routine displacement due to protracted and cyclical armed conflicts in Mindanao has fostered a strong sense of community among Moro women who view care and domestic work as a communal effort. A common coping mechanism involves the sharing of care and domestic work burdens primarily between and among female members of the same family and neighboring communities (Cagoco-Guiam 2013; Margallo 2005). Similar patterns were observed in the aftermath of Typhoon Haiyan in disaster-induced displacements in Visayas. For example, one informant who served in one of the Haiyan humanitarian response teams recounted in our interview, "we heard stories and this was around the first three months after the storm, in the evacuation camps, many lactating mothers breastfed other infants."[11] There was an explicit recognition among women that mutual aid such as collectivizing care work and stretching available relief assistance among themselves emerged as a *mitigating* response to the uneven, limited availability of, or inadequacies in, "external" assistance from the state, local NGOs, or humanitarian response teams.

In both conflict and disaster sites, women's collective social reproductive labor was "the safety net that perhaps was not afforded by the government agencies and local government units. This safety net sustained the internally displaced persons despite the inadequacies of the evacuation centres" (Magcalen-Fernandez 2006: 30). Women's commoning keeps the peace amid brewing rivalries driven by competitive access to the aid economy. In Eastern Visayas, for instance, intra-community tensions emerged as a result of a drastically "changed landscape" where different local and international NGOs flooded communities with their presence post-Haiyan. Shelter and livelihood projects including boats, *pedicabs*, and *sari-sari* stores were embellished with "flashy" international non-governmental organization (INGO) "brands" serving as a new status symbol that stratified locals. Sharing resources, especially food relief and information regarding livelihood assistance, were ways to mitigate local tensions.

Women play a central role in community healing. For example, Moro women contribute to the reproduction and preservation of ethnic and religious traditions that are central to community well-being. Among the Maranao ethnic group, specific women are traditionally tasked with attending to the well-being of the community such that "[T]hey served as *pamomolong* or traditional healers to help community members with afflictions and to safeguard the well-being of the people. They kept the family intact and helped in maintaining peace in the community" (Berowa 2006: xv). This role is seen as part of continuing intangible cultural and religious rituals that bind their peoples, which may have been threatened or disrupted by conflicts too. Another Moro example refers to the community *panday* or *hilot*—women who serve as traditional birth attendants. They render comprehensive reproductive care and assist in household or domestic work while the new mother recuperates. Their service thus offers holistic caring for the new mother's spiritual, physical, and psychological well-being. In Maguindanao, community or village women serve as arbiters who resolve local feuds before they escalate to communal violence. In addition, these same women "also perform roles as traditional birth attendants, officiators of rituals, farmers, community workers/organizers, wives and mothers (average number of children is seven)" (Leyesa 2012). As these Moro women demonstrate, community-level peacebuilding is performed in addition to their social reproductive labor in their families and clans. Maintaining community peace is undertaken consistent with the performance of other cultural functions that benefit women and their community more inclusively, from attending births to officiating reconciliation rituals.

These types of community work are indispensable for social cohesion and genuine post-crisis recovery. However, they are undermined by the broader

[76]   *Politics of Sexual & Reproductive Health*

depletive conditions that structure everyday lives due to the economic devaluing of social reproduction. For example, formal medical services require trained
professionals and time-intensive or sustained provision of assistance—both
of which are already in short supply in camps for internally displaced people
(IDPs) in Mindanao and in similarly remote and rural areas of Eastern Visayas.
Consequently, this health gap underscores the importance of women traditional healers as the pre-existing safety net and crisis shock-absorbers for the
emotional well-being of communities situated within a crisis-prone country.
Community healing is both a pre-condition for and an outcome of healthy
bodies. Yet, it has traditionally taken a back seat in the redistribution of resources in the aftermath of conflicts and disasters that typically prioritizes
formal restoration of physical infrastructures, resumption of market activities, and/or disarmament and amnesties where men tend to be overrepre-
sented and thus benefit more from peace.

The Philippines has been among the many country cases where increasing women's participation in peacebuilding especially at the "grassroots" or
community level is being monitored as part of the global WPS agenda. Moro
women's community peacebuilding efforts have been nationally recognized
as contributing significantly to preventing the occurrence and escalation of
armed conflicts (Arnado 2012; Torres 2014; O'Reilly, Ó Súilleabháin, and
Paffenholz 2015). A male country representative of an international organization observed, "[the Philippines] is a very matriarchal society, women are
the ones leading in the camps, in recovering from crisis."[12] The discursive recognition of women's contributions at the community level is a positive development but this needs to be matched by the availability of material inflows
that sustain women's health and well-being such as comprehensive SRHR
and political economic transformations that materially replenish community
caring labor. For example, women's initiative to lead within IDP camps is in
addition to the labor they are already expected to perform in their households
characterized by crisis-intensified care burdens. Consequently, it becomes
very easy for community work—from *pandays* to BHWs—to be feminized as
"motherwork" or labor that is "unskilled" and "costless." Without accounting
for gendered divisions of community labor, women's leadership will be narrowly understood as "informal" leadership. It will also be harder to challenge
how and why many women continue to be barred from pursuing other forms
and types of leadership beyond feminized ones precisely because the performance of caring duties remains deeply unequal.

Without material inflows, pushing for greater involvement in community
among women will deliberately draw upon notions of female altruism and
instrumentalize community work as gendered sacrifices women are expected
to take on for the sake of the collective. The role of the state, and local and
international crisis responders, in resourcing community peacebuilding must
also be improved and strengthened. Furthermore, changing the feminization

of community work must be included in the foundational reforms undertaken as part of post-crisis recovery and reconstruction. Broader community participation for different groups of women is dependent on stemming the rates of bodily depletion among the most vulnerable of IDP populations. Which women will be around to build and enjoy peace after conflict or disaster, when many of them become ill and overburdened from servicing both family and community, or are dying due to largely preventable sexual and reproductive health complications?

Gendering Filipino *Bayanihan*

In times of crises, Filipino communities are routinely valorized and idealized as innately resilient by the Philippine state. Similar representations of community resilience are increasingly globalized too amid the internationalized response to large-scale disasters that have impacted the country and elsewhere. Disasters, for example, are memorialized by crediting the efficacy of built-in or indigenous disaster early warning and coping mechanisms such as practices of *bayanihan* or *kapwa tao* among Filipinos.[13] *Bayanihan* is defined as an ancient or pre-colonial practice of mutual aid and cooperation underpinned by deep cultural value placed in altruistically "toiling on another's behalf and assuming another's burden" (Bankoff 2007: 26; Ang 1979). Former President Benigno Aquino III (2015) in his commemoration speech of the Haiyan tragedy stated: "May the memory and lessons of that time inspire us to persevere in *building back better*, and in living up to the solidarity, resilience, and generosity of Filipinos from all walks of life demonstrated not only then, but in all times of challenge and adversity." International media coverage of the disaster, notably from the US CNN reporter Anderson Cooper, similarly reproduced references to the inherent strength and resilience of Filipinos in the aftermath of Haiyan (Macaraig 2013; Su and Mangada 2016; Sherwood et al. 2015).[14]

Representations of *bayanihan* in the context of crisis aftermaths serve as a consistent basis of national hubris and exceptionalism. For example, in another speech, Aquino emphatically exclaimed, "*Alam nating walang bagyong maaaring magpaluhod sa Pilipino kung tayo'y magbabayanihan*" (No storm will make the Filipino get down on his [*sic*] knees as long as we help each other) (Cupin 2013). Amid the tremendous challenges for recovery and rehabilitation post-Haiyan, affected communities were widely praised for their resilience or "self-recovery efforts" in what would otherwise have been an even more devastating disaster (Su and Mangada 2016; Mangada 2016). Similar rhetoric has been used to depict internally displaced communities in Mindanao such that cooperation among members of the community provides not only a deep source of pride but the very will to survive. For example, the United Nations

[78] *Politics of Sexual & Reproductive Health*

High Commissioner for Refugees (UNHCR) reported, "[A]rmed conflict may have disrupted the dreams of Zamboanga City's displaced children, but their families remain resilient and hopeful that their situation can get better soon despite the prolonged hardship of having their normal lives uprooted" (UNHCR Philippines 2016). At the same time, Filipino resilience is increasingly "abused and taken for granted" and can turn into a source of fatigue. As noted in another report from Zamboanga displacements, "[T]he IDPs are holding on, even in the midst of unfulfilled commitments and unexplained circumstances. With incomplete information on their status and their future, they accept what their camp managers tell them, '*Maghintay lang*' (Just wait)" (Asian Institute of Journalism and Communication 2015: 33).

Disasters and crises more broadly have occurred with routine frequency in the Philippines such that the threats they pose are already integrated into the schema of Filipinos' daily lives. According to Bankoff's (2003) historical research on the Philippines, "cultures of disaster" are evident in how the physical environment plays a vital role in shaping norms and values, which in turn impacts the design of political and economic institutions. He stresses that disaster resilience in the country is rooted in a "long history of formal and informal networks committed to individual and community welfare that enhance people's capacity to withstand the magnitude and frequency of daily misfortune as experienced in the archipelago" (Bankoff 2015: 431). Building on this point, I argue that cultures of disaster are embedded within the gendered political economy of community social reproduction. This means questioning when and in what contexts *bayanihan* is inclusive of, or detrimental to, women's bodily autonomy. Crisis narratives that celebrate Filipino resilience, even as they may be well intentioned, such as in boosting morale of crisis responders and uplifting spirits among the disaster affected, become complicit in myth-making because the presence of local customs and indigenous social networks does not automatically guarantee that these ties will be activated toward mobilizing resources in gender-inclusive and transformative ways.

Bayanihan fosters a myth that communities are automatically "safe havens" (Smyth and Sweetman 2015), thus obscuring "communities of harm" (Rubio-Marin, Sandoval, and Diaz 2009). In conflicts and disasters, caring communities co-exist with communities of harm, whereby violence that is physically inflicted on an individual is nevertheless experienced as immediate, symbolic, and inflicting long-term harms by the assemblage of people with whom the victim is enmeshed within (Rubio-Marin, Sandoval, and Diaz 2009: 215). The concept of "communities of harm" can draw attention to harms that are not just experienced collectively but also enacted through the community. For example, while women were contributing more to the survival of households by taking on both productive and reproductive labor, these contributions were valued less. In the case of fishing and farming communities in Haiyan-affected areas, "[l]abor is counted and paid in cash only when it is considered 'hard work' such as land preparation and hauling—work that is usually taken by men or assigned to them" (Novales 2014: 31). The many value-added, time consuming, and direct contributions of women—such as sourcing capital, harvesting and selling produce, equipment maintenance, and of course caring for male farmers and fisher folk—are underpaid and uncounted, which also means that these contributions are rendered invisible in the context of long-term post-crisis recovery. Consequently, post-disaster livelihood assistance in farming and fishing tended to reinforce these gendered divisions through assumptions that designate men as primary beneficiaries (Novales 2014).

In the case of Mindanao, Moro women may not speak up about the particular harms inflicted on them by Moro men because they prioritize the needs of the Bangsamoro above their needs as women. Calculating the collective harms that reporting of sexual and gender-based violence (SGBV) cases may inflict on the Bangsamoro cause, Moro women make strategic decisions to remain silent in order not to vilify or betray their *own* Moro men and community from the state and dominant society (see Chapter 4 for further discussion). This can be most pronounced in Moro communities where *rido* or communal revenge killings are practiced, such that women's silence constitutes an invisible cost of maintaining community social cohesion and peace. These forms of "cooperative" behaviors viewed through the twin lens of social reproduction and bodily autonomy unveil the dangers of romanticizing the community.

The economic devaluing of care labor in the Philippines overlaps with deeply ingrained cultural-religious definitions of family and marriage. For example, the family is defined in heteronormative terms, and this is carried over in humanitarian program assistance. Social reproductive contributions by lesbian, gay, bisexual, and transgender (LGBT) people are typically invisible within representations of the Haiyan disaster (and far more invisible in Mindanao's conflict settings). Still, there were a few positive exceptions of post-Haiyan assessments that have begun to render visible LGBT contributions specifically among *bakla* ("effeminate" straight men and gay men) in post-disaster relief recovery (see Oxfam 2016). Among the insights are the multiple and compounded social reproductive contributions of LGBTs, particularly *bakla*, due to their socially constructed identities that combine masculine breadwinner and feminine caregiver roles (Oxfam 2016). LGBTs are also subjected to particular forms of exclusion, discrimination, and violence, often beginning with their own families, which may become particularly intense in times of emergencies. These harms range from being the last to eat in the family to being excluded from family relief assistance.

The myth of *bayanihan* occludes the violence and discrimination experienced by sexual minorities who are also important contributors in social reproduction by "performing" the role of mothers, wives, and daughters in providing care for families and communities. According to McSherry et al. (2015: 35), in post-disaster contexts:

[80] *Politics of Sexual & Reproductive Health*

young *bakla* often spontaneously walk around the village to collect and distribute relief goods amongst their neighbours. Along with this, *bakla* youth usually care for younger children and cook meals for their family or in temporary shelters. In spite of these contributions, when evacuated to those shelters, *baklas* must endure a lack of privacy, reporting discomfort being isolated amongst either women or men in gender-insensitive settings.

Further, they add that "while *kabaklaan* may be visible and unremarkable in the everyday Philippine context, during disaster times and their aftermath, *bakla* and other sexual and gender minorities elsewhere in the world become increasingly invisible to and unheard of by the dominant society" McSherry et al. (2015: 33). Their contributions are rendered invisible precisely because they do not meet dominant or heteronormative representations of female altruism and the Filipino family. Consequently, LGBTs were not equally entitled to share in the material redistribution post-crisis, while they remain "unwanted but needed" in the continuance of family and community life (Oxfam 2016).

Oxfam (2016: 7) reported that same-sex couples were more likely to be given less priority in the granting of housing in permanent relocation sites post-Haiyan. Same-sex couples faced barriers in accessing relief assistance, which is distributed according to family or household units, because their unions are not formally recognized in national laws to begin with. Moreover, as McSherry et al. (2015: 34) corroborate:

Such was the dilemma faced by some *bakla* evacuees after Typhoon Haiyan hit central Philippines. In such instances, community members who are *bakla* are placed in a double bind. They were not given relief goods without documents, and when they had their documents with them, relief goods were given to them but not without some of them experiencing ridicule and harassment.

LGBTs in general would have been excluded in livelihood assistance if not for the initiative, resistance, and audacity of those who demanded a space for themselves. According to a male informant who works for an international development organization, "[I]n the case of LGBTs, we had no programs specifically for them. Some gays who really wanted to be included were joined in the women in carpentry program."[15] Without access to livelihood and economic opportunities, same-sex households experienced heightened depletion as a result of the disaster even as their communities reaped the benefits of their care labor.

The problem, however, is the cyclical impact of exclusions such that the invisibility of LGBTs in humanitarian relief assistance feeds into the lack of empirical data around the extent of bullying, discrimination, and hate crimes perpetrated against them, which can also be expected to escalate just as other forms of SGBV have in crisis settings.[16] And because there are typically no "hard facts" on LGBTs' experiences, it is much harder to design gender-inclusive emergency response and aid programs unless these specifically respond to prevailing silences around their needs. The valorization of crisis-affected communities as characterized by mutual aid and cooperation must be tempered by intersectional analysis of structural inequalities that influence how crises from conflicts to disasters are differentially experienced.

WOMEN-FRIENDLY SPACES

Among the very few markers of success in promoting gender-responsive crisis interventions was the introduction of the community women friendly spaces (WFS) program implemented through the gender-based violence protection cluster in the Haiyan case study. Increasingly, community WFS programs are now being mainstreamed as part of emergency and humanitarian responses in other conflict-affected communities in the Philippines and by the United Nations Population Fund (UNFPA) in other parts of the world (UNFPA 2015). In 2013, the post-Haiyan WFS program was conducted through the partnership of UNFPA, the Department of Social Welfare and Development (DSWD), UNHCR, the United Nations Children's Fund (UNICEF), Oxfam, and the International Organization for Migration. Primarily, "the idea behind women friendly spaces is that women's distinct needs do not stop in emergency situations."[17] In these spaces:

> Pregnant and lactating women were the beneficiaries. Missions are organised for localities with high demand for repro [reproductive health] missions. There will be several stations that the women go through where they receive info sessions, medical consultations, and at the end they receive the dignity kits. So the second component to the reproductive health assistance aside from the medical missions is the dignity kits.[18]

Through a focus group discussion on WFS facilitated by the DSWD in September 2014, women from Leyte and Eastern Samar evaluated WFS centers as a facility "where they learn about many things, one of which is about their rights as women," as a "place to run to when abused or afraid of their husbands," and which "provides Cash for Work, Livelihood programs, sessions on Health and Hygiene, Women's Rights, Gender Based Violence, Child Trafficking and Child Abuse." The women also indicated that among the many benefits of participation in the WFS initiative were better marital relationships due to women knowing their rights and discussing them with their husbands and stronger community bonds among the women (DSWD 2014). The WFS program prioritized reproductive and maternal health needs, which was innovative and much needed at the time. Still, its presence revealed by

[82] *Politics of Sexual & Reproductive Health*

comparison the absence of efforts to promote broader SRHR for sexual minorities, elderly women, and young adolescents. This is because the program was circumscribed within existing cultural-religious norms and legal barriers to SRHR in the country (see also Chapters 4 and 5).

As part of mainstreaming gender-responsive programs at the community level, an all-female watch group was also set up and credited with success in stemming potential SGBV threats in the IDP camps and transitional shelters. According to a male country representative for an international organization:

SGBV under normal circumstances is already a sensitive issue, in exceptional circumstances the stigma is intensified. The PNP [Philippine National Police] and DSWD brokered a deal on a standby agreement for a cadre of policewomen to also serve as camp managers. In Yolanda [Haiyan], we were able to put this in practice and we were successful. The visibility of women in uniform was key to stemming SGBV . . . Women would be more open to talk to other women as representatives of the state.[19]

According to him, "the efforts put into trainings have started bearing fruit. For example in the Yolanda case, we did a lot to disseminate information on SGBV."[20] The influx of various humanitarian contingents, each designating themselves to particular areas and communities of IDPs, allowed for a wider presence and visibility of security personnel.

While the WFS program was able to address specific post-disaster needs of women and girls through the accessibility of hygiene kits, it was viewed as rather less successful in addressing wider issues of violence and insecurity. One informant, however, was critical of how WFS programs aligned in terms of humanitarian protection goals saying that primarily it "was about toilet segregation in the displacement camps and ensuring that access to water was safe by lighting collection areas."[21] Others noted that the presence of more and varied actors on the ground—state and non-state agencies—contributed to the obfuscation of referral pathways when SGBV cases were identified. As pointed out by a male informant:

UNFPA's program on Women Friendly Spaces involved training partners in reporting and monitoring crisis-related gender-based violence. It sought to coordinate and strengthen referral pathways to protect victims and ensure they are safe and can access justice. However, referral pathways are already problematic even outside of disaster settings.[22]

A female government representative stated too that with more NGOs responding in the disaster-affected areas, "their addition has made more complicated the different referral pathways in place for cases of VAWC [violence against women and children]."[23]

MYTHS OF COMMUNITY SURVIVAL [83]

The WFS program, which emerged as part of crisis response, cannot be divorced from the pre-existing state of community infrastructure in the country. Gaps in assistance and protection are acutely revealed for communities in remote areas and those most volatile to localized conflicts. As discussed earlier, many communities lack access to basic health and protection mechanisms at the *barangay* level, which women in crisis situations are in most need of. Women and girls especially are let down at the basic unit of state support, which is the *barangay* before, during, and after crises. For instance, according to one informant: "We found in Eastern Samar that many LGUs and local police were not even aware of RA 9262 [national anti-VAWC legislation].[24] Among the ten municipalities we surveyed barely 1 percent had issued barangay protection orders. Many did not even know how to issue one."[25] As noted by Oxfam Philippines, "out of 52 health facilities, [only] 22 provided sexual violence and rape management services and 35 provided referral service" (Novales 2014: 29). The compounding harms that victims of violence suffer due to failures in frontline response is captured in an anecdote shared by another female informant:

> There was a case of a woman in Tolosa, Leyte where she ended up seeking help via protection order from the *barangay* three times because they were unable to adequately help her or prevent further violence from the husband on two accounts.[26]

The Haiyan disaster was crucial in exposing the failings of state protection services, which directly compound the violation of women's rights. Their interrelationships are clear in that reporting goes hand in hand with accessibility of medical services for victims of SGBV. Similarly, as pointed out by informants on Mindanao: "[G]etting actual reports or data on sexual violence or rape is very difficult but it is a common knowledge that such violence is perpetrated by all groups. The proliferation of guns or small arms is also relevant to this issue. Many *barangays* also lack police stations and health centers."[27] This means that before and after a crisis, victims of SGBV are not guaranteed access to adequate health treatment, protection, and redress. Such gaps create an environment conducive to impunity for perpetrators, allowing them to thrive especially at the community level. They also mutually exacerbate the material and socio-cultural norms that undermine women's and girls' bodily autonomy and well-being (see also Davies, True, and Tanyag 2016).

Women and girls are least likely to report and seek assistance when doing so entails surmounting significant barriers that undercut the fulfillment of their social reproductive roles for their families especially in the face of multiple care obligations post-crisis. In extreme cases, those in geographically remote areas do not even have the option to report given that they are typically not reached by these initiatives and consequently remain without access to

[84] *Politics of Sexual & Reproductive Health*

protection measures prior to and after a crisis (Novales 2014). These everyday gaps in state protection services, therefore, undermine the gains that have been achieved from reporting and monitoring efforts like the deployment of all-female watch groups and gender-responsive disaster contingents and in the WFS.

CONCLUSION

This chapter has shown how restrictions to bodily autonomy especially for women and girls arise at the community level where unpaid care and domestic work is once again expected to fill in the gaps for various crisis-specific programs and assistance. This reliance is not simultaneously matched by health and social welfare provisioning necessary to replenish and renew the bodies that labor for the community. Instead, women through their community roles bear the intensification of care provisioning necessary for community survival during times of crisis but at great cost to their health and wellbeing. Drawing on the case of displacement sites in the Philippines, I highlight an important factor driving individual bodily and community depletion. Material restrictions on the rights of the body to health and security are enabled by discursive representations of survival, which can mythologize the extent of mutual aid, resilience and altruism among communities.

First, while communities of care do exist and often become central in crisis situations, social reproductive costs need to be accounted for as an indispensable step in reversing current trends in the depletion of bodies in pursuit of community survival. SRHR and more equitable household division of labor must be promoted within the context of post-conflict and post-disaster reconstruction as indispensable to fostering truly caring communities. Second, the "paradoxical effects" of care work is such that it "both limits and enhances traditional forms of civic engagement . . . that unpaid care work, in and of itself, constitutes a vital form of civic activity" (Herd and Meyer 2002: 669). Recognizing care and domestic work done at the household and within communities as civic and political engagement matters for fundamentally reframing current modes of allocating resources and authority during and after crises. Unless broader political and economic transformations occur to value community labor away from an overemphasis and overreliance on feminized sacrifice and altruism, initiatives that promote women's inclusion, participation, and leadership in a range of community-based activities will likely exacerbate and multiply the numerous pre-existing care responsibilities women already bear within their households and communities. Furthermore, there are positive cascading benefits to economically valuing community services for promoting inclusive SRHR, stemming SGBV, and strengthening everyday access to justice.

By examining how bodily autonomy is situated within communities of harm and care, this chapter demonstrated why gender is not separate from the political economy of crisis response across conflict and disaster settings. Bodily autonomy is indispensable for challenging the growing ubiquity of community survival myths particularly through the hegemonic deployment of resilience narratives in crisis settings. Such narratives, when they are complicit in reproducing the invisibility of women's labor, exacerbate experiences of violence and inequalities in post-crisis recovery and reconstruction. The myth that communities not only survive crises but are even capable of thriving through self-reliance creates opportunistic spaces for legitimizing state abrogation of responsibilities specifically in the reallocation of resources for strengthening community infrastructures. This is most evident in representations of Filipino communities' inherent ingenuity and innovation when stretching available resources, all the while made possible by the intensification and feminization of community work deliberately harnessed in crisis response and in the day-to-day functions of the state. As the case of crisis-affected communities in the Philippines shows, there are real dangers to "happy-washing" post-conflict and post-disaster recovery in the absence of material inflows to sustain SRHR and social reproduction more broadly. When left unchallenged, we are likely to see more and more of these survival myths globalized. Representations of self-help, mutual aid, and cooperation come at the cost of depleting bodies, and long-term community civic engagement and participation sacrificed for immediate but uneven survival.

[86]   *Politics of Sexual & Reproductive Health*

CHAPTER 4

Patriarchal Bargains and Nation-building in the Aftermath of Crisis

INTRODUCTION

Crises are critical junctures to a long and ongoing nation-building project. They place in sharper focus on how depletion operates most intensely for those deemed to challenge or transgress national identity. This chapter examines how women's bodies are integral to the symbolic and biological reproduction of the nation and how as a result, the political and economic stakes over the control of women's bodies may become higher during and in the aftermath of crises. Sexual and reproductive freedoms have always been at the heart of authoritative struggles over claims on how society and the roles and relationships within it ought to be (Yuval-Davis and Anthias 1989; Yuval-Davis 1997). Building on the analysis of depletion of households and communities discussed in previous chapters, here I draw out their continuum with the accumulation and cascading effects of depletion at the national level.

Seeing crises as constitutive of national and global politics of bodily autonomy, reveals fundamental answers to questions of who is served by, and who services, nation-building during and in the aftermath of a crisis. Who gets to decide what is on the security agenda? Paradoxically, despite how acceptance of, and support for, gender equality has never been more global, maneuvers to diminish the importance of gender issues, especially sexual and reproductive health and rights, also heighten where and when the need for gender equality matters the most. All too often, across various levels of crisis decision-making, gender is relegated to what Cynthia Enloe (2004) calls the patriarchal time zone of "later." This tyranny of urgency translates to how

---

The Global Politics of Sexual and Reproductive Health. Maria Tanyag, Oxford University Press.
© Oxford University Press 2024. DOI: 10.1093/oso/9780197676332.003.0005

gender is believed "to come after" or become relevant only when the "real" work of crisis response and reconstruction has been done. By doing so, it is assumed that gender equality will automatically follow when political and economic order is restored. Yet, as Maria Libertad Dometita, former Oxfam Haiyan Response Gender Coordinator argued, "gender cannot wait until a subsequent phase of the [crisis] response. We could not delay it. If we fail to identify gender specific needs then women will find themselves with less time, less money, less resources. Power, insecurity, and gender inequalities will be further perpetuated" (Oxfam 2015: 35).

The quality of daily human life reproduction and collective pursuits of a nation are interdependent with the health and well-being enjoyed by people and the labors they enable. The denial of this interdependence is reflective of patriarchal political and economic *ordering*. Crisis narratives have the power to sequester the appropriateness of gender interventions across multiple temporalities and spatial realities. Feminist analysis therefore entails resisting the seductions of such narratives to reveal how competing state, non-state, and international actors *routinely* intervene, regulate, and instrumentalize sexual and reproductive freedoms especially during and after crises, in a bid to retain or redefine who constitutes the nation. It asks when and how are material and ideological conditions to bodily depletion weaponized against those who are deemed marginal to, and displaced from, nation-building?

While there are power imbalances in how crises are embodied at the national level, it is important to note that this process is itself a site of struggle and negotiation and that women are not passive victims upon whose bodies national contestations are merely enacted. Rather, as demonstrated by the experiences in the Philippines examined in this chapter, women's bodies are the most immediate resource at their disposal through which they can make material and symbolic bids in pursuit of individual and collective interests within a global neoliberal logic of depletion. Women thus regularly bargain with patriarchy in their households, communities, the state, and transnationally both during and in the aftermath of crises in order to strategically optimize their life chances within a set of gendered "rules of the game" defined by class, race/ethnicity, religion, age, sexuality, and geographic location (Kandiyoti 1988). Patriarchal bargains reveal that bodily autonomy is *relative autonomy* for women as they calculate and employ different coping mechanisms in response to varying sets of material and cultural-religious constraints, which are themselves fluid and constantly renegotiated (Kandiyoti 1988: 286). Analyzing how women are differently positioned vis-à-vis nationhood provides rich insights for explaining ambivalences and disconnections between the proliferation of gender-responsive global and national agendas that inform crisis response and reconstruction on the one hand and, on the other, everyday realities for women's health and well-being during and after crises.

This chapter is divided into three parts. The first section examines the Philippines as a model country and regional leader for pioneering achievements in meeting gender equality indicators of global security and development agendas. The country's global performance and reputation in gender equality rankings and indexes inform and validate representations of national exceptionalism vis-à-vis Filipino women's political participation and leadership. The second section analyzes Filipino women's participation and leadership as patriarchal bargains in post-conflict and post-disaster settings to make visible how women are brought into spheres of crisis political decision-making in limited but legitimizing ways for the symbolic and biological reproduction of the nation. The third section draws out the linkages between women's patriarchal bargains in times of crisis and the everyday political economy of sexual and reproductive freedoms in the Philippines. Pre-existing gendered inequalities among various groups of Filipino women differently position them in post-crisis nation-building. Although siloed from political negotiations and economic brokerage of peace, women's sexual and reproductive bargains ensure survival of a nation constantly responding to multiple crises. Finally, the concluding section provides critical reflections on the quality of post-crisis national rebuilding achieved at the expense of bodily depletion. It questions to what extent women's participation can live up to the promise of durable peace within prevailing logics and conditions of state-sanctioned depletion. Can short-term gains achieved through patriarchal bargains lead to long-term peace?

REPRODUCING EXCEPTIONALISM AND THE PHILIPPINES AS A "MODEL COUNTRY"

Exceptionalism is part of Philippine everyday nationalism simultaneously constructed and negotiated from within and without. On the one hand, the country is entangled within a global hierarchical order among states such that advancing women's status in society is now a widely accepted norm in pursuit of international standing (Towns 2010, 2014). Within this hierarchical order, developing countries such as the Philippines have the incentive to innovate and "pioneer" on the fulfillment of gender equality metrics in a bid to perform, maintain, or "move up" in global rankings. On the other, as Angeles (2020) points out, generations of Filipina feminists, from the American colonial period to the present, have been adept at navigating, utilizing, and resisting discourses framing Philippine exceptionalism. This included anticolonial and nationalist construction of "exceptionality" used by Filipina feminists to frame difference from Western states in terms of women's status as part of anticolonial and postcolonial nation-building projects. This discursive strategy affirmed variants of postcolonial feminist critique from women scholars and

PATRIARCHAL BARGAINS AND NATION-BUILDING [89]

activists in Asia of "idealised precolonial life" to illustrate how colonialism drastically altered the status held and privileges enjoyed by women during precolonial times (Angeles 2020: 232; see also Jayawardena 1986; Edwards and Roces 2004; Mohanty 2003). Contemporary claims of Philippine uniqueness range from "Asia's 'first republic,' 'only Catholic country,' 'only former Spanish colony,' or 'leading English-speaking country'" as well as: "Asia's 'first country to systematically decentralize' with the 'strongest history of democratic decentralization' in the region. The Philippines is also heralded as the 'most gender-equal country in Asia' consistent with a popular view that Filipinas are among the most liberated women in Asia and in the world" (Angeles 2020: 230). Indeed, as noted in an International Peace Institute report, "in 1981, it was the first Southeast Asian nation to ratify the Convention on the Elimination of Discrimination against Women (CEDAW)" (O'Reilly, Ó Súilleabháin, and Paffenholz 2015: 20). Moreover, the country has been recognized as a global and regional exemplar for promoting gender across peace and security and disaster risk reduction and climate change agendas.

Women's bodies are central to reproducing a country's global status. In the case of the Philippines, representations of exceptionalism co-exist within the same gendered political economy dynamics that position Filipino women as having a comparative advantage in care and sexual economies on the basis of essential maternal attributes (see Chapter 1). Markers of national gender equality achievements are steeped in contradictions when restrictions to bodily autonomy also exist. There is a risk that a country's exemplary global standing in peace, security, and development agendas contributes to the depletion of women's bodies in the absence of material inflows to address the embodied costs of, and gaps fostered by, exceptionalism. What the case of the Philippines alerts us to is that social hierarchies among states are constituted within a particular global political economy—one that sustains and operates on a logic of depletion through the occlusion of long-standing barriers in sexual and reproductive health.

Women, Peace and Security (WPS) Agenda

In 2010, the Philippines became the first country in the Asia-Pacific to have adopted a national action plan for UN Security Council Resolution 1325 (UN Women 2015: 241). This has been widely celebrated as a model for monumental achievements and for showing the world "what works" and "how it can be done" in gender-inclusive peace processes (O'Reilly, Ó Súilleabháin, and Paffenholz 2015; UN Women 2015). Drawing on the Bangsamoro peace process, it has been regarded as an "outlier" for global women's participation in peace processes and strong civil-society orientation in contrast to elite and military-driven peace processes where key figures all come from military

[90] *Politics of Sexual & Reproductive Health*

backgrounds (O'Reilly, Ó Súilleabháin, and Paffenholz 2015: 9; UN Women 2015). On March 27, 2014, the Comprehensive Agreement on the Bangsamoro (CAB) was signed between the Moro Islamic Liberation Front (MILF) and the government of the Philippines. The CAB became a historic peace agreement for signaling the end of a forty-year conflict and 17 years of negotiations between the two sides.

Prior to the Bangsamoro peace deal, there had been several peace agreements that resulted from distinct but interconnected peace processes between the government and two main factions of Moro rebels, the MILF and the Moro National Liberation Front (MNLF). All of them largely failed to generate political commitment and action and did not progress to the same extent as CAB.[1] By contrast, the success of CAB was largely credited to a number of key political factors. First, the full support of former President Benigno "Noynoy" Aquino III and the military played catalytic roles. The Aquino government made the Bangsamoro peace process central to its national agenda and brought to bear the full political commitment of the executive branch (Transitional Justice and Reconciliation Commission 2016). This commitment continued after the signing of CAB, with Aquino pushing for the enactment of a Bangsamoro Basic Law that would implement provisions in CAB until the end of his presidential term. Second, the agreement was strongly anchored in the Moros' right to self-determination and pursuit of political and economic autonomy. The peace process was viewed favorably and had the popular support of the Moros who believed that the signing of a peace agreement between the negotiating teams might truly secure lasting peace in Mindanao and for the country as a whole. Indeed, CAB was considered a fundamental step for advancing Moros' historical grievances, which had been ignored or erased by previous governments (Transitional Justice and Reconciliation Commission 2016). In the preamble, CAB states:

> Underlying the CAB is the recognition of the justness and legitimacy of the cause of the Bangsamoro people and their aspiration to chart their political future through democratic process that will secure their identity and posterity and allow for meaningful self-governance . . . The Parties . . . commit to . . . reduce social, economic, and political inequalities; correct historical injustice committed against the Bangsamoro; and remove cultural inequities through the agreed modalities aimed at equitably diffusing wealth and political power for the common good. (Comprehensive Agreement on the Bangsamoro 2014: 1)

It also provides a framework for revenue generation and wealth-sharing, power-sharing between Bangsamoro authority and central government, and a normalization plan addressing socio-economic development and transitional justice and reconciliation. With the signing of the peace deal, armed encounters between the government and the MILF were significantly lessened and conflict deaths declined (International Alert 2014). According to the Internal Displacement Monitoring Centre, "the total number of people displaced by conflict and violence reached its lowest level since 2011" (IDMC 2015b: 1).

Third, the success of the Bangsamoro peace process was attributed to strong women's leadership and participation in and outside of the formal peace process, which enabled high levels of engagement among civil society groups and relatively gender-balanced negotiations. The Bangsamoro peace process became historic for having the world's first female chief negotiator—Miriam Coronel-Ferrer from the government panel—to sign a peace agreement. According to the global report of UN Women (2015: 45), between 1990 and 2011 and across 31 peace processes that the UN was involved in, women represented just 2% of chief mediators, 4% of witnesses and signatories, and 9% of negotiators. In the case of Mindanao, women represented 50% of the government's negotiating team and 25% of the signatories. Women were present from both sides of the negotiating table and throughout the peace negotiation process (see also O'Reilly, Ó Súilleabháin, and Paffenholz 2015). This level of representation was built incrementally and at critical junctures by pioneering women who, after inclusion in the formal peace process, lobbied for and included other women.

In 1998, Dr Emily Marohombsar (*Manila Times* 2013), a Moro from the Maranao[2] ethnic group, was the first and only female member of the government of the Philippines negotiating panel for the MILF peace process. Subsequently in 2001, with the appointment of Irene Santiago, the number of women increased to two. Since 2004, both the numbers and roles of women increased such that, by June 2014 at the Global Summit to End Sexual Violence in Conflict held in London, the Philippines with its majority-female delegation was recognized as a "success story" or a model for women's participation in peacebuilding (Republic of the Philippines Department of Foreign Affairs 2014). Filipina feminist and then-Presidential Adviser on the Peace Process Teresita Quintos Deles underscored the global significance of the Bangsamoro peace process: "The Philippine government has blazed a trail, ahead of many other countries, for women's participation in its peace processes" (OPAPP 2014: 1). For her part, Coronel-Ferrer credits deliberate decisions to include women and gender in the peace process, including Deles's leadership in influencing Aquino to consider her as the "right person for the job" despite his initial hesitation. Eventually she was "glad another woman kept the faith in [her] and that the President too kept his faith on two women to see through a concern that is very important to him" (OPAPP 2014: 6).

Women's presence on the peace panel enabled the creation of high-level opportunities for drawing attention to the gendered consequences of armed conflicts and for substantively integrating gender in peace and security. Throughout the Bangsamoro peace process, Coronel-Ferrer noted that "windows of opportunity" opened for them unexpectedly:

> On the item on non-discrimination based on sex, creed, race, ethnicity and so on, then MILF panel member Datu Michael Mastura moved to use "gender" instead of sex which he deemed a controversial subject. Qualifying that he is not saying that there is no sexuality in Islam, he nonetheless cautioned that the *ulamas* are wary of the *s* word. We heartily agreed to replace it with the even better alternative word that he had proposed. (OPAPP 2014: 4)

The unlikely route to the inclusion of the word "gender" in the Bangsamoro peace deal instead of the word "sex," which was understood narrowly as sexual intercourse, reflects the propitious spaces afforded to women negotiators. These advances—regardless of how fraught with misconceptions—establish precedents which can allow for structural reforms that stem the disproportionate bodily depletion of women in conflict situations. Still, these opportunities would not have been possible, let alone actually harnessed in pursuit of gender equality outcomes, if not for women negotiators who championed gender. As pointed out by an informant, "relative to other peace negotiations, MILF has made significant adjustments to accommodate 'gender' or women's perspectives due in part to the presence of female negotiators."[3] In addition, the MILF's position on women's participation in the peace process had to respond to growth in domestic and international pressures over the years, especially from civil society organizations mobilizing under Resolution 1325.

Civil society networks, notably the Women Engaged in Action on 1325 (WE Act 1325), built on pre-existing strong feminist and peace activism in the country to ensure that the Bangsamoro peace process was strongly aligned with the global WPS Agenda (Trojanowska 2019). Civil society engagement was sustained from the signing of CAB through to lobbying for its enactment as law. Women's direct participation and leadership in the peace process cascaded to broader and more diverse participation from interest groups and constituencies even after the signing of the peace agreement. Moreover, according to the Office of the Presidential Adviser on the Peace Process, the Philippine government in negotiating with the MILF conducted and participated in 553 consultations with various stakeholders including non-Muslim indigenous or Lumad elders (see Figure 4.1). Consequently, this strong inclusion of various stakeholders corresponded with trust and approval especially among communities in the Bangsamoro territories even as episodic violence led to a decline in national support for Bangsamoro autonomy and threatened to derail the peace process (Social Weather Stations 2013, 2015).[4]

Research by Krause, Krause, and Bränfors (2018) examined the relationship between women's participation in peace negotiations and the quality and durability of the resulting peace. Drawing on their analysis of peace agreements, they found that "*linkages* between women civil society groups and female signatories positively impact accord content and implementation" (2018: 987, emphasis in the original). In the Philippine case, linkages between women

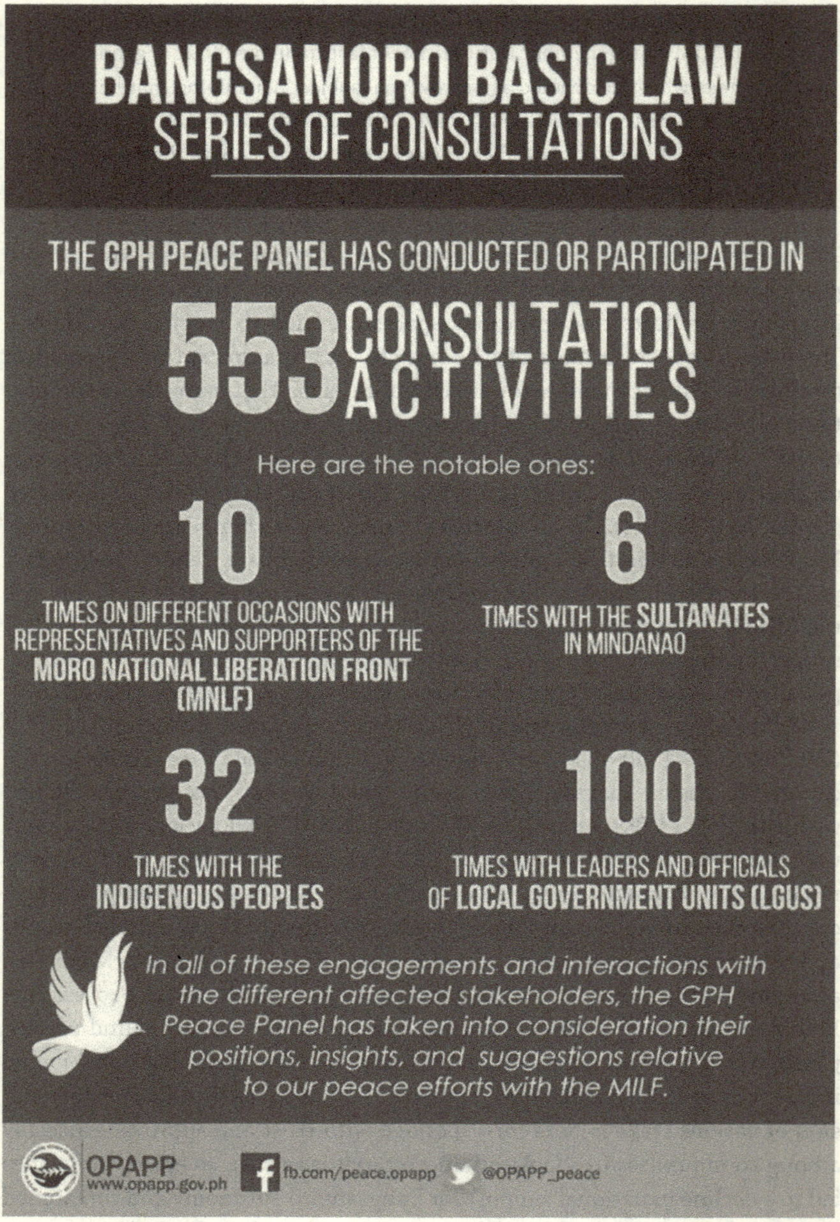

Figure 4.1. Civil society participation numbers in Government of the Philippines (GPH) Peace Panel consultations
Source: OPAPP.gov.ph

[94] *Politics of Sexual & Reproductive Health*

from both sides of the negotiating parties with civil society organizations such as WE Act 1325 indeed enhanced the legitimacy and representativeness of the peace process and resulting peace deal. The CAB and Bangsamoro Basic Law reflected broad-based socio-economic reforms including gender-responsive provisions in addition to power-sharing and territorial provisions. This is illustrated strongly in the 2012 Framework Agreement on the Bangsamoro, a precursor to CAB, which explicitly guarantees the *"meaningful political participation of women"* post-conflict and "protection from all forms of violence" (Framework Agreement on the Bangsamoro 2012, emphasis added). Similarly, in CAB, women-specific provisions in the peace agreement and succeeding annexes include: (a) at least 5% of Bangsamoro official development funds must be set aside for supporting women through a gender and development plan (*Annex on Revenue and Wealth Sharing 2013*); (b) the Bangsamoro governance structure shall consist of a council of elders where women and other sectors will be guaranteed representation (*Annex on Power Sharing 2013*); and (c) there will be targeted socio-economic assistance for decommissioned MILF women auxiliary forces (*Annex on Normalization 2014*) (Global Network of Women Peacebuilders 2014; O'Reilly, Ó Súilleabháin, and Paffenholz 2015: 24).

The Philippine national action plan on 1325 has been "localized" or implemented as concrete programs in conflict-affected areas in the Philippines including the Bangsamoro areas of Mindanao (Global Network of Women Peacebuilders 2014; WE Act 1325 2016). The local implementation of the national action plan alongside the peace process strengthened civil society linkages further by building trust in the peace process at grassroots levels and ensuring that peace reforms were already strongly tethered to post-conflict recovery and long-term development needs in Mindanao. The national action plan is implemented primarily through the government's *Payapa at Masaganang Pamayanan* (peaceful and prosperous [also resilient] communities, PAMANA) program. PAMANA serves as "a complementary track to peace negotiations, [it] aims to extend development interventions to isolated, hard-to-reach, conflict-affected communities to ensure that they are not left behind . . . PAMANA remains as the government's flagship program for conflict-vulnerable and affected areas in the country." Further, it "aimed to implement the NAP [national action plan] WPS through PAMANA as part of its own gender mainstreaming strategy. As a result, there had been efforts to include women in post-conflict normalization and community development and peace process" (WE Act 1325 2016: 19). The program consisted of allocation of priority funding for agricultural (e.g., farming assistance) and community infrastructures (e.g., improving roads and water supplies) and community engagement through focus group discussions among Bangsamoro women, the first of which was held in December 2011, prior to CAB.

The focus group discussions identified the following as priority gender-related concerns: lack of livelihood opportunities and poor literacy rates in Basilan, the plight of internally displaced women in Lanao del Sur, human trafficking in Maguindanao, a "cycle of violence" in Sulu, and human trafficking and deportation in Tawi-Tawi (We Act 1325 2016: 55). Subsequently, these forms of community engagement were regular conduits between women negotiators and Moro women on the frontlines of conflict. As one of the few cases globally, the Philippines substantiates why women's participation matters for the quality and durability of peace (Krause, Krause, and Bränfors 2018; UN Women 2015). Moreover, although still uncommon at a global level, it showed that where there is an inclusion of gender perspectives and women's participation, "agreements with female signatories included a maximum of provisions with regard to political, social, and economic reform" (Krause, Krause, and Bränfors 2018: 1001; see also True and Riveros-Morales 2019; Bell and McNicholl 2019). Indeed, PAMANA and the national action plan 1325 consistently raised the socio-economic dimensions of armed conflicts, which in turn were translated into the actual peace agreement.

Disaster Risk Reduction and Climate Change Agenda

In the area of disaster risk reduction and climate change, representations of exceptionalism emerge in response to the Philippines being ranked as among the most disaster-prone countries in the world. Based on the 2016 Global Climate Risk (GCR) Index by GermanWatch, it was among the top countries identified as extremely vulnerable to climate change risks both in terms of exceptional catastrophes and continuous threats (Kreft et al. 2015). The GCR Index quantifies the impacts of extreme weather events in terms of direct fatalities and indirect or long-term socio-economic losses sustained as a result of a disaster. According to two datasets—one examining risks for 2014 and a more longitudinal analysis from 1995 to 2014—the country has consistently topped in both rankings, along with other primarily developing countries in the Asia-Pacific region such as Thailand and Myanmar. However, the Philippines is distinct in that it is shown to recurrently experience extreme catastrophes within a 20-year period, such as super typhoon Haiyan in 2013, and for consistently having an average of 8–9 typhoons per year (Kreft et al. 2015: 8).

The frequent occurrence of environmental disasters in the country means that disaster-induced displacements are also a regular rather than exceptional experience for millions of Filipinos. According to the Internal Displacement Monitoring Centre's Disaster Displacement Risk Index, the country is ranked second in terms of the highest relative risk of disaster-induced displacement, with approximately 21,000 per million Filipinos at risk per year (IDMC

2015a: 23). This index also predicts future displacement trajectories based on historical data from the 1994–2003 period on the frequency and intensity of displacements in a given country, thus corroborating findings on the Philippines in the GCR Index. Because of routine exposure to mega-disasters and compounded climate risks, the Philippines is also at the frontline of developing national policies on disaster risk reduction and climate change in the Asia-Pacific region (ARROW 2014). Special Representative of the UN Secretary-General on Disaster Risk Reduction Margareta Wahlstrom considers the country's laws as the "best in the world" and indicates "a proactive stance in addressing disasters" (quoted in IDMC 2015a: 30).

One of the pioneering legislations is the Climate Change Act of 2009 (also known as Republic Act 9729).[5] This law paved the way for two key reforms: the creation of a Climate Change Commission and the adoption of a National Climate Change Action Plan (2011-2028). Climate change reform, according to the Commission, is in response to globally acknowledged rising temperatures and locally recorded climate changes such as the "slight increase in the number of cyclones in the Visayas during 1971-2000 compared with the 1951 to 1980 and 1960–1990 periods" (Climate Change Commission 2011: 2). The Climate Change Act sets forth the building of a "climate-resilient and climate-smart Philippines with highly adaptive communities" as a national priority. To this end, climate resilience policy must "incorporate a gender-sensitive, pro-children (*sic*) and pro-poor perspective in all climate change and renewable energy efforts, plans and programs" (Section 2). Under the law, the Commission must be composed of four commissioners, at least one of whom should be a woman (Climate Change Commission n.d.). In the climate change action plan, "gender and development" is explicitly defined as "cut[ting] across strategic priorities and sectors" such that "gender-responsive" approaches are mainstreamed across all levels and areas of climate policy-making (Climate Change Commission 2011: 6). Commission resolution no. 2019-002 mandates the need to create sex-disaggregated data as part of gender analysis and gender-responsive climate change governance.

Another landmark piece of legislation called the National Disaster Risk Reduction and Management Act of 2010 (also known as Republic Act 10121)[6] seeks to:

> [a]dopt a disaster risk reduction and management approach that is holistic, comprehensive, integrated, and proactive in lessening the socioeconomic and environmental impacts of disasters including climate change, and promote the involvement and participation of all sectors and all stakeholders concerned, at all levels, especially the local community. (Section 2, Article d)

It promotes the mainstreaming of disaster risk reduction and climate change in development processes across the policy areas of agriculture, water, health, education, and poverty (Section 2, Article g). The Act enabled the creation of the National Disaster Risk Reduction and Management Council, which serves as the chief coordinating body for monitoring, evaluating, and preparing for disasters in the country. The Act also stipulates that the development and implementation of a National Disaster Risk Reduction and Management Plan (NDRRMP) must be founded on partnerships of national and local governments in building disaster resilience (Section 2, Article e). It guarantees that "disaster risk reduction and climate change measures are gender responsive, sensitive to indigenous knowledge systems, and respectful of human rights" (Section 2, Article j). It even recommends the need to "enhance and implement a program where humanitarian aid workers, communities, health professionals, government aid agencies, donors, and the media are educated and trained on how they can actively support breastfeeding before and during a disaster and/or an emergency" (Section 2, Article o). The NDRRMP for 2011–2028 provides indicators, expected outcomes, and obligations of state agencies down to the *barangay* level in creating "safer, adaptive and disaster-resilient Filipino communities toward sustainable development" (National Disaster Risk Reduction and Management Council 2012).

The Philippine Commission on Women, which is the primary policy-making and coordinating body on women and national gender equality concerns, forms part of, or is institutionally represented in, both the Climate Change Commission and the National Disaster Risk Reduction and Management Council. Nationally, it serves as the focal point for ensuring gender is incorporated across all governmental decision-making and is a prime mover for the Philippines to meet its international gender equality obligations. Similarly, civil society representation, including from local women's organizations, is required both by the National Disaster Risk Reduction and Management Act and Climate Change Act. In addition to these crisis-specific legislations, pre-existing gender equality laws in the country recognize the distinct and disproportionate impacts of natural disasters on women and girls. They serve to reinforce the strong recognition of gender in the national laws on climate change and disaster resilience.

The Magna Carta of Women (also known as Republic Act 9710)[7] includes Section 10 on "Women Affected by Disasters, Calamities, and Other Crisis Situations." It guarantees that:

> Women have the right to protection and security in times of disasters, calamities, and other crisis situations especially in all phases of relief, recovery, rehabilitation, and construction efforts. The State shall provide for immediate humanitarian assistance, allocation of resources, and early resettlement, if necessary. It shall also address the particular needs of women from a gender perspective to ensure their full protection from sexual exploitation and other sexual and gender-based violence committed against them. Responses to

disaster situations shall include the provision of services, such as psychosocial support, livelihood support, education, psychological health, and comprehensive health services, including protection during pregnancy.

The same law provides the Philippine state's related obligations to women in conflict situations. Under Section 29:

(a) Increase the number of women participating in discussions and decision-making in the peace process . . . (b) Ensure the development and inclusion of women's welfare and concerns in the peace agenda in the overall peace strategy . . . (e) The recognition and support for women's role in conflict prevention, management, resolution and peacemaking, and in indigenous systems of conflict resolution.

Finally, the Responsible Parenthood and Reproductive Health (RPRH) Act of 2012 (also known as Republic Act 10354), which took almost two decades to enact, stipulates key provisions on advancing sexual and reproductive health including the relevant assistance on comprehensive emergency obstetric and newborn care in disaster contexts (see also Chapter 1). Importantly, Section 4.15 of the implementing rules and regulations of the RPRH Law entitled "Maternal and Newborn Health Care in Crisis Situations" provides that:

The LGUs [local government units] and the DOH [Department of Health] shall ensure that a minimum initial service package[8] for reproductive health, including maternal and neonatal health care kits and services as defined by the DOH, shall be given proper attention in crisis situations such as disasters and humanitarian crises. The minimum initial service package shall become part of the DOH response to crises and emergencies.[9]

Referencing the lessons learnt from the 2013 Typhoon Haiyan experience, the DOH issued Administrative Order 2016-05 in February 2016, which provides further policy guidance on minimum initial service packages and dignity kits in emergencies and disasters, consistent with the RPRH Law (Senate of the Philippines 2016). The administrative order mandates that dignity kits must be "pre-positioned," especially in disaster-prone areas such as Visayas. Moreover, LGUs, given their direct relationship and proximity to communities, are tasked with playing a lead role in ensuring reliable and timely access to emergency health services, as opposed to the national government. This reinforces provisions in the National Disaster Risk Reduction and Management Act that stipulate local governments of every province, city, and municipality down to basic units of the *barangay* should have disaster risk reduction and management committees and offices. Further, these local units must ensure that "there is an efficient mechanism for immediate delivery of food, shelter and medical supplies for women and children, [and] endeavor to create a special place where internally-displaced mothers can find help with breastfeeding, feed and care for their babies and give support to each other" (Section 12c, 16). These laws and policies demonstrate that the Philippines has made progress in gender mainstreaming across national disaster risk reduction and environmental and climate change governance. They reflect the presence of strong and pre-existing gender perspectives and institutions sustained by Filipino women's activism in the country.

Global research on the Environment and Gender Index measures country performance in relation to a number of gender, environment, and sustainable development indicators. In particular, the Index ranks countries based on multi-country data categorized under six themes: livelihood, ecosystem, gender-based rights and participation, governance, gender-based education and assets, and country reported activities that refer to inclusion of gender in Conference of Parties reports. Findings from the Index show that "countries which take seriously their commitments to advancing gender equality in environmental arenas are making strides toward long-term wellbeing for all their citizens" (IUCN 2015: 2). Consequently, countries working toward gender equality are also more likely to achieve climate justice (IUCN 2013, 2015). Building on the Environment and Gender Index, one report examined case studies of women in environmental decision-making in Ecuador, Liberia, and the Philippines. Its key findings indicate that the Philippines is "the strongest performer from a policy standpoint" on gender inclusion in environmental decision-making. Moreover, it "has been a leader, especially within Southeast Asia, for enacting gender-sensitive policies and other policies pertaining to women's rights since the late 1980s" (Luna et al. 2015: 7). These in turn translate to an overall strong performance in Filipino women's representation in international environmental delegations, especially women from civil society organizations.

The report, however, also noted that the country has had "mixed success" due to the gap between world-leading legislation and substantive participation and leadership on environmental decision-making, especially at higher positions in governance. For example, Filipino women remain the minority in the government, making up only 20% of Philippine ministers and 36% of vice-ministers of the environment (Luna et al. 2015: 30). Women's environmental leadership tends to be more visible at lower levels of governance and in non-governmental organization (NGO) spaces, while those in geographically remote, poor, and crisis-affected areas face the most barriers to participation and representation. In the case of post–Typhoon Haiyan Philippines, the creation and subsequent implementation of Women Friendly Spaces in disaster settings and women-led gender-based violence patrols and relief distribution teams as well as the coordination of women's organizations in crisis response and planning nationwide through the Women in Emergencies

[100] *Politics of Sexual & Reproductive Health*

Network (WeNet Philippines) are all evidence of Filipino women's frontline everyday leadership in times of emergencies (ActionAid International 2016). These examples help fuel and sustain national narratives of exceptionalism—constructed internally by local feminists and women's activists, and externally through global gendered hierarchies of order—that the Philippines and in particular Filipino women are among the best in the world when it comes to promoting gender in crisis-related policy-making.

CRISIS AND BARGAINING WITH PATRIARCHY

Women's bodies are sites of struggle over the reproduction of the nation (Yuval-Davis 1997; Stevens 1999). Violent competition, largely by and among men for national political and economic resources, also represents competition over the control of women's labor, their mobility, and wider access to political decision-making and economic opportunities. As Jindy Pettman (1996: 186) argues, "violence demonstrates the boundaries of belonging, as well as, who owns the territory." During and in the aftermath of crises such as conflicts and disasters, ongoing processes of boundary-making more intensely inscribe national political and economic order on women's bodies. At the same time, the politics of bodily autonomy reveals how women strategize around, resist, and renegotiate patriarchal structures and ideologies that govern their everyday lives.

Bodily Autonomy and Self-determination: Two Sides of the Same Coin?

Peace negotiations are negotiations over the gender order. Minority group rights to self-determination are embodied and reproduced by women's bodies and labor; hence, peace agreements symbolically and materially reflect whose bodies serve as carriers of tradition and markers of difference (Yuval-Davis 1997). Coronel-Ferrer recounted an anecdote of the Bangsamoro peace negotiations:

> MILF Panel Chair Mohagher Iqbal said his piece. Speaking from his heart, he believed that women and men cannot have absolute equality because they are different physically, biologically and even emotionally . . .
>
> [To which Coronel-Ferrer replied] Yes we are different, biologically, socially. Men traditionally carried arms, women gave birth. But equality is not about sameness. It is about relationships founded on mutual respect and the dignity of both persons. It is no different from what the MILF wanted for the Bangsamoro—parity of esteem. The same "parity of esteem" or mutual respect

that is desired between the majority and the minority population is desirable as well between men and women. (OPAPP 2014: 4–5)

In the case of the Bangsamoro peace process, the political stakes for Moro self-determination and political autonomy are interrelated with Moro women's bodily autonomy. Integral to Moro political and economic autonomy is the freedom to practice Sharia. In the Philippines, Moro societies in Mindanao have plural legal systems: Moros are subject to Sharia law for personal and family relations, and they may also settle grievances through customary laws. Under Presidential Decree 1083, also known as the Code of Muslim Personal Laws (CMPL), the Code shall prevail over national laws that conflict with its provisions. It was enacted in 1977 as a deliberate strategy by then-President Ferdinand Marcos to appease Muslim separatists (Chiarella 2012: 228; Solamo-Antonio 2015: 83). The Code predates the country's signing of the CEDAW and other national laws on gender equality. Furthermore, it has not been reviewed since its enactment, despite a growing clamor to update the Code's provisions to equally reflect changing behaviors and values among Muslim communities (Solamo-Antonio 2015: 98). Notably, in the UN CEDAW Committee's concluding comments to the combined 5th–6th Philippine CEDAW reports:

> The Committee expresses its concern about the precarious situation of rural and indigenous women, as well as the Muslim women in the autonomous region of Muslim Mindanao, who lack access to adequate health services, education, clean water and sanitation services and credit facilities. The Committee is also concerned about women's limited access to justice in cases of violence, especially in the conflict zones, and the lack of sanctions against the perpetrators of such violence. The Committee is furthermore concerned that the practice of early marriage is persistent among Muslim women. (CEDAW 2006a: 6)

The combined 7th–8th Philippine CEDAW reports identify discriminatory provisions in the CMPL as those relating to early marriage, polygamy, divorce, and unequal inheritance rights (CEDAW 2015b: 8). According to a female representative from a government commission:

> Muslim women specifically face issues on early marriage and polygamy. In our consultations with them for the CEDAW reporting, they maintained that their religion sanctions these practices. The long-term solution is to really increase the rank and file membership of Muslim women in positions of leadership. The CMPL for instance was put together by a predominantly male congress and thus privileges the consultative role of Muslim leaders who are also primarily male.[10]

And yet, in the peace process, the MILF panel had been all-male too, with the exception of Raissa Jajurie, a Moro woman lawyer who led their legal team.

[102] *Politics of Sexual & Reproductive Health*

The CAB expands and further entrenches Sharia law under the envisioned autonomous Bangsamoro region.

In the cases of the CMPL and Sharia law, we see how the Moros' group right to self-determination has been articulated primarily from the vantage point of male Moro rebels. It perpetuates a male-centric ability to practice traditional laws and customs. Many of these traditions relate to regulating the family and prescribing appropriate sexual relations and reproductive practices. For example, in the case of early marriages, the CMPL stipulates that marriage is allowed for any Muslim male at least 15 years of age, while for Muslim females it states the "age of puberty." Based on a survey conducted by Nisa Ul Haqq Fi Bangsamoro,[11] the reasons cited for early marriage among young Moro women were shaped by different factors, although "religious beliefs ranked highest, with women saying early marriage was in accordance with their religion." Indeed, according to Solamo-Antonio (2015), in one Sharia district court, it was found that the youngest age of marriage was 7 years for a girl and 11 years for a boy. Yasmin Busran-Lao, executive director for Nisa Ul Haqq Fi Bangsamoro and former member of the government negotiating panel, suggests that a strong obstacle to addressing early marriages among Moros, in addition to religious beliefs, is that marriage registration remains uncommon especially in remote areas (quoted in *New Humanitarian* 2010). Early marriages become prevalent when the state cannot keep track of what unions occur, especially in conflict-affected areas with pre-existing weak social welfare and public administration. The state is neither present nor "felt" in Moro communities.

Early marriage also comes as a distinct consequence of protracted displacement. Another key finding from the survey is that due to a lack of privacy in the evacuation camps, parents resort to forcing their children into marriage particularly to protect the girl's chastity and, by extension, family honor. They do so to prevent the likelihood of pre-marital sexual relations occurring among adolescents, which are strictly forbidden in Islam. Further, early and forced marriages have an economic basis in the context of displacement. "In the evacuation centre, each family is entitled only to one food coupon for basic relief goods. Girls and boys are married off by their parents to create new families and qualify for more food coupons" (*New Humanitarian* 2010; see also Global Network of Women Peacebuilders 2014: 10). According to a female informant from an international development organization based in Mindanao:

> In evacuation centers we worked with, food pack distribution is by family, in situations where conflict and relief response have been routine . . . there is really a push for survival to just get married at an early age to secure relief packs. This may also help explain why there is a population boom too after calamities.[12]

Hence, the strategy of humanitarian relief assistance that targets families as beneficiaries incentivizes Moro communities who have been displaced over a prolonged period of time to use early marriages and adolescent pregnancies for economic survival.

These forms of patriarchal bargains are not "conflict-specific," but rather emerge from the same conditions that undermine women's bodily autonomy in the everyday. Unless pre-existing cultural sanctions for early marriages are transformed, they will continue to negate any interventions to promote broader political and economic participation among Moros in peace processes and post-conflict reconstruction. The Bangsamoro peace process, much like the CMPL, subordinates substantive gender reforms, including the promotion of sexual and reproductive health, to that of more "political" goals within nationalist struggles. This occurs precisely because male MILF rebels serve to benefit from, and so try to protect their interests in, the carving-up of political authority. As Graça Machel, the co-mediator for the 2008 Kenya peace negotiations puts it, "when you give prominence to the warring parties at the expense of consulting and involving the majority of people, you are giving them rights to decide on behalf of the others, in essence rewarding them for having taken up arms" (quoted in O'Reilly, Ó Súilleabháin, and Paffenholz 2015: 14).

The success story behind women's direct participation in the Bangsamoro peace process was more apparent in the case of women on the government panel rather than the MILF panel. By and large, the "MILF leadership is still very patriarchal and this was made evident throughout the peace process."[13] Overall, the MILF side of the negotiating table has never had a Moro woman negotiator despite the contributions of the Bangsamoro Islamic Women Auxiliary Brigade (BIWAB), the MILF's women auxiliary forces (Global Network of Women Peacebuilders 2011). Although the numbers of Filipino women involved in various roles in the peace process gradually increased, Filipino Moro women were limited to indirect consultations and community participatory efforts spearheaded by the government panel (OPAPP 2014; O'Reilly, Ó Súilleabháin, and Paffenholz 2015). According to a female representative of an international organization involved in promoting women's peacebuilding work, "we were unable to access BIWAB. The MILF leaders were very protective of them and would not let us meet."[14]

The invisibility of Moro women at peace negotiating tables reproduces popular conceptions that Moro women only ever figure as the conflicts' *victims*. National imaginaries of the peace process inevitably portray Moro resistance as a masculinized and all-male resistance. Yet, as BIWAB commander Ling Gumander stated in an interview, "How do you suppose the battle raged on for days and weeks if there was no BIWAB to support the men fighting?" (Cabusao 2019). There is a danger therefore that given the celebratory national and global reputation of the Bangsamoro peace process, the various active roles, including leadership by Moro women for the Moro struggle and how they are situated in the frontlines of both conflict and peacebuilding, become forgotten. Crucially, without asking where the Moro women are in the national peace process, we lose sight of the complex ways in which they have had to regularly bargain with patriarchy in order to strategize and navigate spaces for bodily autonomy.

Moro women's lack of direct participation is itself a patriarchal bargain and is tied to other strategic "silences" that inform the Bangsamoro peace process. Because the negotiations were only between the government and the MILF, peace in relation to intra-state conflicts was negotiated while discussions on other forms of conflict, particularly clan and community forms of violence such as *rido*, were absent. Armed conflicts in Mindanao escalate or morph into different permutations of conflict from *rido* or clan feuds to non-state armed conflict between different armed groups, and intra-state conflict (International Alert 2014: 28; see also Torres 2014). *Rido* predominantly occurs in Bangsamoro areas of Mindanao such as Lanao del Sur and Maguindanao (International Alert 2014; Torres 2014). These clan feuds tend to be intractable and many remain unresolved.[15] Dominant accounts of violence and insecurity in Mindanao tend to reify intra-state conflict between Moro rebels and state armed forces as the most crucial manifestation of escalating conflict (International Alert 2014; Paredes 2015). However, while "Muslim-Christian conflict in Mindanao dominates the attention of international and local media, clan conflicts are actually more pertinent in the daily lives of people" (Torres 2014: 5). Indeed, as one informant noted, "the frequent occurrence of *rido* is to many communities just a 'normal' or everyday reality. It is normalized violence and also part of the structure that many communities deal with."[16] *Rido* is treated as separate from the national peace process and is instead relegated as an issue to be resolved "internally," even as evidence strongly establishes the causal mechanisms between *rido* and intra-state conflicts in Mindanao.

Clans serve social, political, and economic purposes for nation-building.[17] In terms of advancing political and economic interests, families are effective vehicles through which power is solidified in the Philippines (McCoy 2009). A clear example is the ubiquity of "political dynasties" where several members of a family simultaneously occupy different government positions within a given locality (McCoy 2009; Teehankee 2007). It is through political clans that Filipino women, and women in Asia more generally, have been able to secure public office (Derichs and Thompson 2013). However, it is also through powerful clans that the more pernicious forms of violence occur in the country. In the case of the Ampatuans of Maguindanao, powerful clans have managed to amass weapons and build private armies to advance their political and economic interests and quell opposition.[18] In conflict-affected areas of Mindanao, Cook and Collier (2006: 38) observe that "individual clans can be simultaneously represented in local politics, local military commands and local insurgency commands." What this means is that clans and ethnic tribes blur separation of the different spheres between the government, military, and rebel groups such that it is possible for *rido*, which is technically just war among clans or tribes, to eventually "escalate" into violence between the MNLF and the MILF when key members of these respective groups belong to the feuding parties. These "conflict strings," as Steven Rood (2005: 6) argues, occur when "what begins as a dispute between families can end with organised armed forces clashing, as parties to the dispute persuade others to become involved or the Philippine military can mistake a clan clash as a separatist operation and intervene on its own."

Conflict strings suggest that the exercise of authority—whether local politics, the military, or within insurgent groups—is embedded within the historical and present relationships among clans and ethnic groupings in Mindanao. Yet, anthropologist Anne Marie Hilsdon (2009: 358) argues that "the general framing of 'war' and 'conflict' in terms of declarations, ceasefires and peace negotiations, however, interrupts the contemporary social process and facilitates a 'hands off' approach by the government, which relegates forms of community violence like *rido* to culture." The omission of clan and community-level violence within the national peace process conveniently erases the responsibility of the state in addressing such forms of violence, including holding the MILF to account for its role in perpetrating violence against Moro and Lumad civilians. It also reinforces related silences on the absence of "within-group" sexual and gender-based violence, distinctly experienced by Moro women as Moros, in the peace negotiations and agreement. This invisibility underscores how the control of women's bodies is precisely what is fought over—rather than being merely "collateral damage"—due to the centrality of family and intimate relations in exercising the right to self-determination.

Rido is fundamentally linked to the deep importance given to ethnic, clan, and kinship identities and the cultural role of family in providing protection and retribution of insults to honor. Conflicts arise as families, clans, or ethnic groups struggle to protect their group's honor when it is deemed insulted or disrespected by the offending party. Honor or *maratabat*, a term which originates from the Maranao ethnic group, is inscribed within the Moro cultural code as something that must be defended strongly if not violently when it is slighted. The unfortunately common outcome is a cycle of recurrent revenge killings owing to the deep emotions involved (Torres 2014). Honor is gendered through cultural and religious norms that allocate a different set of expectations between men and women. Discourses and symbols of the masculine protector and feminine protected inform the dynamics of clan feuds. State militarization in response to Moro separatism is a source of broader frustration, rebelliousness, and circulation of firearms in Mindanao. Violence in general has presented opportunities for Moro men to assert masculinity and perform the male protector identity. As Claribel Bartolome argues, "*maratabat* which exists on all sides of nationalist conflict, similarly ignites both *rido* and 'war' between the government and

Muslim insurgencies" (cited in Hilsdon 2009: 354). Involvement in armed conflicts compensates men's inability to become breadwinners in the family and the fulfillment of the protector role is even more salient in the face of historical underdevelopment and limited economic opportunities for Moros. Importantly, to be a protector, Moro men must have a family to protect. For women and girls, this means the intensification of their role as biological and cultural reproducers to enable men to attain, perform, and secure their masculine identity. While clan feuds can be triggered by land disputes and political rivalries (in some cases even simultaneously), perceived sexual misdemeanors committed against women are a common trigger for clan feuds (Bartolome, as cited in Hilsdon 2009: 353).

Moro women are the designated bearers of clan and ethnic identity and thus "arranged marriage, divorce, polygamy and its related activities all offer many opportunities for family honour to be besmirched and for its *maratabat* to be threatened" (Hilsdon 2009: 353). Specifically, "offenses against the *maratabat* of [a] woman are deemed more serious than those committed against male *maratabat*" (Montillo-Burton et al. 2014: 133). That is, while the feminine *maratabat* is offended in so far as the offense undermines family and clan honor, it takes on a graver offense precisely because it challenges the masculinity of male relatives as protectors. Montillo-Burton et al. (2014: 132) add further that "there is a popular belief among Meranao that when the causes of a *rido* are land and women, they are hard to settle and involve much loss of lives and property." Consequently, in addition to being even more intractable than "regular" *rido*, cases involving women can be particularly emotionally intense, "irrational," and violent, thereby influencing the unwillingness of state authorities to intervene or for such cases to go "under the radar." According to a police officer in Mindanao:

> Crimes against chastity, if it happens here, is more than *rido* that is why they get settled immediately in the traditional way . . . . They have this tradition of *maratabat* or the pride of the men who are relatives of the victim and the pride of the women in connection with her male relatives that makes things very complicated—that is why these incidents are settled immediately and no longer get to us. (quoted in WE Act 1325 2016: 53)

Rido erupts to reclaim honor—specifically honor tied to Moro masculinity—since male members of the family are expected to exact retribution through violence.

The everyday patriarchal structure enforced by *maratabat* cultivates gendered expectations of self-sacrifice such that women and girls victimized through rape or sexual violence typically "opt" to remain silent about the violence they have experienced in order to avoid *rido* between the woman's clan and the perpetrator's clan thereby also preventing an escalation of violence.[19]

PATRIARCHAL BARGAINS AND NATION-BUILDING [107]

Women and girls subordinate their bodily integrity by "internalizing" sexual and gender-based violence inflicted against them out of a sense of duty to protect family and/or clan honor. This act of self-sacrifice is particularly acute among internally displaced persons who have limited or no access to protection from powerful and armed clans, rendering them "easy" targets. As one informant observed, "Not speaking up is a way by which they protect others— their own family (children), or communities from further violence. They would rather be individual victims of sexual violence than allow loss of life through clan wars."[20] Another informant explained:

> They just can't report because of *maratabat* . . . they will go to channels of elderly women . . . then mediation occurs to prevent bloodshed through *rido*. The normal reporting channel is to go to the barangay or police and then DSWD [Department of Social Welfare and Development]. But with Moro areas, the preference is to course through indigenous mechanisms where mediation occurs.[21]

Failure to account for women's strategic silences as patriarchal bargains has far-reaching implications for reproducing partial if not distorted accounts of the dynamics of conflict and insecurity in Mindanao. For example, based on 2014 nationwide crime statistics, conflict-affected areas ironically appeared as the most peaceful regions in the Philippines despite also being where *rido* is especially rife (Vargas 2014). A high-ranking police official explained the severe underreporting of crimes: "because of culture, people will not report (crimes) to the police, they consult their village chiefs because once they report it to the police, it is tantamount to a declaration of war" (quoted in Vargas 2014). Self-sacrifice in this regard is motivated by cultural perceptions, as well as actual accessibility, of appropriate institutions for redressing sexual and gender-based violence.

Globally, when law enforcement is weak and criminals are rarely brought to justice, women and girls are less likely to report crimes committed against them to state authorities (UN Women 2011). And yet, non-reliance on state justice systems in Mindanao further empowers customary laws and tribal justice systems that may not necessarily be effective in protecting women and girls (Musawah 2009). Moro grievances, including those relating to sexual and gender-based violence, are redressed in a manner that exposes women and girls to further harms, such as through forced marriage (including dowry) and other forms of indigenous settlement arrangements, which means victims continue to interact with perpetrators in their daily lives. Early and forced marriages are strategies to appease feuding clans.[22] For instance, "daughters are offered for marriage to appease warring clans. Marriage is seen as one step in repairing damaged relationships but still grievances are understood to be deeper or more enduring. So *rido* can still occur despite the sacrifice of

[108] *Politics of Sexual & Reproductive Health*

daughters."[23] This therefore goes back to how pre-existing structures such as the CMPL fails to adequately protect Muslim women and girls when deadly clan feuds erupt (Solamo-Antonio 2015).

The general lack of gender-based crime reporting in Bangsamoro areas feeds into the lack of accessibility of sexual and reproductive health services that address complications of rape and sexual violence including treatment for sexually transmitted diseases and HIV/AIDS and post-abortion care, among others. This occurs, first, when victims do not report to state authorities. They therefore cannot access the appropriate medical treatment guaranteed by law to all victims of rape and sexual violence in the country, which includes a health professional administering post-exposure prophylaxis for HIV infection after sexual assault and use of emergency contraception (Center for Reproductive Rights 2016). Second, low statistics on rape and sexual violence mean that there is little data to support the allocation of budget for comprehensive sexual and reproductive health services that meet the needs of rape and sexual violence victims. In principle, the state cannot likely estimate the quantity of supplies and personnel that may be needed due to historically weak sexual and reproductive health–seeking behavior. These barriers to justice accumulate and compound one another and drive victims of sexual violence in Mindanao to "disappear" from the legal system and over time women in these communities have learnt that silence is an effective strategy to maintain community and national security at their bodily expense.[24]

The interplay between masculine protector and feminine protected embedded in *maratabat* affords relative space for women's agency including in facilitating peace. O'Reilly, Ó Súilleabháin, and Paffenholz (2015: 20), for example, highlight that in the context of Mindanao, women have served as mediators between feuding clans because they are rarely targeted in clan disputes and revenge killings (see also Dwyer and Cagoco-Guiam 2012). They argue that because their physical security is less threatened than men's due to a "feminine protected" norm, their mobility allows them to facilitate peace by means of collecting retribution payments and hosting reconciliation feasts. However, as Gemma Bagayaua of Maguindanao points out in her recounting of *rido* incidences involving Moro women:

> "What makes women crucial in peace-making is the concept of maratabat," says Coco Lucman, a son of Princess Tarhata. "It is an insult for the family of a man if he is the one to initiate peace talk," Lucman says. "It's like losing your *manly pride*." It is a lot easier if a woman initiates the talks, he explains. (quoted in Torres 2014: 277)

This indicates the gendered expectation of female altruism or the culturally and religiously enforced self-sacrifice of women whose pride, as the above quote suggests, is secondary if not altogether dispensable compared to men's. Women in conflict situations initiate peace and line up for relief assistance, but they do so, rather than Moro men, because these actions are feminizing (see Chapter 2). This also partly explains why there are relatively more spaces afforded to Moro women at the clan and community levels of peacebuilding compared to the national Bangsamoro peace process.

Women's peacebuilding roles are welcomed in so far as they do not challenge the gender order that privileges Moro masculinity. Thus, the exclusion of Moro women at the national level from the Bangsamoro peace process serves to maintain Moro women's subjectivity as in need of protection, whose best interests can only be articulated by their protectors—male MILF leaders at the negotiating table. The resistance of the MILF to include women within their ranks, even as they may negotiate with women from the government, is shaped by this deeply embedded norm of Moro masculine pride. Consequently, the peace process maintained an artificial separation between the high politics of Moro self-determination and "everyday" issues of gender equality *within* Moro clans and ethnic groups. From maintaining silence on rape and sexual violence to avoid *rido* to towing the official MILF line in order not to betray the Moro political cause—it is women's patriarchal bargains that makes post-conflict nation-building possible.

POST-DISASTER SEX ECONOMY

Women's patriarchal bargains secured post-disaster national recovery in the aftermath of Typhoon Haiyan too. The surge of humanitarian contingents and foreign resources created economic opportunities just as much as they enabled new forms of inequalities and spaces for gendered exploitation. As Ong (2015) points out, post-Haiyan recovery was bifurcated between "two Taclobans"—a metaphor for the deepening of economic inequalities causally related to the humanitarian effort. The influx of aid itself contributed greatly to the economic recovery of Eastern Visayas where many of the poorest provinces in the Philippines are located. For example, as one informant noted, "Particularly in the case of INGOs [international NGOs], their presence made the disaster a profitable business. You can see it even in Tacloban, all of a sudden SUVs are so ubiquitous. Of course these big INGOs can afford them. The car companies were among the biggest winners in the disaster."[25] Indeed, during my field visits to Tacloban between March 2015 and April 2016, I noted hotels and accommodation had proliferated, major car companies had opened, and a new shopping mall had been built. Among many other visible signs of economic recovery were the increased number of cafes, restaurants, and bars that provided employment for many Taclobanons. I distinctly recall a remark made by one informant that after Haiyan, Tacloban seemed to have acquired a taste for

[110] *Politics of Sexual & Reproductive Health*

coffee because before the typhoon, a cup of coffee was worth 80 pesos whereas afterward, different "café" style coffee ranged in price from 150 to 300 pesos.

The impact on the economy was particularly stark in that even just six months after Haiyan struck, Ong (2015) noted:

> Five times a week from 10 pm, a "booze truck" parks outside Burgos Street near posh Hotel Alejandro, local headquarters for the United Nations, and attracts an odd assortment of foreign aid workers, religious volunteers, and curious locals toasting to Heinekens and Red Horses. Here people are friendly and chatty, though weary from the day's work.

There was a separate Tacloban for those who brought in aid and economic resources and those who directly benefited from their arrival. Another Tacloban existed for those who continue to be in protracted displacement and were further impoverished by a lack of access to the growing post-disaster economy. Prior to Haiyan, the two main regions severely affected by the disaster—Leyte and Samar—reflected poor levels of human development. Table 4.1 shows that prior to the disaster, the level of human development in Eastern Samar was almost half the national average, and only more than one-third of the human development level in the urban region of Metro Manila, where the capital is located, in 2012.

Under the "mantra" of building "disaster resilience," which has gained currency among national and international actors in the Philippines, women's "self-reliance" in crisis and emergencies—as patriarchal bargains—flourished in order to meet the gaps resulting from the confluence of inadequate state disaster relief assistance and pre-existing chronic levels of underdevelopment. After the Haiyan disaster, "funding [came] from three main actors: national government, local governments, and INGOs."[26] As one informant claimed,

Table 4.1. HAIYAN-AFFECTED PROVINCES AND 2012 HUMAN DEVELOPMENT INDEX SCORES

Provinces	Human Development Index 2012
Philippines	0.644
Metro Manila	0.829
Biliran	0.568
Eastern Samar	0.389
Leyte	0.586
Northern Samar	0.432
Southern Leyte	0.533
Western Samar	0.452

Source: Human Development Network (2012-2013).

"NGOs were meant to just fill in the gaps . . . but in reality NGOs have ended up doing more and the government has less and less role or presence."[27] Another informant expressed the same sentiment, "INGOs are at the forefront of service provision on women in terms of the Haiyan response. The government just played a secondary role, had little initiative apart from a focus on infrastructure building."[28] A majority of the non-state actors deployed to assist in the relief and rehabilitation process were constrained within the parameters of emergency assistance and limited to a select number of beneficiaries at the community level (Commission on Human Rights Philippines 2016).

Post-disaster economic transformations went hand in hand with the emergent sex economy in Eastern Visayas. According to a female informant, "it is well known that immediately after the storm, the first to open back up are the 'parlors' [massage parlors] and hotels."[29] Hotels are integral to prostitution and sex trafficking. Yet in the aftermath of Typhoon Haiyan, these private spaces were regarded as separate if not safe havens amid the devastation, and therefore economic transactions that occurred within them went "under the radar." In the words of an informant, "in the immediate aftermath, hotels were not part of coordination on protecting minors from sex work and they continue to be excluded in protection efforts."[30] Another informant argued that, "Tacloban has its sex industry even before the storm. It is the center of Visayas and among the most industrialized or developed."[31] The arrival of foreign and local military contingents created a huge clientele such that women from outside Samar and Leyte were rumored to have migrated to the area. The sex industry had been particularly economically rewarding as suggested by informants such that "in Western Samar, one local mayor is known to have encouraged sex work from his female constituency. [He said] *Mabuti pa magprosti kesa tambay*! [better to be a prostitute than homeless]."[32]

In the long wake after the mega-disaster, the boundaries between dependency for economic resources and physical protection were very blurred especially for young women. According to another informant:

> In our work immediately after the storm, there were several incidences wherein the Philippine military soldiers were found to have kept young girls as their girlfriends. The girls were found together with the men in their camps/bunk beds . . . the girls claimed they were just charging their cellphones since the military camp had generators . . . They [soldiers] said the girls insisted on going inside their camps . . . and that they were just there to charge their phones. The men said they could not resist. In the case of the girls, you know because of culture . . . many would just say it was their fault . . . they are "*pikat*"[33] or flirts.[34]

Illicit affairs between local women and Filipino and foreign nationals who responded to the crisis supposedly thrived and contributed to the range of

[112]   *Politics of Sexual & Reproductive Health*

social reproductive transactions that rebuilt the economy of Eastern Visayas. Stories of post-disaster relationships, however, cannot be separated from the political and economic structures that already defined these women's lives. Data prior to the disaster indicates that many young women, especially in Eastern Visayas, had a sexual experience before age 15 (see Table 4.2). They comprise the second highest percentage of reported early onset of sexual activity at the national level. Higher fertility rates among Visayan women and women from the urban regions that constitute Metro Manila were also recorded (Philippine Statistics Authority 2014).

The post-disaster sex economy would not have easily emerged without the material and ideological drivers already in place that condition self-sacrificing behaviors that deplete women's bodily autonomy and well-being in the everyday. Labor migration had already been a key economic strategy in the absence of employment opportunities in many impoverished provinces in Eastern Visayas. Exporting Filipino women's labor is viewed as providing a path out of household poverty and into post-crisis recovery. For example, Haiyan-affected communities were reported to have been able to withstand devastation for several weeks before any official state assistance arrived because of remittances from overseas and urban Filipino workers. Built-in "care chains" typical of many "left-behind" families in the Philippines also stepped in. As one informant pointed out, "remittances by migrants—local and international—have been crucial to disaster relief and recovery" (see also OCHA 2015e). He also noted that, "in the case of Tacloban, relatives were the first respondents to victims."[35] This observation was corroborated in Samar and Leyte provinces where people were not only coming out of disaster zones,

Table 4.2. AGE AT FIRST SEXUAL INTERCOURSE AMONG YOUNG WOMEN

Region	Percentage of women (15–24 years) who had sexual intercourse before age 15	Percentage of women (18–24 years) who had sexual intercourse before age 18
National Capital	1.7	14.4
VI—Western Visayas	2.0	21.3
VII—Central Visayas	2.9	22.2
VIII—Eastern Visayas	4.0	21.0
IX—Zamboanga	1.3	20.0
XI—Davao	5.2	27.1
Autonomous Region in Muslim Mindanao	3.1	23.5

Source: Philippines Statistics Authority 2014: Table 2
Note: Davao registered the highest nationally and Eastern Visayas ranked second. Religious and cultural barriers may mediate under-reporting.

but also coming in to search for families and friends, to rescue and offer assistance (IOM, DSWD, IDMC, and SAS 2014).

Through the aid of mobile technology and pre-positioned remittance services nationwide, important financial resources were wired to affected families. This ensured survival for some families and communities. However, the national reliance on remittances reinforced pre-existing socio-economic inequalities and created new ones. According to a female informant based in the remote town of Guiuan, Samar, "OFWs [overseas Filipino workers] and private remittances contribute to the unequal recovery after the storm. So you can see concrete houses amidst nipa huts. Those with relatives working overseas received assistance to rebuild including to start a new livelihood."[36] This point is crucial because Eastern Samar, Samar, and Leyte provinces in the Eastern Visayas region were found to have the largest proportion of individuals with social vulnerabilities and special needs, "possibly [as] a result of the higher impact from the typhoon, continued displacement and consolidation of households as well as pre-existing economic vulnerability" (IOM, DSWD, IDMC, and SAS 2014: 18).

Aside from labor migration, remittances are generated through intermarriage with foreign nationals. The connections between crisis, remittances, and women's bodies are clear to one informant. Speaking from her experience as a local of Leyte, she stated that "in remote areas in Eastern Visayas, it is normal for multiple female members of the family to be paired with foreigner husbands through referral or match-making."[37] For a country where national and local economies are built on the backs of women's and girls' care and domestic work, foreign marriages as a way out of poverty and "insurance" in times of crisis are not exceptional. Hence, as the same informant explained:

> [S]ecuring a foreigner husband is [an] important economic strategy because it is the ideal male/masculine provider that allows whole families to be lifted from poverty. The whole family of the girl will benefit from the exchange rate and remittances. Some families have been fortunate to find a good man who has clean intentions and actually help the family, but this is not always the case.[38]

The same global circuits of mobility that enable Filipino women to secure employment overseas and foreign marriages as economic strategies for their families also lead other women to violence and exploitation. It was believed that "in the aftermath of Yolanda, illegal recruiters really targeted the region especially unaccompanied minors (those who lost their families in the disaster). They were brought to Cebu and then also to Paranaque [in red light districts]."[39]

Various state and non-state actors, consequently, were on high alert to monitor and prevent human trafficking through the gender-based violence protection cluster. In Eastern Visayas, as an informant stressed, "trafficking

[114]   *Politics of Sexual & Reproductive Health*

has occurred even before and the region is already high risk. Trafficking in light of the disaster raises even greater challenges for identification of cases, orientation and training of teams."[40] In some cases, they were able to "rescue" women and girls. However, a reported barrier is that "recruiters do not recruit for sex work outright. They will normally say to parents like they will send the girls to school, or arrange for them to work as a domestic helper in exchange."[41] Many women and girls likely faced intensified pressures to take on illicit or "quick fix" routes to secure employment in urban areas such as Manila, often with the intention of securing further employment overseas at great personal or bodily cost.[42]

The Haiyan disaster response—in meaningfully implementing the *build back better* slogan—could have been leveraged in instituting strong state accountability and coordination measures. This approach is vital in bridging development gaps among affected communities in the long run. The Philippine state, instead, was regarded as having taken a "backseat" in relief and reconstruction while non-state actors ended up taking the lead (see also Mangada 2015, 2016). A "rolled back" state during crisis poses distinct consequences for sexual and reproductive health and well-being post-disaster. For instance, in a public hearing convened by the Commission on Human Rights in Tacloban in April 2016, some participants noted that "INGOs were more active in delivering RH [reproductive health] relief and services [including contraceptives]" but that "in the coastal areas, women did not have access to contraceptives donated as aid."[43] Meanwhile, others reported that communities in geographically remote areas indeed received assistance including RH services from international and local NGOs. Many therefore would not have had access to such services if not for the disaster. Still, this sort of "ad hoc" health and social welfare delivery contributed to uneven recovery post-disaster (Commission on Human Rights Philippines 2016).

While the Philippines is leading the way for climate change adaptation and disaster resilience through its globally recognized national policies and initiatives founded on the principles of gender inclusiveness and responsiveness, we see from the experience of Haiyan humanitarian and development interventions that disaster resilience remains built on the backs of women and girls through the neglect of their bodily autonomy. As one female informant lamented, "after disasters such as Haiyan, it opens the best opportunity for substantive change. But this was not capitalized on fully in the Haiyan experience . . . if there was an effort to be transformative it came belatedly."[44] The national project of building disaster resilience is implicated in how the vast majority of women and girls are kept politically and economically marginalized from broader decision-making and leadership because the depletive conditions that structure their everyday lives remain unchanged, and in some cases even worsened post-disaster.

Dominant discourses on building national disaster resilience may in effect exonerate the state from its primary obligation in providing sustainable and comprehensive post-disaster relief and rehabilitation assistance through mobilizing "self-reliant" communities in times of crisis while keeping women's patriarchal bargains normalized. People dealing with constant environmental crises learn to practice mutual aid and support precisely because they are left to their own devices as a result of geographical remoteness, have had a weak state presence historically, or both. Building disaster resilience in this manner aligns with the neoliberal state project of progressively opening spaces for private or non-state actors in the provision of social welfare services. Within this juncture, I demonstrate in Chapter 5 the gendered costs of humanitarian organizations, particularly faith-based groups, playing a crucial part in reaching remote communities where the state has had little presence or authority.

CONCLUSION: (RE)BUILDING A NATION ON WOMEN'S PATRIARCHAL BARGAINS

In this chapter, I analyzed the paradox of limited but legitimizing ways in which women are brought into national post-conflict and post-disaster processes to maintain the gender order. The Philippines may have a global reputation in key security and development agendas as an exemplar of gender equality, but this status is enabled by immediate and long-term consequences of the patriarchal bargains that women make in the service of, or to contest, nation. What become invisible against a backdrop of world rankings and narratives of exceptionalism are disparities within the country and paradoxical gender equality outcomes among diverse groups of women particularly those in crisis-prone areas. Disaggregating gender equality issues and accounting for restrictions to bodily autonomy reveal how a strong national record in gender mainstreaming and Filipino women's political and economic participation are actually built on inequalities in social reproduction. Thus, unless markers of gender equality progress are reconciled with the political economy of bodily autonomy, they keep hidden an array of interlinked costs that deplete both the substance and longevity of women's participation.

Interrogating women's patriarchal bargains have significant implications not just for the inclusivity and durability of the peace agenda in the Philippines, but also in exposing how state-level violence and insecurity are linked to gendered constructions of masculinity and femininity that underpin the family or clan dynamics before, during, and after crises. Inclusive peace suffers when varied patriarchal structures that govern Filipino women's lives, such as the discriminatory provisions in Sharia law and economic pressures to generate remittances, are assumed as separate from political and economic processes of rebuilding nation in the aftermath of crises. Without understanding the political economy conditions that complicate experiences of peace and security, we fail to see the kind of "patriarchal bargains" women make in their everyday

[116] *Politics of Sexual & Reproductive Health*

lives that are costing their well-being (Kandiyoti 1988). Indeed, we similarly miss out on how these bargains may also come back to undermine women or to retain male-dominated spaces. For instance, Coronel-Ferrer recounted her experience while serving as chief government negotiator and one of a handful of women in the Bangsamoro peace process, "our facilitator chided us for bringing in 'kitchen economics' into the talks. 'Beware of the housewives,' he joked, 'They are after the kitchen money'" (OPAPP 2014: 7).

Ultimately, meaningful political participation by broader groups of women is dependent on ensuring bodily autonomy for all. This requires a strong role for the state in overhauling legal barriers and cultural or religious norms that take root in the family, clan, and ethnic groups. Women's participation matters because, as studies have shown, their inclusion at the peace and environmental decision-making tables leads to more gender-responsive outcomes and is more strongly correlated with the advancement of gender equality goals. However, it is not just women's presence alone that matters but rather substantive and inclusive participation. This can truly occur when participatory approaches in national peace processes and disaster resilience programs lead to replenishing the full extent and value of women's social reproductive contributions in ensuring post-crisis survival. Importantly, women's health and well-being are a pre-condition for the sustainable flourishing of a nation. Transformative change that tackles the gendered roots of vulnerability and resilience involves fundamentally recognizing that sustaining the well-being of households and communities post-crisis is contingent upon ensuring the bodily autonomy of women and girls across all spheres of social reproduction, from the household to the state and globally.

The next two chapters of this book are dedicated to examining further the global drivers to the politics of bodily autonomy, which structurally and ideologically connect experiences in the Philippines and elsewhere. Continuing the multi-scalar analysis the book employs, I turn to how sexual and reproductive health, as a global agenda and human right, has been fiercely contested transnationally. I explain how and why taking seriously this contentiousness is important for fully understanding global configurations of power and in reimagining a new feminist international politics.

CHAPTER 5
The Global Crisis of Religious Fundamentalisms

INTRODUCTION

On April 23, 2019, Resolution 2467 was adopted by the UN Security Council amid intense debate and controversy. The Resolution, then a recent addition to the growing number of resolutions under the Women, Peace and Security (WPS) Agenda, expressed deep concern over the slow progress in eliminating continued high prevalence of sexual violence in situations of armed conflicts. It reiterated previous resolutions by stressing that "sexual violence in conflict occurs on a continuum of interrelated and recurring forms of violence against women and girls" and is exacerbated by the underrepresentation of women in decision-making and leadership roles, insufficient financing on WPS, discriminatory laws and harmful social norms among other prevailing gender inequalities (UN Security Council 2019a). To this end, the Resolution recognized national ownership and accountability in addressing the root causes of such violence while also maintaining that responses must be "survivor-centered." This entails establishing the varied and distinct needs and well-being of survivors as central to the pursuit of ending impunity and inaction as well as across conflict prevention, resolution, and peacebuilding measures. It places an emphasis on the interlinked human rights protection of victims of sexual violence in conflict settings and children born of rape.

The development of Resolution 2467, however, was fiercely contentious in large part due to the threat of a US veto over language relating to sexual and reproductive health and rights (SRHR) (UN Security Council 2019a). Together with China and Russia, the United States also strongly opposed a proposal to

---

The Global Politics of Sexual and Reproductive Health. Maria Tanyag, Oxford University Press.
© Oxford University Press 2024. DOI: 10.1093/oso/9780197676332.003.0006

develop a formal Working Group of the Security Council on sexual violence in conflict and SRHR (Allen and Shepherd 2019). The Resolution was eventually passed with 13 affirmative votes and abstentions from China and Russia.[1] In the end, language explicitly referring to SRHR was excised from the resolution document to the expressed regret of countries including Belgium, France, South Africa, the United Kingdom, Spain, and Uruguay (UN Security Council 2019a). In several statements, country representatives were vocal on how the opposition to the language of SRHR and its subsequent removal were inimical to the broad aims and commitments set out in the Resolution when the document itself so prominently references a "survivor-centered approach." Indeed, to center the survivor is to promote the survivor's right to bodily autonomy and self-determination.

The politics surrounding Resolution 2467 mobilized far-reaching international and social media attention and prompted wider discussions on the difficulties of bridging SRHR and WPS spaces. In the immediate aftermath, feminist and human rights groups were divided over the political significance and consequences of the removal of SRHR from the outcome document. For example, one side of the debate argued that the removal of specific references to SRHR does not equate to rights being eroded. Chinkin and Rees (2019) noted that Resolution 2467 already references existing international legal obligations, particularly the Convention on the Elimination of All Forms of Discrimination against Women (CEDAW) and its Optional Protocol. They point out that "CEDAW—the international blueprint for the legal guarantee of women's human rights—has only rarely been expressly referenced in earlier WPS Resolutions. Inclusion of CEDAW within an operative paragraph in Resolution 2467 means that it is stronger than previous WPS Resolutions in this respect" (2019: 5). Furthermore, they stress that the textual inclusion of SRHR in previous Resolutions 2106 and 2122 remains enshrined and since "the language is still there . . . an intelligent approach is to use the full range of entry points to assert these rights" (16). Rees wrote further, "the US should be challenged on its stance on this (and many other issues) every day until it changes, and many others have rightfully done so. But focusing on this as the only issue takes too much energy from the room whilst there are other things to which we should direct our efforts" (Women's International League for Peace and Freedom 2019).

Another side of this debate emphasized the significance of the removal as not simply a "squabble over a few words" but rather symbolic of the place of gender within the Security Council. For example, analysis by Allen and Shepherd (2019) drew the connections between Resolution 2467 and the uncompromising anti-feminist pushback from the United States during President Donald Trump's administration. They this signifies that "Council members made a calculated decision that removing sexual and reproductive health for women who had been raped in conflict was justifiable" and the removal of

SRHR from the specific resolution sets a dangerous precedent for the WPS agenda and exposes the need for an "iron-clad defence." Thus, Resolution 2467 (re)exposed differences within feminist movements regarding the type of strategic response needed in addressing resistances to women's rights, and specifically to bodily autonomy at the global level. In weighing the significance of the politics surrounding Resolution 2467, I argue that the lens to employ is not that of the WPS but the longer one of SRHR.

This chapter examines how the politics of women's bodily autonomy is driven at the global level by a neoliberal economic logic of depletion and the complementary expansion of religious fundamentalisms especially in crisis settings. It situates definitional disputes over sexual and reproductive freedoms within the sustained influence of globally orchestrated political forces that first coalesced in global human rights and development conferences particularly in the 1980s and 1990s. Threats of backsliding and actual reversals within the WPS agenda on account of SRHR are not exceptional but rather symptomatic of widely deployed political strategies from the so-called unholy alliance formed by the Vatican, conservative governments, and religious fundamentalist non-state actors. To develop this analysis, this chapter is structured as follows. First, I demonstrate how the emergence of a truly global religious fundamentalist backlash was precipitated by CEDAW and at UN Conferences in the 1980s and 1990s. From then, religious fundamentalists have continued to manifest and proliferate their own counter-agenda framed through the language of "pro-life," "traditional values," and "protection of the family" at global and national levels. Second, I turn to how religious fundamentalist forces have taken to crisis and emergencies as vital fronts in ideologically opposing sexual and reproductive freedoms. Drawing on evidence from the Philippines, I trace how Filipino Catholic fundamentalist forces with their political economic ties to a global Christian Right, have been afforded windows of opportunity to promote a "pro-life" agenda and thereby restrict rights to bodily autonomy. Last, the chapter concludes with reflections on feminist strategies, within and beyond the WPS agenda, for overcoming the imbrication of neoliberalism and religious fundamentalisms in an increasingly crisis-prone world. To prevent the global threat and impacts of religious fundamentalisms, it is imperative that there be a recognition that the battle over SRHR is not a "side issue" for gender, peace, and security. Rather, it is *the* cornerstone issue upon which significant gender equality gains and losses are fought over.

THERE AND BACK AGAIN: CEDAW AND GLOBAL RELIGIOUS FUNDAMENTALIST BACKLASH

The lead up to and eventual adoption of CEDAW represented a watershed moment for women's and human rights movements across the world. It was the

[120] *Politics of Sexual & Reproductive Health*

outcome of labors and commitments by women pushing to move beyond a non-binding declaration in advancing women's rights.[2] However, it is also in the birth of CEDAW that both the emergence and the subsequent ossification of the religious fundamentalist backlash can be found. Research from feminists and human rights activists typically situate the rise of a counter-movement to transnational women's movements in the UN Conferences of the 1990s (see Chappell 2006; Petchesky 1995; Corrêa 1994; Berer and Ravindran 1996). I argue, however, that we need to go farther back and historicize global religious fundamentalisms and particularly anti-feminist backlash in relation to CEDAW for two main reasons.

First, CEDAW remains the primary binding treaty on women's rights, upon which by default, new agendas, resolutions, and frameworks are anchored. This treaty status creates the impression that CEDAW is and has since been a "settled" issue. Indeed, as already discussed above in the context of Resolution 2467, the presence of CEDAW was referenced as *mitigating* whatever impact the removal of SRHR has on the implementation of WPS agenda as a whole. Yet, State Parties' reservations regarding CEDAW, though often taken for granted or assumed not to exist, are animated by shared ideological resistances to bodily autonomy, well-being, and pleasure. CEDAW reservations demonstrate the continuity of religious fundamentalist counter-movements in the 1990s and contemporary forms of backlash and anti-feminist resistance.

Second, religious fundamentalisms generate interlinked and concerted impacts that constitute physical, structural, and symbolic harms to women's bodies. Making visible the common and continuing thread across CEDAW reservations and contemporary religious fundamentalist backlash can inform a rethinking of feminist strategies at present and for the future. As an important driver to the global politics of SRHR, examining religious fundamentalisms contributes to a more comprehensive account of the fragmentation of feminist agendas and why they tend to be implemented in a piecemeal manner. Resistance to sexual and reproductive freedoms represents an integral issue upon which to examine how political compromises employed in feminist agenda-setting and implementation have also enabled religious fundamentalisms to gain ground in multi-scalar ways and in crisis settings.

CEDAW Reservations

CEDAW was adopted as treaty in 1979 and entered into force in 1981; it is the foundational legal instrument for promoting and protecting women's rights globally as it seeks to end *all* forms of discrimination. In 2020, it had 189 State Parties with recent accession from South Sudan (2015) and the State of Palestine (2014) (UN Treaty Collection 1979). The convention also established a Committee comprising 23 independent experts on women's rights

GLOBAL CRISIS OF RELIGIOUS FUNDAMENTALISMS [121]

from around the world tasked to monitor the implementation of CEDAW. However, despite the truly global reach of CEDAW, it is among the main UN Human Rights treaties with the highest reservations made by State Parties.[3] Its full implementation has been continuously thwarted and undermined because of longstanding reservations to core provisions. Additionally, the CEDAW Committee observed that State Parties "have entered interpretative declarations" which in fact constitute general reservations on the basis that they seek to modify the legal effect of the Convention (UN General Assembly 1998: 47). Treaty reservations are permissible unless they are incompatible with the object and purpose of the treaty or convention (UN Treaty Collection 1969). Reservations to CEDAW overwhelmingly relate to Articles 2, 16, and 29. Article 2 stipulates that "States Parties condemn discrimination against women in all its forms, agree to pursue by all appropriate means and without delay a policy of eliminating discrimination against women." Article 16 refers to the elimination of discrimination "in all matters relating to marriage and family relations." Article 29 relates to accountability and dispute resolution whereby "[a]ny dispute between two or more States Parties concerning the interpretation or application of the present Convention which is not settled by negotiation shall, at the request of one of them, be submitted to arbitration" (UN General Assembly 1979).

Among these, Article 16 is the subject of most State Party reservations. State Parties enter reservations to Article 16 on marriage and family relations typically in combination with reservations to Article 2, the provision on undertaking measures and actions toward elimination of all forms of discrimination. This combination renders these reservations more suspect (De Pauw 2013: 58; see also CEDAW 2006b). Reservations to Articles 2 and 16 indicate which aspects of gender equality are most contested, on what basis those oppositions are made, and by whom. I argue that essentially, these reservations are about the control of women's bodily autonomy and well-being. They reveal how State Parties "accept" CEDAW except when it relates to fundamentally addressing the control of women's bodies in the primary spheres where they are more likely to experience direct subjugation and loss of autonomy—in the family and community. They sign or accede to CEDAW but only insofar as this is in broader service of, rather than transforming, those who benefit from specific configurations of state or national identity.

The CEDAW Committee has reiterated that Articles 2 and 16 are core provisions and as such any reservation relating to these are neither permissible nor compatible with the object and purpose of the treaty. They further stress that these reservations "perpetuate the myth of women's inferiority and reinforce inequalities in the lives of millions of women throughout the world" (UN General Assembly 1998: 3). Predominantly, these reservations are made on the basis of blanket claims regarding conflict with Islamic Sharia Law; customary rights on monarchic succession and inheritance of chiefly and traditional titles; customs and traditional practices; and/or national laws regarding the regulation of women's status within the family such as their ability to retain or bestow family name and citizenship, inherit property, and access social welfare. Therefore, while reservations to Article 29 are permissible, those relating to Articles 2 and 16 are not, and these raise serious and ongoing concerns.

For example, reservations from Monaco and Malta are made explicitly on the basis that Article 16 might be interpreted to legalize abortion. In response, the Committee has stated unequivocally that "[n]either traditional, religious or cultural practice nor incompatible domestic laws and policies can justify violations of the Convention. The Committee also remains convinced that reservations to article 16, whether lodged for national, traditional, religious or cultural reasons . . . should be reviewed and modified or withdrawn" (UN General Assembly 1998: 3). The CEDAW Committee has also expressed concerns that very few reservations to Article 2 have been withdrawn and even fewer in the case of Article 16.[4] On the contrary, there is evidence indicating that reservations to Article 16 remain intractable and have even increased in number among recently joined State Parties.

Research by De Pauw (2013), which analyzed trends in CEDAW reservations, observed that the percentage of State Parties formulating a reservation upon accession increased from 38% between 1980 and 1990, to 50% between 2002 and 2012. The latter decade is characterized by a greater inclination to formulate reservations driven by the "application of discriminatory customary law or religious norms in the group of States that have ratified the treaty" (2013: 60). Moreover, while some of the reservations have been partially withdrawn or modified, states may still have de facto limitations in place (Keller 2014). For example, among the recent modifications to a CEDAW reservation is the case of the Kingdom of Bahrain, which on June 1, 2016, notified the Secretary-General that it has made "editorial amendments" such that it will now implement Articles 2, 15 (paragraph 4), and Article 16 but "without breaching the provisions of the Islamic Shariah." Generic references to Sharia or any other system of law without clearly defining areas of incompatibility raise doubts over whether and to what the extent a State Party genuinely commits to and intends to fulfill its treaty obligations. Crucially, these reservations overwhelming speak to how through them domestic political struggles over women's bodies play out in the symbolic and biological reproduction of the nation. CEDAW reservations, for instance, can be leveraged for domestic political bargaining such as in consolidating support from specific constituencies or pressure groups (Keller 2014; see also Chapter 4 on the Code of Muslim Personal Laws in the Philippines).

The CEDAW Committee has employed a range of mechanisms to repeatedly urge concerned State Parties to review, modify and/or gradually withdraw reservations to Article 2 and 16 as part of its treaty obligations and for national-level implementation (CEDAW 2006b).[5] First, these consist of constructive dialogues with State Parties via the periodic reporting processes, especially in the CEDAW concluding comments where such calls are typically made. Second, the Committee has provided guidance on the meaning, intention, and scope of specific provisions through issuance of General Recommendations. Through these recommendations, the Committee has sought to explicate the inextricable links between Articles 2 and 16 and other provisions of CEDAW. CEDAW reservations have been the subject of a number of general recommendations, namely: no. 4 (1987) Reservations; no. 20 Reservations to the Convention (1992); no. 21 (1994) Equality in Marriage and Family Relations; no. 28 (2010) The Core Obligations of States Parties under Article 2 of the CEDAW; no. 29 (2013) Article 16—Economic Consequences of Marriage, Family relations and their dissolution (see also De Pauw 2013). That reservations have thematically featured in the general recommendations issued by the Committee for more than three decades attests to the deep contention over and recalcitrance to reform women's status within the family, which is most directly linked to sexual and reproductive rights.

Third, the Optional Protocol to CEDAW serves to facilitate a complaints procedure for women's rights violations, particularly those relating to discriminatory national laws that conflict with CEDAW. The Optional Protocol entered into force on December 22, 2000, and has 114 State Parties (UN Treaty Collection 1999). The protocol stipulates that "communications may be submitted by or on behalf of individuals or groups of individuals, under the jurisdiction of a State Party, claiming to be victims of a violation of any of the rights set forth in the Convention by that State Party (Article 2)" and, on the basis of reliable information, to conduct its own confidential inquiry (Article 8). During the drafting of the Convention, a complaints procedure had already been proposed but subsequently challenged because it was believed by some state delegates that "complaints procedures were needed for 'serious international crimes' such as apartheid and racial discrimination, rather than discrimination against women" (UN Women 2009a).

Despite the initial resistance, the Optional Protocol has since been widely used including in the case of the Philippines. The Protocol enables the CEDAW Committee to recognize widespread and systematic violations where they arise and in so doing, prompt measures toward reform from the offending State Parties.[6] This mechanism, while important in promoting national-level implementation, is unlikely to make significant impacts on State Parties with pre-existing reservations to CEDAW who have also refused to sign or accede to the Optional Protocol. It is politically expedient for these State Parties to resist opening themselves to the Protocol precisely because of the factors and motivations that drive their retention of CEDAW reservations.

Finally, the CEDAW Committee has forged cooperation with a number of other international bodies to strengthen its work in developing guidance,

[124]   *Politics of Sexual & Reproductive Health*

communications, and inquiry procedures. These include partnership with the Special Rapporteur on Violence Against Women through sharing information regarding rights violations and guidance on the elimination of discrimination and violence against women (OHCHR 2018). The Commission on the Status of Women through its separate communications procedures also provides relevant information for the work of the CEDAW Committee (UN Women 2009b). In 2010, the Working Group on Discrimination Against Women and Girls[7] was established out of a deep concern expressed by the Human Rights Council "that women everywhere are still subject to significant disadvantage as the result of discriminatory laws and practices and that de jure and de facto equality has not been achieved in any country in the world." Cooperative mechanisms between CEDAW and national human rights bodies enhance existing instruments for eliminating harmful laws and practices that State Parties' reservations protect by default.

These mechanisms for ensuring CEDAW implementation can be effective in generating "quiet" but incremental gains that wear away resistances to women's rights and gender equality. For example, local non-governmental organizations (NGOs) in the Philippines used the Optional Protocol to make the state accountable for violations to sexual and reproductive freedoms. The Optional Protocol inquiry was specifically prompted by a joint submission against a local executive order issued by a former Mayor of Manila in February 2000. This order declared Manila—one of the most densely populated cities in the Philippines—to be "pro-life," which translated to a public ban on contraceptives. Subsequently in 2007, the succeeding Manila mayor continued this ban by issuing his own executive order ruling that the city was "not [to] disburse and appropriate funds or finance any program or purchase materials, medicines for artificial birth control" (quoted in CEDAW 2015a: 4).

In 2015, the CEDAW Committee's findings and recommendations were released, and it was concluded that the Philippine state is accountable for various grave and systematic reproductive rights violations in the country. Specifically, the committee stressed the role of the Philippine state in perpetuating cultural and religious stereotypes of women's primary role as child bearers and child rearers to undermine and constrain their bodily autonomy and well-being (UN CEDAW Committee 2015a). This outcome catalyzed the establishment of a national inquiry by the Philippine Commission on Human Rights the following year, which found similar executive orders and de-facto contraceptive bans in other provinces and regional areas in the Philippines (Commission on Human Rights Philippines 2016). It also reaffirmed the importance of eliminating barriers to accessing sexual and reproductive health in the country especially for the urban poor, those in geographically remote areas, and those situated in crisis settings. What the Philippine case shows is that the CEDAW Committee can and does lend global legitimacy to national-level initiatives that seek to eliminate barriers to SRHR.

However, the growth and proliferation of CEDAW mechanisms have not corresponded to a similar pace in the modification and withdrawal of reservations. Quite the opposite, resistance to women's rights and specifically rights to bodily autonomy on the basis of preserving religion, tradition, and family values has not only persisted but has also skillfully adapted to the modalities afforded by neoliberal globalization. When CEDAW was first opened for signature and ratification and even during the drafting of the convention itself, it was already apparent that fundamentalist interpretations of religion would be used not for a wholesale resistance to the gender equality agenda but to "bracket off" sexual and reproductive rights to retain women's subordinated status in marriage and family relations.

The period leading to and after CEDAW would be the "canary in the coalmine" for how the beliefs of a very narrow set of national-level actors can be globalized to export harms to bodily autonomy, health, and well-being. The next decade will be marked by alliance-building of political forces seeking to preserve women's subordination. For example, by 1987, DAWN, a transnational women's organization representing Africa, Asia, and Latin America, was already signaling the alarm on "a crisis of culture" driven by "a sharp upsurge of fundamentalism in most major religions," but particularly by US-based "fundamentalist Christian churches [that] provide finance, personnel, and ideas to the extreme right wing's attacks on women" within their own country and abroad. DAWN situated the impacts of fundamentalisms within the intersection of growing worldwide militarization and violence in women's everyday lives particularly as "attacks on their control over reproduction" (Sen and Grown 1987: 74). Fundamentalists drum up in a carefully orchestrated manner "popular fears over the breakdown of traditional family structures and culture" to enforce the subordination of women and their exclusion from decision-making processes (Sen and Grown 1987: 75).

The UN Decade for Women and the Rise of a Counter-movement

The period from 1976 to 1985 was proclaimed by the General Assembly as *the United Nations Decade for Women: Equality, Development and Peace* (UN General Assembly 1975: 95). This was followed by the 1990s when key UN conferences on women and gender equality were held, and landmark documents such as the Cairo Programme of Action and Beijing Declaration and Platform for Action were produced (UN Women 2020; see Table 5.1).[8] The period from the 1980s to the 1990s was revolutionary in that world conferences provided local women's movements hitherto unavailable opportunities to circumvent the State, which was seen as a main barrier to women's rights and a source of insecurity. These national movements would respond by forging transnational

Table 5.1. SRHR AND KEY GLOBAL CONFERENCES

Year	Conference	Location
1975	World Conference of the International Women's Year (First World Conference on Women)	Mexico City
1979 CEDAW		
1980	World Conference of the United Nations Decade for Women	Copenhagen
1985	World Conference to review and appraise the achievements of the United Nations Decade for Women	Nairobi
1993	World Conference on Human Rights	Vienna
1994	International Conference on Population and Development	Cairo
1995	World Summit for Social Development	Copenhagen
1995	Fourth World Conference on Women	Beijing

alliances, identifying shared and systemic oppressions, as well as deploying their activism in multi-scalar ways, within and beyond the UN.

As catalytic as the UN conferences have been for women's activism, so were they for the very same actors and ideas that underpinned State Parties' reservations to CEDAW's Articles 2 and 16, and which would then manifest and reappear on the global stage. The UN conferences provided the impetus and political opportunity for the "seeds of backlash" to be sown on a global scale, which will continue to define and (re)direct feminist activisms in the new millennium (Ferree and Tripp 2006). During this period, a transnational reactionary force more popularly referred to by activists and academics as the "unholy alliance" emerged from a loose network of states and non-state actors that have come together on a shared goal of resisting, undermining, and reversing change toward gender equality in the name of religion and tradition (Petchesky 2003; Chappell 2006). This alliance brought together what would otherwise appear as unlikely bedfellows—for instance in the case of government representatives from the United States, Egypt, and Iran. It also included activists and NGOs, many of which were funded by or affiliated with the US Christian Right and coordinated with and received support from conservative governments across both the Islamic and Christian blocs[9] and international religious actors that have permanent non-member observer status at the UN, namely the Vatican and Organization of the Islamic Conference (OIC).

Chappell (2006: 498–499) argues that this alliance is best understood as a counter-movement. Drawing insights from literature on transnational social movements, Chappell explains that there are three main facets to how counter-movements operate. In the first place, they try to prevent issues from being defined as "problems." However, if an issue has been socially constructed as a problem, they will then prevent it from being included in a political agenda. But, if an issue does get put on an agenda, they will seek to

GLOBAL CRISIS OF RELIGIOUS FUNDAMENTALISMS [127]

undermine, neutralize, or depoliticize its status within that agenda. Thus, "instead of counting success in terms of effecting change, the measure of counter-movements is their ability to prevent their opponents' frames from being recognised or demands from being met" (Chappell 2006: 498). The global counter-movement became evident through their shared patriarchal values and deliberate focus on contesting the language and framing of women's rights at the UN conferences. Various accounts of the debates over the Cairo and Beijing outcome documents corroborate the idea that the formation of "pro-life" or "pro-family" counter narratives was influential in determining which gender equality language gets included and how (Chappell 2006; Petchesky 2003; Corrêa, Germain, and Petchesky 2005).

While the most substantive definition of sexual and reproductive health and rights has been enshrined in the Cairo and Beijing outcome documents, they were nevertheless *negotiated* outcomes and can be read as records of political contestations and compromises over what sort of discourses and entitlements could be put on the agenda during that time. The outcome documents of Cairo and Beijing in particular matter because following Chappell's analysis, "it signifies which frames and which framers have been (un)successful in the battle to define the meaning of women's rights" (2006: 496). Language matters because it also has material consequences through the ability to "freeze" or "lock in" configurations of power relations. For instance, Petchesky and Corrêa, both pioneering sexual and reproductive health and rights scholar-activists, recount how the resulting agenda secured in Cairo and Beijing deviated from the more holistic and integrated frames initially put forward by the global women's movements, especially by those from the Global South (Corrêa, Germain, and Petchesky 2005). Because of the fierce opposition raised by a conservative counter-movement, the SRHR agenda in the 1990s fell short by failing to incorporate abortion in the agenda and in its limited reference to sexual rights. This meant that the resulting agenda remained discursively circumscribed within traditional representations of the family and by heteronormative and maternalist frames. Sexuality, pleasure, and desire—all embodiments of agency—were excised from the emerging framework on bodily rights.

The retention of maternalist frames associated with reproductive health appealed to the counter-movement, which did champion protecting women's rights, though insofar as they conform to their traditional social reproductive roles especially within the family. Consequently, rather than a decisive victory, the Cairo and Beijing agendas created ambivalent positions on the rights of LGBT persons and sex workers, despite clear and common political ground, because they transgress "acceptable" forms of femininity. Similarly, a narrow agenda created dangerous alignments with conservative political forces who sought to benefit from framing women as victims lacking sexual agency, because this is used to justify masculine protection. As Petchesky notes for

[128] *Politics of Sexual & Reproductive Health*

example, sex trafficking was considered one of the "favourite human rights" issue by the US Christian Right and in later years by the United States under the Bush government for it dovetailed effectively with the US War on Terror and its tactic of deploying protection narratives to legitimize state militarism (2005: 308). Negotiated outcomes were seen as inevitable because the trans-national women's movement at the time had to pragmatically consolidate different perspectives, whenever possible and even within their own coalition, and to compromise on other issues in order to avoid a bigger loss in terms of a rejected UN agenda.

In the case of DAWN, there was a deliberate decision not to dismiss or vilify the ways women work within their own cultures and traditions to enhance individual and collective autonomy especially in navigating everyday social reproductive demands. Cultural critiques, in the absence of material redistribution of resources and labor, cannot fully account for the complex web of power relationships women find themselves in. This includes for example recognizing how polygamy has served in the easing of household burdens and the sharing resources among women—allowing relative freedom from marital servitude to pursue non-caring activities in their days (Corrêa 1994: 80–81). Moreover, Corrêa explained that "ambivalences and gaps are a result of political conditions and the balance of forces existing at the time." It was acknowledged that pragmatism was necessary in order to build broader coalitions and to sustain a political movement in the long run. She added further "we didn't have the strength at that point to address abortion as a human right; we must now focus on building that strength" (Corrêa, Germain, and Petchesky 2005, 110).

In the aftermath of these global conferences, networks of feminist activists and scholars have had to find the language to define and make sense of the counter-movement or anti-feminist backlash they were coming up against. They have had to discern the frames, organizational structures, and political strategies their opponents were employing while also navigating and learning about newly opened UN processes and institutions (see Sen and Grown 1987; Corrêa 1994; Petchesky 2003; Berer and Ravindran 1996). The conferences in Cairo and Beijing made even more apparent what was incipient during the CEDAW drafting and ratification process—that feminist activism incurs cost and reprisal. Over the next decade, it became increasingly crucial to begin mapping how this backlash was systematically undermining their advocacy across multiple geographies and at different levels of governance. In 1996, the journal *Reproductive Health Matters*[10] devoted a Special Issue to fundamentalism and reproductive rights. The then editors, Marge Berer and T.K. Sundari Ravindran wrote, "given the extent of the influence of politically-motivated fundamentalism internationally, not least at the Cairo and Beijing conferences, this seemed an important moment to focus on the influence and dangers of the many faces of fundamentalism for women and women's rights" (1996: 7).

GLOBAL CRISIS OF RELIGIOUS FUNDAMENTALISMS [129]

Berer and Ravindran observed then that the term fundamentalism—or more accurately *fundamentalisms*—was being used to describe "a range of movements and tendencies in all regions of the world which aim to impose what they define as tradition—whether religious, national, cultural or ethnic—on societies they consider to be in danger of straying from the fundamental tenets that hold them together" (1996: 7). In this Special Issue, contributors used a number of concepts to define fundamentalism such as anti-women, authoritarian, conservative, patriarchal, nationalist, ethno-religious, and extremist. Analyses of fundamentalism were drawn from within and among different religions and in places as geographically diverse as Iran, Poland, Indonesia, and India. In succeeding years, the term *religious* fundamentalisms would become more commonly used to emphasize the driving ideology and growing influence of religious non-state actors such as the US Christian Right. Post Cairo and Beijing, there was an observable shift from the limited use of religion by the state as a tool to restrict progress on gender equality to religious actors who can actively weaponize state power and hold hostage decision-making processes in order to advance a regressive and anti-feminist agenda despite themselves constituting a minority in global politics.

In 2007, a survey entitled "Resisting and Challenging Religious Fundamentalisms" was conducted by the Association for Women's Rights in Development (AWID) with more than 1,600 women's rights activists from 160 countries and found that religious fundamentalists have "have grown more visible, strategic and aggressive." What this survey showed is that, while there are debates over the right terminologies to use, activists do find the concept of "religious fundamentalisms" useful for their work, meaningfully capturing what they encounter and understand in the varied spaces they operate (AWID 2008a, 2008b, 2011, 2016). While many of the activists agreed that religious fundamentalisms deploy different political tactics and manifest in varying levels of influence and formations, their espoused ideologies share a common goal of reinforcing patriarchy through an emphasis on family, traditional gender roles, and moral purity and superiority. Based on the responses, 76% believe that the strength of religious fundamentalisms has increased globally, while 60% reported an increase in their respective geographic contexts (AWID 2008a, 2008b), and 8 out of 10 women's rights activists have personally experienced the negative impacts of religious fundamentalisms (AWID 2008b: 7).

What sets fundamentalist forces apart is an intolerance of "diversity and dissent" based on interrelated assertions of moral, ethno/national, religious, and political "superiority." According to one of the activists, Alejandra Sardá from Argentina, "three fundamentalist expressions that dominate the international debates: Islamists, Roman Catholics and Evangelical Christians . . . the only issues on which they agree are those related to restricting the exercise of sexual rights on the part of women, but also of others with non-conventional identities and practices" (quoted in AWID 2008b: 6). This intolerance also

[130] *Politics of Sexual & Reproductive Health*

underpins threats of or actual use of violence by religious fundamentalists in the vilification and "fear-mongering" of the "other." Approximately half of respondents (at 46%) found that the negative impacts of religious fundamentalisms directly relate to SRHR. Women, LGBT, and human rights activists in general have been targeted by religious fundamentalist violence ranging from verbal attacks and insult, which were reportedly most common, to physical and sexual violence, less reported but more serious cases of violent backlash (AWID 2008a, 2008b, 2011).

More recently, feminist scholars and activists have begun to recognize the need to go beyond understanding religious fundamentalists as simply "backlash" or as a counter-movement because doing so risks obscuring how they have adapted to crucial developments in contemporary global political economy (see Sen 2005; AWID 2011). Indeed, while they still operate as a counter-movement, as can be seen consistently in global conferences and forums, religious fundamentalists are not entirely reactionary. They themselves actively construct and constitute political projects at various scales where political and economic decision-making is made. For instance, the Vatican (or Holy See) as a Permanent Observer to the UN has been instrumental in promoting a global pro-life agenda. Additionally, according to a study focused specifically on the gendered impacts of religious fundamentalisms on women's political participation in Asia, religious fundamentalist forces were recognized as increasingly a frightening impediment to democratic governance (Derichs and Fleschenberg 2010).

Case studies from Buddhist, Christian, and Islamic societies of the region demonstrate how religious fundamentalisms constitute "global political projects" that "operate formally through the state or informally through institutions and individuals" (Estrada Claudio 2010: 14–15). They influence not only political discourses and frames but also the manner in which political decision-making is made in order to simultaneously target, undermine, and endanger the work of women in politics. They further constrain broader political participation and full citizenship by denying bodily autonomy through restrictions of sexual and reproductive freedoms. Religious fundamentalists contest power at global and national levels because "[b]y restricting women's reproductive and socialising roles to within the framework of the family, fundamentalists gain the key to directing an entire society" (AWID 2011: 17). Thus, the term religious fundamentalism is also used to "refer to the authoritarian manipulation of religion and use of extreme interpretations of religion by particular State or non-State actors to achieve power, money, and extend social control" (OURs 2017: 8). For these actors, resisting SRHR is *the* agenda because it serves as a gateway for (re)instating their political and moral authority in a rapidly changing world.

Religious fundamentalists seek and exercise power ideologically *and* materially. Part of analyzing how religious fundamentalists operate is understanding their political economy. This includes making visible how they are active drivers of global politics and the social reproductive crisis their very impacts constitute. Yet, the political economic roots of religious fundamentalisms have been underexamined. According to Petchesky, Gemain, and Corrêa (2005), among the shortcomings or missed opportunities in the Cairo and Beijing conferences is the relative absence of a political economy critique. Aside from the eventual downplaying of comprehensive and affirmative aspects of sexual and reproductive freedoms (e.g., LGBT rights, abortion, sexuality, and pleasure), another pragmatic outcome of the UN Conferences was that the then emerging transnational women's alliance sharpened their cultural critique on the neglect of micro- and macro-level analysis of trends and processes enabled by economic policies. Such an oversight was perhaps understandably unavoidable as they were navigating religious fundamentalist resistances, which strongly justified the denial of bodily autonomy on the basis of preserving tradition and culture. However, the trade-off between culture and political economy in the context of SRHR aligns with Fraser's analysis of how "second-wave" feminist movements shifted political claims from "redistribution" to "recognition" just at the birth of neoliberalism. This, as she points out, resulted in the exchange of "one truncated paradigm for another" wherein "the cultural strand became decoupled not only from the economic strand, but also from the critique of capitalism that had previously integrated them" (Fraser 2013: 219).

The cost of losing an integrated feminist critique of political economy was that feminism—and the transformative agenda it represented—became "unmoored" and thus free for resignification. Feminist discourses and activisms thus became the "new spirit" of capitalism that would enable neoliberalism to take root and thrive. First, because a strong political economy analysis was needed in order to account for critical changes particularly in the way the World Bank and the International Monetary Fund (IMF) had taken over the global development agenda (Fraser 2013; see also Sen 2005 and Berer 2011 for examples). Second, building on Fraser's account, I argue that a splintered feminist analysis during this specific historical juncture also helped embolden religious fundamentalists who were vying in ideological competition to appeal to populations who either perceive or experience first-hand discontents and displacements due to global economic transformations. Over time, there will be renewed and stronger calls that "we need both political economy and culture to understand contemporary religious fundamentalisms" (Chhachhi 2014: 263). The need for political economy analysis becomes even more apparent as the period from the 1990s to the present has also corresponded with perverse impacts of market forces in global health and women's rights as well as in the governance of crisis and emergencies (Benatar, Gill, and Bakker 2011; Gill and Bakker 2011).

In the next section, I examine religious fundamentalisms and their role in restricting sexual and reproductive freedoms in crisis settings. How do

[132] *Politics of Sexual & Reproductive Health*

religious fundamentalists operate in enacting and (re)appropriating security in spaces of crisis? The presence and proliferation of religious fundamentalisms in global and national crisis responses demonstrate how these forces have adapted on a global scale to instrumentalize women's bodies for the social reproduction of political and economic order. Crucially, authoritative struggles over bodily autonomy are shifting in the name of security.

CRISES AND THE POLITICAL ECONOMY OF RELIGIOUS FUNDAMENTALISMS

> The rise of religious fundamentalisms must be understood as part of the interrelated crises the world is facing: growing inequality and poverty; failure of states to provide essential services; lack of real democracy and civil liberties; militarism, insecurity, conflict, and displacements; and depletion of energy resources. (AWID 2016: 15)

In 2016, AWID published another report as part of their ongoing analysis of religious fundamentalisms: *The devil is in the details*. The report is aimed at examining the structural drivers of religious fundamentalisms in the context of escalating global violence and uncertainty over the full implementation of the Sustainable Development Goals (SDGs) by 2030. This requires feminist analysis to "understand women's bodies as a site of control for religious fundamentalists, and how this may inform policies and approaches of development actors" from a wide range of geographic and political contexts (AWID 2016: 9). The report showed that development practitioners and policy-makers have many local and global challenges to talk about, let alone, directly address religious fundamentalisms. For example, religion is seen as "too touchy" especially by foreign or external development actors who do not want to be seen as antagonizing local partners and beneficiaries. Such a pragmatic approach is seen as necessary to avoid jeopardizing their ability to deliver aid and other programs. Meanwhile, the report also noted that religious fundamentalisms may be left unchallenged through the misuse and manipulation of ideas such as "cultural sensitivity" and in the context of mainstreaming "gender and diversity" trainings in the development sector (2016: 7).

The insights from the AWID report alert us to how fundamentalists have been able to thrive in many parts of the world by appropriating the language and modalities employed by the development sector and in feminist activisms. Religious fundamentalisms have complicated and deep entanglements with the global economy and transnational feminist activisms. AWID (2016, 2011) therefore argues for the importance of questioning vested material interests that may be served by the uncritical promotion of diversity and the value placed in maintaining harmony above all within the global development agenda. Crucially, as the quote opening this section suggests, we need to pay greater attention how the growth of religious fundamentalisms interrelates with neoliberal crisis responses.

Faith-based Partnerships in Crisis Settings

In the Philippines, religious fundamentalisms have stepped into the spaces opened by state retrenchment and the privatization of social welfare, development, and crisis response. State intervention on women's bodies in the country began around the same time many "population control" policies were being adopted in Asia during the 1960s and 1970s (Herrin and Pernia 2003: 299–300; Corrêa 1994: 25). The population control discourse was so dominant and influential during this period that the 1973 Philippine Constitution stipulated "it shall be the responsibility of the State to achieve and maintain population levels most conducive to the national welfare" (Philippine Constitution 1973). Following an economic rationale, then President Ferdinand Marcos launched a National Policy on Family Planning in 1969. Subsequently, the Philippine Commission on Population (Popcom) was created in line with the justification that a working population program is necessary to attain the country's social and economic goals (Presidential Decree No. 79 1972; Republic of the Philippines Commission on Population n.d.). Part of the Commission's mandate is to "promote a broad understanding of the adverse effects on family life and national welfare of unlimited population growth" (Presidential Decree No. 79 1972.). With pressure from the IMF and funding from the U.S. Agency for International Development USAID, Marcos's policy was narrowly focused on the reduction of fertility; and was widely regarded as successful at this (Fabros et al. 1998: 226; David 2003:18–21).

From the 1970s, contraceptives in the country had almost exclusively come from USAID, the United Nations Population Fund (UNFPA), and other international organizations and so the need for government procurement was negligible. In particular, USAID contraceptive donations accounted for 80% of the country's total supply requirement at that time (Tanyag 2015). Historically, as for many developing countries at that time, accessibility was heavily dependent on foreign donations of family planning supplies. However, beginning in the late 1990s, the US government decided to systematically stop being the main provider of family planning supplies in a bid to make developing countries "self-reliant" with regard to their family planning programs (Brune 2005).

In 2007, the global withdrawal of USAID contraceptive supplies fully came to effect in the Philippines, creating massive gaps in accessing health care especially for poor women. This occurred because the state neither "stepped in" nor "stepped up" to ensure public provision of contraceptives, choosing instead to pass the burden of self-reliance onto individuals and families. For example, the national government under President Gloria Arroyo (2001–2010) made no effort to publicly provide contraceptives (Tanyag 2015). This approach proved detrimental to poor women who were most reliant on state welfare support. Those with resources can still procure contraceptives "out of pocket" and in private health facilities and pharmacies. In 2001, the Department of Health also banned Postinor, an emergency contraceptive (EC) pill, in response to the petition of a local pro-life/pro-family group, *Abay Pamilya* (or "In Service of the Family"). The group argued that the pill is an abortifacient and as such, goes against the 1987 Philippine Constitution (Ruiz Austria 2004: 98), which stipulates that the state "shall equally protect the life of the mother and the life of the unborn from conception." Official information from the World Health Organization (WHO) clarifies that the EC pill does not induce abortions. However, the Health Secretary at the time defended his decision by stating that while he respects the standards of WHO, the country need not always follow international standards.[11]

Arroyo's presidency was defined by a firm stance against contraceptives justified by the belief that she was being responsive to the needs of most Filipino mothers who are conservative Catholics and therefore do not use contraceptives (Abinales and Amoroso 2005: 296). This juncture was enabled at the global level too. Under Arroyo, the Philippines was part of a global campaign to protect the unborn (Tan 2004). On March 25, 2004, Arroyo declared a national celebration of "The Day of the Unborn," with the support of the Catholic Bishops' Conference of the Philippines and in concert with many other countries especially in Latin America and pro-life groups overseas (CBCP For Life 2012). A few months after, on April 2, US President George W. Bush signed the Unborn Victims of Violence Act, announcing to the world that "the United States of America is building a culture of life."[12] Sexual and reproductive freedoms in the Philippines therefore began to be significantly undermined through the opening of spaces for Catholic Church leaders, "pro-life" groups, and local government officials, including conservative elite women, to restrict access to contraceptives through the state. Their influence in policy-making drives and exacerbates pervasive restrictions to bodily autonomy from lack of access to contraceptives to the continued criminalization of abortion (Likhaan, Reprocen, and Center for Reproductive Rights 2007/2010).

Neoliberal governance, which promotes public-private partnerships, has also opened spaces for non-state actors such as international funding institutions, transnational corporations, and NGOs in the delivery of social goods (Prügl and True 2014). Gradually, however, NGOs have been delivering more aid than the whole UN system (Ferris 2005). As Ferris points out, faith-based and secular humanitarian organizations are more active, with bigger budgets and more credibility in service delivery than donor governments and related state ministries (2005: 311). Faith-based groups have a long history in humanitarian and development spaces. While a minority, NGOs at the UN that articulate a pro-life or "traditional" or "family values" agenda predominantly originate from or are based in the United States (Norwegian Agency for Development Cooperation 2013). They reflect a continuity to the historical presence of USAID funding especially in the Global South. Indeed, the US Christian Right has a reach and resources that mirror the legacy of US imperialism. For instance, Human Life International, a US-based NGO, funds and supports satellite branches in other parts of the world, including in former colonies such as the Philippines.

Faith-based organizations are characterized by one or more of these attributes: religious affiliation; explicit references to religion in their mission statement; financial support from religious sources; and governance structures and decision-making based on religious values (Ferris 2005: 312). Religious actors and faith-based organizations are positioned as "development partners" and vehicles for effective crisis response. Faith-based development partnerships are being framed as "front lines" that may have the "local knowledge" and pre-existing community presence even before a crisis such as a disaster or conflict erupts. Indeed, in a special session on religious engagement at the 2016 World Humanitarian Summit, Caritas Internationalis President Cardinal Antonio Tagle, who is also a prominent Filipino archbishop, stated that "faith leaders and faith-based organizations in humanitarian contexts are not only able to deliver critical services during a crisis but to do so with a unique wisdom of compassion and reconciliation" (Vatican Radio 2016).[13]

In the Philippines, the Church and Christian faith-based organizations are typically among the first in the civil society sector to extend aid owing to their pre-existing social, political, and economic networks in a country where approximately 80% of the Filipino population are Catholics. Structural adjustment programs, care labor as a "cheap" export, and the resulting remittance-driven national economy all mean that development has been uneven. NGOs do not just "fill in the gaps" in social welfare and emergency relief provisions in the country. In poor, remote, and rural areas in the country, they are more visible and reliable than the state and thus, have clear infrastructural and logistical advantages in responding to any crisis. There was a clear sense among the NGO representatives I interviewed that faith-based response is a permanent fixture in national crisis-response. A rural women's NGO representative noted that "the Church in the Philippines in many parts of the country, especially rural areas, functions as the State. The church has long looked after the welfare of IPs [indigenous peoples] in this country while the state has largely been absent."[14] For example, the Church has administrative regions that constitute dioceses and parishes throughout the country. Its organizational structure parallels that of the state such that several *barangays* will typically have one parish. At the primary level of this structure are the

[136] *Politics of Sexual & Reproductive Health*

Basic Ecclesial Communities (BECs) also formerly known as Basic Christian Communities (BCCs).

Through leadership by the parish priest of BECs, the Church is able to mobilize civic volunteerism and participation as well as economic resources among communities crucial for a crisis-prone country. As a result:

> The Catholic Church has an infrastructure that matches, if not surpasses the network of government. Even in the most remote places, the church can reach because they are already there even before the calamity or crisis with pre-existing relationships and history of charitable assistance. Along with faith-based groups, the Catholic community is thus really helpful for relief and rehabilitation.[15]

Moreover, another informant claimed, "[a Catholic NGO] is among the fastest to respond in times of disaster due to its strategy of working with the Church which has an expansive network. Unlike the government which is typically delayed by bureaucratic processes even in times of crisis."[16] Churches—as in the physical infrastructures themselves—serve as evacuation sites:

> In times of crisis (and even in normal situations), parish priests and local churches have always played an important role for many Filipinos. Filipinos seek refuge in churches. Historically, churches served as sanctuaries in times of disasters—they offer temporary shelter and provide donated relief mobilised through charitable institutions.[17]

Consequently, as Bankoff argued "people may rely more on church-based networks and religious leaders to see them through times of crisis when social security provisions are rudimentary or non-existent" (2015: 434). This applies too for international donors and response teams who cannot but tap local religious leaders and the vast network of BECs in order to deliver immediate relief assistance.

Feminist scholars point out that the turn toward neoliberal governance has adversely impacted feminist movements by means of NGO-ization. In the long-run, NGO-ization has de-radicalized their impact and objectives by fragmenting feminist critiques and funneling them into bureaucratic systems characterized by tech-fixes and marketization (Kandiyoti 2015; Fraser 2013). Feminist movements have also been impacted by the related rise of religious groups in crisis or humanitarian spaces and by the latter's broadening presence, which is contributing to normalizing cultural norms and practices that deny bodily autonomy. For example, AWID cites how donations initially collected for disaster response were used for Hindu Right's organizing by a charity organization (2016: 27). Moreover, consolidating insights from AWID's networks, "there is some evidence that at least some religious organizations have used services and relief to introduce narrower interpretations of religion and adoption of rigid gender roles, heteronorma-tivity, conservative dress codes and behavior" (2016: 27). Some have also used crisis settings as spaces to proselytize and convert despite standards set by the International Red Cross and Red Crescent Movement prohibiting these practices (2016: 28). Faith-based partnerships in the Philippines sug-gest similar gendered costs to crisis responses with a strong Catholic "pro-life" and "pro-family" agenda.

Based on the national inquiry conducted by the Philippine Commission on Human Rights (2016), "RH goods and services" are not considered a priority during times of crisis. The lack of access to SRHR in times of crises is perhaps unsurprising given pre-existing weak public health systems. However, the issue of accessibility is not easily addressed by making supplies and services available. In the post-disaster case study, for example, there were reports that the accessibility of EC pills was restricted *through* the Typhoon Haiyan human-itarian response itself. According to a female informant:

> UNFPA rape kit donations had EC pills [morning-after] but some members of UNFPA-Philippines decided to take them out claiming that these are unregis-tered in the country. However, WHO standards already provide that the delivery of unregistered products can be allowed under emergency situations.[18]

This telling incident was corroborated in the Commission Inquiry held in Tacloban City where it was reported that "development partners distributed rape kits but allegedly took out EC pills. This [issue] was raised at a meeting in the regional office in the aftermath of Yolanda."[19] In this example, the in-fluence of religious fundamentalist beliefs in faith-based partnerships risks undermining emergency assistance because "when health service is framed through a particular religion the services offered will be limited or not the most appropriate for patients."[20] This concern should not be construed as devaluing in general the tremendous contribution of churches and faith-based groups in saving lives during crisis and emergencies. However, in cases of rape and sexual violence, the consequences of religious fundamentalists' influence in restricting access to SRHR may constitute grave violations of rights and can lead to compounded and intergenerational harms. This demonstrates the importance of ensuring state responsibility and accountability in crisis and emergencies especially for core obligations that cannot be divested to religious groups or other private actors alone.

In Haiyan-affected areas, the majority of which are rural, the Catholic Church and faith-based groups were pivotal in reaching out to far-flung com-munities to provide relief assistance and initiate post-disaster livelihood projects. However, the Church and religious actors are not beholden to their constituencies in the same way as governments are made accountable through democratic institutions and processes. As pointed out in my interviews:

[138] *Politics of Sexual & Reproductive Health*

Unlike the state, the Church has less mechanisms for accountability. It is still very feudal. Bishops exercise tremendous power in a given locality. Diocesan priests are financially dependent on the generosity of the communities they are assigned in. Local elites financially support priests.[21]

At local levels, these political and economic alliances become evident wherein conservative politicians and Church leaders can and have been able to effectively restrict public health access to SRHR based on their own religious fundamentalist beliefs. The case of the Philippines demonstrates how faith-based partnerships may thus come at the cost of comprehensive sexual and reproductive health services and supplies. When the fundamentalist views of the Church and other religious groups translate into definitions of sex and reproduction that underlie crisis responses, in effect these will be exclusionary toward adolescent sexuality, abortion, and LGBT rights.

Where access to contraception and other vital sexual and reproductive health services have been routinely denied to women and girls on the basis of fundamentalist interpretation of the Catholic religion, it is clear that the necessary measures for comprehensive health service delivery and protection mechanisms in emergencies require material redistribution of wealth and authority. Yet, the national Responsible Parenthood and Reproductive Health (RPRH) Law had been challenged on constitutional grounds by the pro-life lobby. The Supreme Court upheld provisions that protected (a) requiring parental and spousal consents for accessing services and supplies and (b) conscientious objection by private and public health providers (except in an emergency or life-threatening condition) (Melgar et al. 2018). The difficulty here, as one informant noted, is that:

> Under the RPRH Law, conscientious objection on provision of services was recognised but it is stipulated that they must still provide the appropriate referral to where services may be accessed . . . In emergency contexts, conscientious objection is problematic because SRHR is fundamentally part of emergency care.[22]

The broader issue the informant raised regarding implementation is that the provision of contraception and other SRHR supplies is not typically considered part of emergency response. Ongoing resistance through the courts and "on the ground" means that the deeply held beliefs and prejudices of local community partners will continue to serve as a crucial barrier in promoting comprehensive SRHR programs. While the RPHL Law mandates access to contraceptive information and services to people in situations of sexual and gender-based violence and crises, there remain complex challenges in its implementation. For example, as Melgar et al. (2018: 7) point out, "legal restrictions to minors and the use and availability of emergency contraception are still in place."

Another example is in the case of the lack of crisis assistance to LGBTs. A male country representative of an international organization reported that:

> LGBTs and anti-discrimination against LGBTs remain controversial [among local partners]. Compared with other countries, Philippines shows a higher degree of acceptance. [We] do not really have specific programs supporting others outside of the violence against women program. Most work being done is around gender-based violence on *women*. We just do not have the capacity to take on another challenging area. We also do not have the expertise. But that is certainly the next area we should be focusing on.[23]

What this tells us is that SRHR gaps will persist, to the detriment of diverse groups of women and girls in crisis settings and even with the best intentions of international response teams and private donors, in the absence of domestic-level reforms. In some cases, counter-intuitive power asymmetries between local authorities and foreign or external organizations mean that international NGOs (INGOs) may not always be in a position to challenge conservative views when doing so can prevent "access" or open themselves to pressures to leave the community or country. Local religious fundamentalist influence can take deeper roots due to the constant vulnerability of crisis-affected populations and given the cultural weight of gratitude as an obligation in the face of charity.[24] Different gender equality issues are hierarchically constructed and negotiated in spaces of aid before, during, and after crises.

Rights versus Needs?

Religious fundamentalisms provide the legitimating discourses and ideologies that complement and further enable political economic processes on a global scale. Religious fundamentalisms are linked with development and humanitarian crises in that these forces seek to appeal to populations particularly from two major religious groups—Islam and Christianity—that have been displaced and dispossessed by the global economy. Beginning at the UN conferences, religious fundamentalists challenge not just the universality of women's rights but also their supposed contradistinction with people's "basic needs" (Petchesky 2000). In the case of Christian fundamentalists, Petchesky traces the dichotomization between "basic needs" and "human rights" to a position first adopted by a pro-life NGO called the Caucus for Stable Families during the ICPD + 5 review process in 1999 (Petchesky 2000). This narrative, which was espoused by Christian fundamentalist actors and the Vatican, represented their cross-cutting critique of development "gone astray" as a result of the dominance of Western or Global North countries in both the global economy and within feminist activisms. This critique allows them to frame

[140] *Politics of Sexual & Reproductive Health*

specific issues as prerequisites to human survival under the category of "basic needs" while dismissing sexual and reproductive health as "'flawed' priorities [that] reflect a Western agenda (read, of Western feminists) with a blatant disregard for the genuine needs and priorities of women in the South" (Petchesky 2000: 17).

The dichotomization between "rights" and "needs" re-emerged in a 2013 campaign by the US-based INGO Human Life International as part of mobilizing protests to the Women Deliver global conference. This triennial women's health conference has been financially supported by the Bill and Melinda Gates Foundation. Thus in their campaign entitled "No Controversy? Facts for Melinda Gates," Human Life International claimed that what women (particularly young women from the Global South as their YouTube video portrays) *really* need are "better schools, better hospitals, better roads" instead of "drugs" (Human Life International 2012). From their viewpoint, development is narrowly understood as provisioning infrastructures for water, food, and shelter, which in turn are basic needs that must take precedence especially in the face of poverty (Petchesky 2003). Not surprisingly, Catholic NGOs in the Philippines are typically active in the WASH (water, sanitation, and hygiene) cluster of international humanitarian and local disaster response.[25] It is important to note that this dichotomization does not challenge health as a basic need per se, rather, it is informed by a fine-tuned opposition to sexual and reproductive health. Behind this logic is conceptualizing development without bodily autonomy in the same manner that we see Catholic fundamentalists bracket off SRHR from inclusive and durable solutions to peace and post-crisis recovery. The "basic needs" rhetoric indeed can become even more compelling in crisis settings where narratives of emergency relief and resource scarcity collide with the tyranny of urgency. It resonates with global economic trends such that SRHR receive among the lowest budget allocations in official development assistance to conflict-affected countries (Tanabe et al. 2015; Chynoweth 2015; Patel et al. 2009). For instance, "only about 50 per cent of the UNFPA global humanitarian appeal is achieved each year" which leaves millions of displaced women and girls without adequate access to sexual and reproductive health (UNFPA 2019).

The Catholic fundamentalists' "rights versus needs" discourse is initially convincing because it mobilizes the language of rational prioritization to global and national resource allocations and dovetails with feminist critiques to North-South political economic divides. First, this position ostensibly urges governments in developing countries with thinly spread resources to resist economic domination by developed countries and to respond to the "genuine" concerns and priorities of Global South women. Second, part of their strategy in resisting SRHR has been the appropriation of feminist resistance to global and national population control measures including against neo-Malthusian approaches that frame fertility rates among the Global South as drivers of global instability and environmental degradation.[26] As Petchesky observes, "Northern and industrialized countries, particularly the U.S., surely do champion certain reproductive and sexual health rights to the virtual exclusion of health infrastructure needs such as safe water and sanitation" (2000: 19). Thus, it gains ground, including among conservative national governments and elites who are intent on quelling domestic feminist and human rights movements. In effect, deploying the discourse of "basic needs" was a bid to build common cause on global inequalities obscuring the transnational women's movements behind SRHR. It also capitalized on a particular juncture when feminist energies were directed at resisting culture while political economy critiques waned (Sen 2005; Petchesky 2000; Fraser 2013).

From a critical feminist perspective, the "rights versus needs" discourse allows Catholic fundamentalists to appear progressive while ultimately keeping religious decision-making male-dominated and exclusionary. Its continuous deployment serves to contest and establish who has the authoritative voice on the "real world" problems of poor "Third World" or "Global South" women. By professing to champion the Global South, they can appear critical of global economic and gender inequalities while retaining the foundational gendered material relations that guarantee them moral authority to dictate what is good in politics, society, and economy. This self-image of the Catholic Church has its roots in liberation theology, which draws from Marxist political thought but with an important distinction in recognizing the potential of religion to "liberate as well as oppress." Liberation theology grew to prominence in the 1970s as it catalyzed activism among the Catholic clergy and laity across Latin America and Africa, before gradually reaching the Philippines. Post–Vatican II, the Catholic Church shifted its exclusive focus from divine salvation in the afterlife to serving the world as a champion for the oppressed by directly contributing to addressing underdevelopment and poverty in the here and now (Cooper 2015; Holden and Nadeau 2010).[27] Liberation theology is aimed at reconstructing "modernization processes from the vantage points of victims: the poor and those who have been displaced by development" (Holden and Nadeau 2010: 91).

The localization of liberation theology in the Philippines brought the Church into alliance with anti-Marcos dictatorship and social justice movements. Church activism reached "grassroots" level through the social infrastructure of BECs. In the words of one informant, BECs embodied "how the Church undertakes community organising. It started in Mindanao and reflects the conscientization of the religious order."[28] BECs have been on the frontlines of assisting peasants and rural communities around land-rights reform as a core advocacy. However, as a female informant who is a leader of a faith-based NGO pointed out:

> The Catholic Church in the Philippines is at the forefront of social issues . . . they are part of mobilisations on climate, poverty, corruption, governance . . . The

[142] *Politics of Sexual & Reproductive Health*

Church was also a key player in toppling the Marcos dictatorship through Cardinal Sin. It is even convening a Workers' Congress. So the Church is a strong advocate for a lot of social issues but never supportive of women's groups when it comes to SRHR.[29]

This view suggests that the Catholic Church champions social justice based on normative positions regarding the "worthy" poor and on the role of women in the family and society. For example, Roces' (2009, 2012) historical analysis of women's movements in the Philippines demonstrated that constructions of the Filipino woman as self-sacrificing "martyr" and "victim" have been more effective in mobilizing political alliances between women's groups and Catholic nuns and religious groups. This alliance was activated in pursuit of legal reform on the issue of prostitution and sex trafficking. It was possible because violence against *hetero* women did not challenge the Church's paternalistic authority and fundamentalist interpretations of sex, sexuality, and ideal femininity. The violence against women (VAW) and anti-prostitution campaign in the country portrayed women as victims in need of protection, which in turn aligned with the Church's pro-family agenda and the kind of "social justice" issues it can champion. The Church is thus willing to promote the interests of Filipino women when they embody these core traits: "virginal until married, fertile when married, and long suffering until death" (Roces 2009: 272).

By contrast, issues relating to SRHR that clearly promote sexual agency among all individuals activate different doctrinal politics, thereby being framed as anti-life and anti-family (Htun 2003; Htun and Weldon 2018). Rights relating to contraception, abortion, and same-sex relationships are perceived as threats to the institutions of marriage and the family. For instance, Filipinos For Life, a globally connected pro-life group with strong conservative women's membership, opposed the RPRH law and argued that it is they who represented "*true* women's health" (emphasis mine, Tanyag 2015: 69). Filipino pro-life women contend that promoting access to contraception "only empowers those who wish to take advantage of us without having to worry about consequences" (Tanyag 2015: 69). Absent from this narrative is the possibility that women themselves and all individuals can find empowerment in and do take pleasure from sex. Employing the same masculine protection narratives used by the Church, they cast women's health in the limited light of either victimhood or maternal virtue. Moreover, as pointed out by an informant in an interview, decisions relating to and interpretations of Catholic religious doctrine remain exclusively made by men, and this explains why "many priests though lack awareness or are out-of-touch with the issues when it comes to SRHR . . . rather than promoting 'informed choice' they insist on 'blind obedience.' Reproductive health is not a stand-alone issue. It is connected with other social justice issues."[30]

Doctrinal contestations within the Catholic Church have moved away from the radicalism found in liberation theology to a more conservative position and one that renders it complicit in the reproduction of neoliberalism. In the case of Christian organizations and the Catholic Church, they have sought to maintain a presence in global economic and security debates by infusing a "moral style" to neoliberalism (Muehlebach 2013). Catholic fundamentalism "sacralises" the neoliberal economy by offering complementary ideological principles on love, charity, and self-sacrifice. As neoliberal economic policies were restructuring care and social reproduction more broadly, the Catholic Church animated these changes with the language of virtue and volunteerism. Christian teaching in general is framed as providing the necessary values to reign in market excesses rather than reform market fundamentalism per se (Muehlebach 2013). Embracing the prevailing economic order is seen as providing fertile ground for individuals to be "tested" for their capacities in sin, sacrifice, and redemption. According to Muehlebach (2013: 460), a Catholicization of neoliberalism made values of mutual help and charity central to smoothing out both societal and market imperfections while leaving material relations and distribution of resources intact. Labor expressed as gift or sacrifice mobilizes volunteerism and "self-help," thereby conveniently complementing the rolling back of state responsibility and redistribution. This, Muehlebach (2013) argues, is precisely the kind of moral subjectivity that legitimates neoliberalism.

Indeed, the BECs in the Philippines, though initially catalyzed by liberation theology, now function more like agents in normalizing neoliberal governance and crisis response. First, BECs work with communities to be "self-reliant" in meeting their own needs as a marker of resilience. This form of resilience is limited in addressing structural and large-scale development reforms as well as effective crisis response. Catholic valorization of volunteerism and mutual help among communities serves to legitimate existing unequal material relations because it does not challenge gendered division of labor. Volunteerism is thus borne heavily by women. Second, Catholicized neoliberalism rests on mobilizing charity among elites, and indeed in the Philippines local philanthropy and remittances from extended kinship networks ensure survival in a country beset my multiple forms of crises. In the words of a female representative from a prominent faith-based group, "charity is an integral part of Catholic teaching. Churches are even present in the most far-flung places in the country . . . in times of crisis and calamities, Catholics are very visible in selflessly extending their hand. The values on charity and love are there."[31] At the same time, these Christian actors represent an influential bloc in global governance whose "influence does not reflect their number but is largely due to a striking ability to build alliances across religious boundaries as well as elicit the support of religious communities around the world" (Norwegian Agency for Development Cooperation 2013: 1).

[144] *Politics of Sexual & Reproductive Health*

Contradictions emerge because women are simultaneously asked to "step in" and "to hollow out" their selves in mitigating global economic harms. For instance, Pope Francis (2015), the leader of the global Catholic religious community, noted that "often the readiness of mothers to make sacrifices for their children is taken advantage of so as to 'save' on social spending." Still, he relies on the same "martyrdom of mothers" as an antidote to the contemporary "self-centredness of societies." In his words, "motherhood is more than childbearing; it is a life choice entailing sacrifice, respect for life, and commitment to passing on those human and religious values which are essential for a healthy society" (quoted in Harris 2015). Whether referring to love, sacrifice, or charity, these virtues are feminized in that most often it is women's bodies and social reproductive labor that mitigate the excesses of states and markets. Extolling maternal virtue must be matched by accounting for how and why "it can waver, dry up, desist, and begin to withdraw from certain kinds of suffering and certain kinds of people" (Muehlebach 2013: 462).

CONCLUSION: RETHINKING FEMINIST STRATEGIES IN THE FACE OF GLOBALIZED HARMS

The capacity of religious fundamentalist forces to globalize or "export harms" became an even more pressing concern as global politics turned to a new period of heightened religious fundamentalist "backlash." In 2017, the election of Donald Trump marked a critical juncture for demonstrating the fragility of feminist and human rights gains. In other parts of the world, a resurgence of authoritarian and hypermasculine leaders—from Bolsonaro to Duterte—would take the global stage. International political decision-making is being shaped by their brazen disregard for gender equality and human rights. Feminist movements would come under direct attack and be vilified as a threat to national and global society. Core institutions such as the UN, Human Rights Council, and WHO, along with the importance of multilateralism, are being questioned. In the face of this intensified resurgence against human rights and specific targeting of feminists, a new global initiative called the Observatory on the Universality of Rights was developed. The Observatory is "a new collaborative initiative that aims to monitor, analyze, and share information on initiatives that misuse religion, culture, and tradition to undermine the universality of human rights" (OURs 2017). At this new juncture, it is important to ask what or why these men's rise to power caught many societies by surprise? Who among us were not surprised? What does hypermasculine leadership—and the complicity of women within it—tell us about global politics at a time when crises from conflicts and disasters to climate change have been cascading harms across multiple scales of social reproduction and affecting multitudes all over the world?

The visceral and visible arrival of "populist" and aggressive world leaders has prompted important and critical reflections from scholars and activists alike. Ongoing scholarly efforts aim to diagnose the macro and micro-processes in political economy, culture, and security driving this emerging global force defined as "cultural backlash" by Norris and Inglehart (2019). There has been a growth of dedicated journal special issues focused on examining the rise of the global far right (Sweetman 2017; Fangen and Skjelsbæk 2020). Research on whether Trump, Bolsonaro, and Duterte reflect disruptions from normal politics or form part of a continuum of anti-feminist resistance promises to generate important insights for feminist political strategies and analytical tools in the face of an uncertain future. The discussions from this chapter suggest that examining the global politics of bodily autonomy reveals the shared roots of authoritarian or hypermasculine leaders and religious fundamentalists.

Future research can examine how religious fundamentalist ideologies help men like Trump rise to power, and vice versa, how hypermasculine leaders further embolden religious fundamentalists, amplifying their impacts on a global scale. On a micro-level, religious fundamentalists can appeal to threatened masculinities through the way they construct and valorize particular forms of subjugated femininities. As Yuval-Davis point out, fundamentalists are compelling in that they promise men, who want to process their own sense of dislocation within the global economy, a sense of control and power through the domination of others. Fundamentalists say, "'we will make you feel good at home; you can control your environment, your women, your children,' and then people will be willing to accept all the changes in society [that fundamentalists want to introduce]" (quoted in AWID 2016: 17–18). On a macro-level, the linkages between hypermasculinity and religious fundamentalisms are evident in the case of the US Christian Right. While Christians and Evangelicals in particular have been powerful in shaping US politics, their capacity to make a global impact becomes particularly pronounced through measures such as the Global Gag Rule (GGR),[32] also known as the Mexico City Policy, which originated under the Reagan Administration and was spurred by the 1984 World Population Conference held in Mexico City. Since it was first introduced in 1984, it has been frequently rescinded or reinstated based on US party lines.[33] The policy was revoked under presidents Bill Clinton and Barack Obama, both members of the Democratic Party, and reinstated under the Republican presidencies of George H.W. Bush, George W. Bush, and once more, under Donald Trump. This US policy places limits on US funding distribution by excluding overseas NGOs that perform or promote abortion and related services such as public information campaigns and lobbying. It becomes a "gag" because the policy primarily affects NGOs from the Global South who are most reliant on foreign aid. Many NGOs are forced to comply or risk losing crucial financial assistance. The GGR exemplifies the capacity of religious fundamentalist forces to tie the performance of religiosity with hypermasculine foreign policy and aid delivery. However, amid representations of "exceptionality" and the dramatic reception to Trump's move to reinstate the GGR just days after taking office, it is equally important not to lose sight of how it is in fact consistent with and a continuation of neoliberal global economic processes.

As I have discussed in this chapter, religious fundamentalisms operate as a counter-movement or backlash and as a global political project. As a counter-movement, their resistances are directed at where feminist activism is and where it is increasingly the strongest—in the WPS agenda. Their tactic of opposing or undoing the language agreed in CEDAW, the UN Conferences and succeeding "Plus Five" processes, crisis settings, and every platform thereafter including what we are seeing now in the WPS agenda is a well-rehearsed and fine-tuned resistance to SRHR rather than to gender equality as a whole. Feminist activism and analyses require looking both ways—backward and forward—to understand the scale and nature of the threat posed by religious fundamentalisms. I have shown that such a strategy of editing out SRHR has been globally deployed before and will continue to be deployed in the security debates on the WPS agenda as well. It is important to bear in mind that though the WPS agenda is attracting significant political traction and funding at present, its backbone, like other gender equality agendas, is in the right to bodily autonomy and well-being.

There remains a lack of consensus on what is truly at stake in the negotiations over definitions and references to sexual and reproductive health at all levels of security and development agenda implementation. As Corrêa notes "the problem is not that these issues aren't in the document; the problem is that the issues have not been resolved in reality" (Corrêa, Germain, and Petchesky 2005: 110). It has been a feminist strategy, thus far, to "soften" or exclude thorny issues of abortion and sexual rights in order to make incremental gains that work around what is/was politically possible within a given time and space. However, it is also increasingly evident that gender equality agendas have had varied and piecemeal outcomes precisely because of such political strategies. The fragile and oscillating status of SRHR in international peace and security is as much an outcome of anti-feminist backlash as the ongoing problem of "compartmentalized" feminist theorizing and political activism (see Elomaki and Kantola 2018). Analyzing gender equality issues in a disaggregated manner reveals how concessions on sexual and reproductive freedoms form part of political processes that have allowed for the nexus of neoliberal economic and fundamentalist ideologies to flourish.

Following Petchesky's (2003: 27) analysis, we need to make sense of the processes taking place regarding sexual and reproductive rights in order to recognize how global power and authority are changing and realigning depending on specific historical conjunctures. Paying attention to how religious fundamentalisms sequester different gender equality issues is increasingly vital to understand how religious discourses have evolved and why fundamentalist forces have thrived in tandem with neoliberalism. It is true that political processes mediate what can be materially and ideologically possible. Often, as we have seen in the WPS agenda experience, treating SRHR as a collateral feminist issue is justified as unfortunate but necessary compromise in order to incrementally advance gender equality agendas. However, both the fragmentation of radical and comprehensive global agendas developed in the 1990s and the depoliticization of feminist goals were by-products of neoliberal piece-meal, market-driven governance (Berer 2011; Fraser 2013). Importantly, in keeping SRHR in brackets, feminist activism itself has unwittingly taken a page out of the religious fundamentalist playbook and further embedded neoliberalism. More to the point, this fragmentation and depoliticization of feminist activism has come at the cost of neglecting the crucial and foundational link that held these radical agendas together—bodily autonomy.

Learning from the long and complicated history of transnational activisms on SRHR, it is important to rearticulate with vigilance why women's bodies and rights to bodily autonomy matter for global peace and security. By considering the foundational significance of sexual and reproductive freedoms, feminist activism will be able to not only counteract backlash but also more robustly articulate its own political projects to reimagine the world beyond a neoliberal logic of depletion. This involves taking stock of how religious fundamentalists are themselves invested in sustaining the neoliberal political project. A critical feminist analysis of religious fundamentalists' doctrinal politics involves analyzing how, through their pro-life or pro-family agenda, they have stepped in and continue to capitalize on material and ideological transformations arising from the privatization and marketization of sexual and reproductive health, social welfare, and crisis governance. The Philippine case suggests the need to pay greater attention to how crises are harnessed to further fundamentalisms in ways that jeopardize both the everyday and future global and national commitments to promoting gender equality. Religious fundamentalisms themselves will constitute a global crisis as faith-based groups become ever more present and influential in humanitarian response as well as in post-conflict and post-disaster reconstruction. As part of reassessing feminist strategies to genuinely support the full range of SRHR, it is important to interrogate global and local donor relationships in ways that ensure conservative views on sexuality, LGBT rights, and abortion do not undermine the delivery of aid in crisis settings.

Feminists cannot seek to end conflict-related sexual and gender-based violence, promote durable peace, and end global inequalities without attending to the mutual imbrication of religious fundamentalist and neoliberal ideologies. Stronger coalition-building is necessary to make visible how SRHR can serve as a powerful thread and common denominator that joins up all other movements across sex workers, LGBTs, HIV/AIDs, development and climate justice activists, and WPS practitioners. Connections can also be drawn with

[148]   *Politics of Sexual & Reproductive Health*

women belonging to faith-based groups and networks who are simultaneously challenging exclusionary and male-dominated decision-making present in all major religious traditions and working to strengthen inclusivity in humanitarian crisis response and peacebuilding efforts. Among prominent examples are the work of Women Living Under Muslim Laws network and Musawah in Islam and the network Catholics for RH in the Philippines. Women's ability to directly interpret religious doctrine and texts is therefore an SRHR issue. Finally, as enshrined in the Cairo and Beijing outcome documents, bodily autonomy is not just about individual choice or "self-help" but rather the full weight of resources directed at providing the "enabling conditions" across social, political, and economic realms for equitable provisioning of care and social reproduction more broadly. The next chapter shows that this means not just promoting access to health and distribution of care resources, but also rethinking the ways in which bodies, desire, and sexuality are renewed and regenerated.

CHAPTER 6
Regeneration and the Politics of Flourishing

INTRODUCTION

Thus far in this book I have discussed the logic and multidimensional conditions of depletion that circumscribe women's health and well-being within their households, community, and state and the global political economy. I now turn to analyzing what alternative politics and pathways there are beyond simply mitigating or reversing depletion. I am convinced that radical alternatives emerge when we examine the anti-thesis of depletion: *regeneration*. This chapter represents my attempt at thinking through the importance of envisioning change as a necessary component to developing feminist critique. I do so by synthesizing insights from different feminist scholarship and in going beyond the Philippine context to join up multiple sites and struggles.

I conceptualize regeneration as a politics of flourishing informed by past, present, and emerging analyses on the linkages across women's bodies, sexual and reproductive health and rights (SRHR), and planetary health. We cannot think about modalities for addressing the bodily impacts of contemporary security issues without reckoning with the causes and consequences of climate change and environmental degradation. Ecological crises are bound up with the crisis in social reproduction, which in turn manifests in a crisis of bodily autonomy. From feminist perspectives, crisis settings provide opportunities for making visible how regenerating depleted bodies is inseparable from the regeneration of social, political, economic, and ecological environments. It is not by coincidence but rather by design that the depletion of women's bodies is occurring at the same time as the rapacious depletion of the environment.

The Global Politics of Sexual and Reproductive Health. Maria Tanyag, Oxford University Press.
© Oxford University Press 2024. DOI: 10.1093/oso/9780197676332.003.0007

As many activists and scholars, particularly ecofeminists, have long pointed out, "all environmental issues are reproductive issues" (Di Chiro 2008: 278; Mies and Shiva 1993/2014; ARROW 2014; Śen and Grown 1987).[1]

I build on my earlier conceptualization of regeneration to more concretely address the logic of depletion based on the inseparability of the politics of bodily autonomy from the well-being of our planet and its ecosystems. Here I define regeneration as an expansive feminist project of eliminating the material and ideological drivers to global systemic crises that deplete both people and planet. In the first section of this chapter, I begin by tracing ideas of regeneration in early Third World/Global South women's transnational coalition movements of the 1980s and 1990s, which articulated the interlinking of women's bodies, peace, and environment. I recognize that there are deep historical and theoretical roots to linking people's health and environment across different disciplines. My focus, however, is in highlighting how these particular feminist and postcolonial perspectives provided radical alternatives to security by making visible through women's lives (1) the interlinking of different forms of oppression and (2) the interdependence of human and non-human flourishing. Second, I bring regeneration in dialogue with contemporary feminist research on climate change and the Anthropocene to show the enduring relevance of and renewed challenges to the global politics of sexual and reproductive health. Regeneration is immanent in the nexus of contemporary reproductive justice and environmental justice movements. Though still largely under-examined, I argue that these alliances continue to hold radical ideas that can inform a post-crisis recovery that is more durable because it is based on creating better conditions for the pursuit of healthy and thriving human and non-human lives. In the last part of the chapter, I discuss key examples of those transformations I envision when regeneration is the organizing principle in the aftermath of a crisis. These examples are not definitive but are intended to open ongoing reflections on the alternative ethics and practices that might be inspired by shifting emphasis from mere survival to abundance in the face of predicted intensification of simultaneous political, economic, and ecological crises. I ask: How can the politics of bodily autonomy radically inform global responses to multiple different crises that allows both human and non-human systems to *replenish* and *renew*?

UNEARTHING REGENERATION IN FEMINIST ENVIRONMENTAL SCHOLARSHIP AND ACTIVISM

According to the depletion framework set out by Rai, Hoskyns, and Thomas (2014), three types of reversal are possible: mitigation, replenishment, and transformation. Mitigation refers to attempts to lessen harms or re-allocate the costs of social reproduction. Mitigation strategies are undertaken either by individuals or collectives. They constitute solutions most immediately available to households and communities and especially women engaged in care and domestic work; and thus, have "built in" inequalities (2014: 99). Typically, women belonging to lower socio-economic status or those at the "bottom rungs" of global gendered and racialized division of labor end up mitigating depletion for other women. Replenishment refers to inflows from state and non-state actors to lessen the effects of depletion. These efforts, as Rai, Hoskyns, and Thomas argue, do not entail structural change and instead "fill in" systemic gaps that hinder the continuation of social reproductive labor regardless of the terms in which this labor is allocated. Transformation, therefore, differs from both approaches in that it fundamentally involves restructuring gender relations and the recognition and valuation of social reproduction (2014: 99). Rai, Hoskyns, and Thomas (2014: 100) suggest that the pursuit of transformation is an ongoing one and can be viewed "not as a single revolutionary event but as a bundle of changes."

Together with Rai and True, I took on the task of specifying what transformation would look like in the context of depletion in post-conflict transitions (Rai, True, and Tanyag 2019). We proposed regeneration as a re-imagination of "new institutional rules and norms and nonstate initiatives to redress inequalities" rooted in the economic devaluing of social reproduction (2019: 574). In this initial conceptualization of regeneration, we focused on the role of the State as "accountable to reverse depletion and reduce the chances for the recurrence of conflict" while also acknowledging that it is situated "within complex and interconnected systems of governance" (2019: 575). A regenerative state rebuilds social welfare infrastructures and the care economy; facilitates inclusive and deliberative decision-making processes anchored on a recognition and valuing of social reproductive labor; and finally, incorporates accountability mechanisms to ensure that state agencies, international organizations, and financial institutions especially shift away from "post-conflict development strategies that emphasize power transitions among elites representing armed groups and distributing authority and resources accordingly" (2019: 579).

Interlinked Systems of Oppression

The process of regeneration has also been thought of more broadly and in different ways by feminist scholarship and activism that emerged in the 1980s and 1990s. Among the critiques developed during this period is how violence against women is driven by the same political economy roots of environmental degradation and that both are situated within the patriarchal matrix of global capitalism, militarism, and imperialism/colonialism. For example, Black feminists in the United States, ecofeminists, postcolonial feminists,

[152] *Politics of Sexual & Reproductive Health*

and women from what was then called the Third World conceptualized a matrix of oppression to reveal how the issues that make them insecure are in fact multiple, structural, and interlinked (Collins 1989; Davis 1983; Sen and Grown 1987; Mies and Shiva 1993/2014). From this perspective, colonization was a crucial process through which land and natural resources were violently appropriated and significantly re-shaped for depletion. Successive waves of colonization, beginning with European imperialist expansion, sowed legacies of slavery and violence, with enduring consequences not only for women's physical security but also for whole ecosystems for which many have developed caring and kinship relations (Haraway 2016). Colonization displaced indigenous peoples and denigrated other ways of being, knowing, and relating with the environment (Lugones 2010). Alternative worldviews that did not conform to the rational, individualistic, and mechanistic model upon which the emerging global economy was based were either suppressed or violently erased. The ruling paradigm was to treat both the environment and women's bodies as a limitless resource to be continuously harnessed in the service of the state and international system.

Scholars note that the environment, especially the term "nature," has been symbolically represented as feminine across different cultures. References to the earth personifying it as "Gaia," "sacred mother," or "motherland" exist in many societies and often form part of indigenous traditional knowledge that views the environment as "life-giving" (Mies and Shiva 1993/2014). These gendered beliefs and symbols structure ways of relating to the environment in everyday life, albeit with varied outcomes for different women.[2] The development of a Western-centric state system and global economy however depended on the "death of nature" (Merchant 1981; Tickner 1993). Rather than ideas that regard the environment as a being or organism, the incipient global economy's expansion was predicated on viewing the environment as "machine." As Tickner (1993: 62) points out, "the rendering of nature as a dead, inert object was essential if fears of violating nature's inner resources through the mining of metals and fuels crucial for the coming industrial revolution were to be eliminated." This mechanistic view of environment supported large-scale resource accumulation and extraction as well as justified the conquest and control of lands, waters, and non-human lives for political power. Environmental domination therefore occurred along a continuum with the global domination of White European men over other human beings and cultures.

Racial oppression was also expressed as domination of nature. This is exemplified in how colonization and slavery were justified specifically by comparing groups of people to animals or less "evolved" humans. This affected both men and women, but violence was gender-differentiated. For instance, in the Pacific, slavery and forced labor perpetrated by White settlers occurred through a system known as "black-birding," involving deliberate acts of deception, duress, and kidnapping of Pacific Islander men to work in plantations that were in service of the British Empire. Women distinctly bore violent interventions to control biological reproduction and the commodification of their fertility. Within this historically defined and overlapping system of oppression, women's bodies and labor were considered cheap commodities as reproducers of slaves and laborers. Population control and eugenicist policies treated specific groups of women as animals; they were explicitly targeted in manufacturing desirable demographic and "genetic" stock in the service of state-building and the global economy (Yuval-Davis 1997). Their bodies served as a testing ground for medical procedures, population control policies, and technologies that were exported to the colonies, and were also used to biologically perfect the metropole (Yuval-Davis 1997; Corrêa 1994). The denial of the bodily autonomy of slaves and colonized peoples is therefore linked to the fullest expression of their dehumanization.

On the other end, White women, particularly those under European fascist regimes, were also subjected to coercive pro-natalist measures based on reproducing racial superiority, with their bodies also situated within multiple projects of "blood and belonging" (Yuval-Davis 1997). Women who embodied desired features or origins of the ruling group were faced with the responsibility of ensuring the purity of their race or nation. This has also meant strict or violent policing of their sexual relations because of harmful beliefs that "if 'one drop of blood' of members of the 'inferior race' is present, it could 'contaminate' and 'pollute' that of the 'superior race'" (1997: 23). Women who were poor, "impure," or disabled were deemed inferior and as such prevented from bearing children through forced sterilization practices. In settler colonial societies such as Australia, the logic was to rapidly out-populate Aboriginal and Torres Strait Islander peoples as a way to push them out or erase all traces of their ways of life in service of the "terra nullius" myth. Where demographic size embodies power, women who are unable to bear children or willfully choose not to end up facing intense pressures, stigma, or violence.

The regulation of women's fertility, particularly how and which type of women need to reproduce and when, has functioned to support military expansion and militarized enforcement of symbolic boundaries of an ethnic group, nation, and empire. In the aftermath of world wars, revolutions, and civil wars, promoting a "baby boom" was seen as vital for replenishing the population. While wars and revolutions would have seen an expansion of women's roles beyond the home, post-conflict reconstruction meant that life could go back to "normal" and as such, women were expected to resume their primary, pre-war responsibilities in the family. Thus, across Europe and in the United States, increasing birth rates were framed as women's post-conflict duty, which in turn corresponded with the broader push to put them back in the "private sphere" of the household and deny them spaces in public life (Corrêa 1994: 10). This is an example of how spaces for bodily autonomy expanded and contracted according to broader shifts in the militarization of society. National borders influenced how women were differentially situated vis-à-vis unequal distribution of costs and rewards of militarism. While White women in Europe and the United States were experiencing constraints to bodily autonomy, women in other parts of the world were denied bodily autonomy in qualitatively different terms.

Nuclear testing and the deployment of bombs in the Pacific Ocean created intergenerational harms to social reproduction among Pacific Islanders (Keown 2018; Teaiwa 1994). Radioactive exposure led to birth defects, miscarriages and pregnancy-related complications, and severe illnesses such as cancer. The bodies of men and women from the Pacific Islands were treated as "collateral damages" in the pursuit of developing nuclear weapons and for national security of countries such as the United States, France, and Britain (Teaiwa 1994). Teaiwa demonstrated the nexus of colonialism and ecological racism in the Pacific region by juxtaposing sexualized and depoliticized fashion with the negation or disposability of Pacific lives and well-being. In particular, she exposed how the bikini as a two-piece bathing suit named after the Bikini Atoll of the Marshall Islands is an artifact rooted in the nuclear and colonial history of Pacific Islands. In her own words:

> [T]he bomb and the bikini reflected a supreme ambivalence in Western thought: the valorization of woman as Nature, the abom(b)ination of nature manifested by military and scientific technology, the naturalization of racial difference, and the feminization or domestication of military technology. (1994: 101)

The introduction of the bikini served to exoticize and sexualize female bodies as well as to appropriate and commodify the specific site of trauma and dispossession experienced in the Pacific.

Radical change, according to feminist perspectives and activism by women of color, means dismantling the matrix of oppressions beginning at the point at which they all join together—in bodily autonomy and well-being. Women situated within the intersections of racial, class, and gender hierarchies have had to contest restrictions to bodily autonomy within and beyond the state. Racial, class, and various other prejudices, themselves legacies of colonialism, continue to underpin the differential treatment of fertility and perceptions of sexuality among different groups of women. Resisting this matrix of domination therefore also began with reclaiming bodily autonomy. As Maria Mies (1993/2014: 218–219) explains, "for women, self-determination meant first, the liberation from occupation, the end of the determination-by-others, by men and by patriarchal social powers. The demand for self-determination was, therefore a defensive one, based on the right to resistance, the right to defend the self." Moreover, "self-determination" or bodily autonomy stems not from

Western individualism but from a deep appreciation of the self in relation to community.

The ability to give and receive care cannot be left to the individual alone and instead must be actively nourished in community and society. This is because what makes women sick and the factors that determine their ability to decide their sexual and reproductive lives are inseparable from the structures that subordinate the group or collective they belong to (see Chapters 3 and 4). As Davis pointed out, it was because of the oppressive conditions of slavery, and not any biological pre-disposition or inherent attributes, that Black women historically resorted to forced abortions and infanticide (1983: 204–205). Women of color—Latinas and Asians—in similarly oppressed positions have had to relinquish motherhood so as not to raise children condemned to a life of violence and servitude (Davis 1983; Corrêa 1994). So bodily autonomy is an integral component for cascading regeneration from self-care to caring relationships, practices, and institutions.

The costs of successive failures to recognize and transform the global systemic interlinking of capitalism, militarism, and imperialism/colonialism are embodied by women too. They manifest as "reproduction failures" that occur predominantly for women and communities especially in the Third World or Global South, and minorities in the Global North. In the 1980s, the feminist organization Development Alternatives with Women for a New Era (DAWN) traced the occurrence of interlinked "food-fuel-water" crises to the absence of integrated development strategies and macroeconomic policies that took for granted the importance of social welfare and environmental sustainability (Sen and Grown 1987). DAWN pointed out that poor women have consequently borne the burden of reproduction failures. Their ability to support whole populations in meeting basic needs is made even more onerous by on-going militarization and violence perpetrated against them including by their own governments. The embodied costs of reproduction failures intensify during periods of crises as Sen and Grown (1987: 57) explain further:

> where women have little earning power or effective control over cash income or land use (and this may be due to both traditional gender hierarchies and biased state policies toward land reform), their own labor time and that of their children (especially daughters) is the only resource over which they have any control whatsoever. Thus, women's work hours, as the only mechanism for attempting to cope with the crisis, lengthen considerably.

When the global material and ideological root causes of these interlinked crises are left intact, there is a recurrent failure in the provision of community or societal basic needs and a compounding of harm to women's bodies, which we still see today. Yet, the very little space for self-autonomy left to women is even vulnerable to restrictions by conservative and fundamentalist forces

[156] *Politics of Sexual & Reproductive Health*

that oppose gender equality on the basis of maintaining the "natural order." Appeals to the "laws of nature" have been deployed as part of anti-gender opposition by transnational religious fundamentalist forces in a bid to preserve traditional or family values (Chappell 2006; Estrada Claudio 2010; see also Chapter 5).

Interdependent Flourishing

Regeneration demands moving away from and beyond piecemeal or siloed crisis responses to a focus on interdependent flourishing. By making visible how gendered insecurities are interlinked, feminist perspectives inevitably also lay bare the interlinking of human and non-human lives as mutually vulnerable assemblages. Because the reproduction of human lives is interconnected with the regeneration of the environment, it makes sense to understand that political, economic, and environmental crises do not occur in isolation from one another. Recognizing ontological claims of interdependence and mutual vulnerability gives rise to ethical principles that are responsive to the politics of care, partnership, and flourishing. This is exemplified by the development of "ethics of care" or care ethics in feminist theory and philosophy, which emerged during the same period as, and in critical dialogue with, transnational alliance movements of Global South women, peace, and environmental activism of the 1980s and 1990s (Ruddick 1989; Tronto 1994; Robinson 2011; Merchant 2017). In care ethics, security is neither hierarchical nor zero-sum. Instead, it is relational and occurs through partnership.

Robinson (2016: 119) explains how care ethics "interrogates the ethical and political implications of the structural and institutional conditions of care arrangements within and across societies . . . it insists on a social ontology of interdependence and relationality, and a picture of human subjectivity as inherently and unexceptionally vulnerable." Moreover, care ethics informs moral deliberations in a multi-scalar manner by drawing attention to the requisite conditions for health and well-being as cascading from individuals to more expansive, global, and ecological relations of care. That is, "as a global ethic of security, care also highlights the deep and intimate interconnections between the level of the household and political-economic structures and processes at the 'global' scale" (Robinson 2016).

The interdependence of micro and macro-level caring processes is evident in Cuomo's (1998) "ethic of flourishing" and Merchant's (2017) "partnership ethic." While neither of Cuomo's and Merchant's works are explicitly positioned within the feminist care ethics scholarship and emerge instead from ecofeminist traditions, their respective conceptualization of ethics responds to women's positionality vis-à-vis the production and reproduction of care in everyday life. Cuomo conceptualizes the notion of flourishing as a value and ethical goal of ecological feminism, albeit one that has not been explicitly articulated as core to a feminist social justice agenda. Human flourishing depends on the flourishing of non-human others, and in the process of considering the flourishing of others, one may re-evaluate one's existing notions of the conditions for flourishing (Cuomo 1998: 65). According to Cuomo (1998: 73), flourishing is bodily—it progressively involves the promotion of bodily health and well-being in conjunction with the intention to "discover what various beings and systems require to thrive, physically and otherwise, and the integrity and stability of a living thing or system 'from the perspective of' that entity, or with its interest in mind."

Flourishing also necessarily entails the process of becoming, which as Cuomo argues is shaped by history and context to account for the variety and complexity of human and non-human lives. That is, knowledge of how one entity might be able to flourish and to know if it is indeed flourishing comes from a sustained investigation of flourishing from multiple scales of time. Lastly, flourishing is intrinsically interconnected and simultaneously occurs in parts and aggregates such that "individual and communal flourishing contribute to each other dialectically" (Cuomo 1998: 74). Bringing Cuomo's ethic of flourishing to bear on women's bodily autonomy and regeneration therefore raises important insights on the urgent need to deliberate what are starting points for the interconnected flourishing of women and the environment amid contemporary forms and processes of depletion.

So where and how does flourishing begin? A possible answer comes from one of my interviews in the Philippines. A female informant who has worked in displacement sites in Mindanao reported that, "women there say that they consider just making themselves presentable a luxury . . . To think about their beauty and care for their own bodies—they could not do that anymore and can't remember the last time they managed to put make-up on."[3] Among the surprising insights from examining women's bodies and social reproduction in times of crisis is a longing for beauty. I found similar views were raised (though not prominently) in primary interviews undertaken by the Mindanao Working Group on Reproductive Health, Gender and Sexuality among internally displaced women. Maintaining beauty and "presentability," which often constitutes the social and cultural reproduction of group identities, requires not just time but also courage to defy the many indignities of being internally displaced. Importantly, this idea, to me, radically challenges prevailing representations around victimhood of women in internal displacements.

On a practical level, the distribution of dignity kits for women and girls in internal displacements helps address crisis-specific barriers to sexual and reproductive health as well as make possible opportunities for flourishing. Dignity kits provide access to hygiene and sanitary supplies so that women and girls are able to care for their own bodies as well as go about their daily lives during menstruation (see also Chapters 4 and 5). These kits also typically

[158] *Politics of Sexual & Reproductive Health*

include culturally appropriate "modesty" clothing which in the Philippines is usually a *malong* or in other countries an *abaya* or *sari*.[4] However, a longing to make oneself beautiful again signals not simply aspirations to weather the crisis, but rather, resistance and hope-filled visions of bouncing back and thriving anew. To strive for renewal of one's beauty and dignity means to confront the realities of conflicts or disasters *beyond* survival. Relatedly, the neglect of SRHR in crisis settings forecloses any possibility of a life otherwise. Deliberate acts of self-care, usually taken for granted in normal times and circumstances, take on a revolutionary significance in crisis situations because it fundamentally upends the incursion depletion in the intimate spaces of their lives. As the quote from the displaced Filipino woman suggests, it is perhaps even more necessary in the face of crisis to aspire for the good life— love, beauty, and regeneration—in order to create possibilities for materially achieving radical transformations in the political, economic, and ecological conditions of depletion.

Flourishing is collective too. Merchant's (2017: 266) work on "earthcare" advances a related ethical principle on partnership, which suggests that the responsibility for regeneration is a shared and balanced one. She argues that, "[a] partnership ethic sees the human community and the biotic community in a mutual relationship with each other. It states that 'the greatest good for the human and the non-human community is to be found in their mutual, living interdependence.'" This means that neither human nor non-human well-being is taken as more superior or having greater precedence over the other. Merchant's partnership ethics stresses the possibility of relationships among humans as well as between humans and nature. Seeing these connections serves as an important beginning for policy decisions that take into account the distinct material consequences of depletion on people and nature, and the unfettered capacity of human activities to "destroy life as we know it" (Merchant 2017: 267). She adds further that partnership ethics enhances the goals of gender equality as it does not yoke women with the responsibility for "'cleaning up the mess' or individual men of creating male-dominated science, technology and capitalism" (Merchant 2017: 267).

From the feminist lens of partnership ethics, both women and men have collective and individual relationships with nature. Women therefore are not assumed to have either an inherent knowledge of nature or innate ability to care for it (Merchant 2017: 273). Like the ethic of flourishing, partnership ethics stems from an understanding of the interdependence of human and non-human lives that is attentive to how different groups of women face disproportionate care burdens when there are environmental crises. It also creates room for recognizing and supporting women's longstanding leadership in advocating for the protection of people and the environment alongside men within their own countries and globally. An epistemology that understands human and non-human *entanglement*, I argue, offers the most viable alternative for developing analytical and transformative pathways in the face of multiple climate-induced crises that define the Anthropocene.

REGENERATION AND THE (M)ANTHROPOCENE

There is now a strong scientific basis that the continued increase in global warming has already started leading to long-lasting, irreversible impacts such as ecosystem loss and species extinction. Climate change constitutes the main threat to all domains of human life: global health, water, food, economy, infrastructure, and physical security. Climate change is already affecting the "durability" of a post-crisis response. The impacts of climate change potentially render short-lived whatever gains are made in post-conflict or post-disaster reconstruction as simultaneous or overlapping conflicts, disasters, and health pandemics are predicted to increasingly define everyday life, especially for regions such as the Asia Pacific. According to the 2018 Intergovernmental Panel on Climate Change (IPCC) special report on the impacts of global warming of 1.5 degrees Celsius above pre-industrial levels, if global carbon dioxide emissions do not start to significantly decline well before 2030, then broad-range risks and cumulative consequences are very likely to be observed. For example, among the report's key findings with "high confidence" (a strong degree of correctness based on scientific evidence and consensus) is that natural and human systems have already been impacted by global warming. Limiting global warming to 1.5 degrees Celsius instead of 2 degrees Celsius could reduce the number of people impacted by these climate-related risks; however, these risks will and are already occurring in multitudes and with amplified effects (IPCC 2018). Moreover, based on one study that specifically undertook projections for simultaneous exposure to or co-occurrence of multiple climate hazards (fires, floods, heat waves, water scarcity etc.), researchers predict that "coastal areas of Southeast Asia, East and West Africa, the Atlantic coast of South and Central America will be exposed concurrently to the largest changes in up to six climate hazards if GHGs [greenhouse gases] continue to rise throughout the twenty-first century" (Mora et al. 2018: 1067). More people and regions will face overlapping vulnerabilities and therefore will contend with higher risks for new and compounded hazards we are yet to envision. Uncertainties in the capacity of post-crisis transitions to adapt to the complex governance that multiple crises require may again mean that social reproductive labor and particularly women's bodies will bear the brunt. However, even the extent to which social reproduction can reliably constitute a "safety net" is uncertain because of ongoing global gendered and health inequalities and the unprecedented security challenges we will face.

Various scholars across multiple disciplines in the natural, physical, and social sciences including in International Relations (IR), refer to the

[160] *Politics of Sexual & Reproductive Health*

current ecological or "climate crisis" as precipitated by and constitutive of the Anthropocene. The concept of the Anthropocene was first widely proposed in 2000 by atmospheric chemist and Nobel laureate Paul Crutzen and ecologist Eugene Stoermer to designate the current geological epoch as one marked by overwhelming human influence on the planet. The acceleration of human activities, beginning with the Industrial Revolution, marks a turning point in the capacity of humans as a species to alter, particularly through damaging effects, other ecosystems on a global scale. Globalization has facilitated the rapid expansion of markets and industries that relied on heightened extraction of environmental resources and intensified GHG emissions. Since then, there has been a proliferation in the use of the concept both as a geological and cultural term in relation to the causes and consequences of climate change. While there has been some engagement in the field of IR, with questions of whether and how the Anthropocene forces a rethinking and reconstitution of the "global," these remain largely in siloed conversations far removed from the mainstream.[5] Yet, the need to revisit foundational concepts of security and the means to achieve it are never more pressing for the discipline than in the face of renewed challenges to our very existence.

Other scholars have proposed alternative concepts to encapsulate the contemporary ecological crisis. For instance, *capitalocene* is used to emphasize how the state and international system are built on, and maintained by, the continued proliferation of nuclear weapons, accumulation of wealth, and overconsumption, all of which threaten the environment.[6] *Eurocene* highlights how "intersectional axes of destruction" are expressed in geopolitical terms as European-led (Grove 2019: 5). *(M)Anthropocene* builds on these critiques but with an emphasis on how the story of the Anthropocene follows the plot of patriarchy (Di Chiro 2017): global economic transformations have occurred in tandem with the spread of knowledge systems underpinning (White) (m) anthropocentrism. These proponents stress the dangers in blanketing all of "humanity" in discussions of the Anthropocene because this obfuscates how not all human beings have had the same environmental impacts throughout history and not all equally share in vulnerability. Furthermore, which referents are included in the "global" or "planetary" is political in that this carries implications for who benefits in the (re)organization of material and ideological conditions necessary in the pursuit of peace and security.

Perspectives of the "global" that privilege or only view a summation of human lives and economic activities completely miss how bodies and worldviews are differently valued across gender, race, and class lines within the existing global political economy. From a feminist perspective, the key drivers of the Anthropocene are gendered processes, in that these actively co-construct material realities and ideologies differently for men and women. While we now have unprecedented availability and access to scientific evidence, the global climate change agenda has been matched not only by political inaction but worse, by resistance in the form of populist denialism and anti-science backlash that have threatened to derail or undo existing collective efforts. Across .countries where political systems vary greatly, such as the United States and Norway, similar patterns have emerged in terms of the rise and intensification of climate change denialism. Research studies on the "conservative white male" in the United States (McCright and Dunlap 2015, 2011) and Norway (Krange, Kaltenborn, and Hultman 2019) have made visible that the height of climate change denialism is linked with patriarchal beliefs and right-wing nationalism. Compared to the broader US population, conservative white males are most likely to endorse climate change denialist views and reject scientific evidence. The stronger the self-reported confidence in their own understanding of global warming is, the greater the degree of denialism among this group of men (McCright and Dunlap 2015, 2011). These studies show that it is not just the causes of climate change that are gendered. The inaction and outright resistance to address this global problem are gendered too and perhaps increasingly so.

Meanwhile, women's bodies are becoming "hypervisible" as both problem and solution to climate change, as for example, in the revival of population control discourses in the context of climate change debates through "population alarmism" (Hendrixson et al. 2019). Bringing back old Malthusian thinking that considers overpopulation as a problem, various scholars from different disciplines have started linking the reduction of population growth as a form of climate change adaptation and mitigation and as requisite for planetary survival (Hendrixson et al. 2019: 2; Ojeda, Sasser, and Lunstrum 2020).[7] Whereas in the past, the idea of "overpopulation" was primarily viewed as either a limit to economic growth or a threat to domestic and international political stability, it is now being re-signified as a catalyst to the climate emergency. Historically, such populationist beliefs argued that unchecked human population growth breeds a range of interrelated political, economic, societal, and environmental ills. Population control had been a dominant, unchallenged framework in international development and national and local policymaking particularly in the 1960s until the 1980s (Corrêa 1994; Hartmann 2016). It would only be supplanted in the aftermath of international development and population conferences in the 1990s with the emergence of a global SRHR agenda (see Chapter 5). While population control measures occurred on a global scale across different national contexts, it was driven by geopolitics and distinctly incorporated as foreign policy by the United States. Extricated from "development" discourse, population control was underpinned by a belief that rapid population growth in poorer regions posed a threat to the economic growth and political stability of developed countries and the maintenance of a particular global order defined by Western hegemony.

For instance, according to the now declassified US National Security Study Memorandum 200 dated April 24, 1974, then–Secretary of State and National

Security Advisor Henry Kissinger stressed the importance of advancing a worldwide population strategy that recognized the links between regional imbalances in population growth and "US security and overseas interests." Importantly, Kissinger's memorandum reflected an awareness of and attempt at managing criticisms of US-led population control efforts, especially from developing countries, by avoiding the image of US views being imposed on others. Thus, it states that "[a]bove all, the problem must be recognized by the developing countries themselves."[8] Yet well into the early 1990s, the World Bank and US Agency for International Development (USAID) withheld loans and aid unless receiving countries enacted national population policies (Hartmann 2016: 108–109). Aid conditionality in the context of heavy reliance on international aid and funding partly explains why domestic population control programs in the "Third World" were driven more by the aggressive pursuit of demographic targets rather than concern for women's rights. Moreover, this US-led population control approach occurred in tandem with the globalizing of an economic model that exacerbated deeply ingrained gender, racial, and other social inequalities within these countries such that the most marginalized women suffered the brunt of coercive fertility interventions and the privatization of health.

Population control as a policy approach has adapted and evolved over time despite its considerable decline in popularity (Bhatia et al. 2020; Sasser 2017, 2014). Yet, it has retained and carried over to the climate change agenda the same underpinning assumptions and biases while instrumentalizing social justice, gender equality, and human rights goals and agendas (Hendrixson et al. 2019). For instance, old forms of target-driven programs on fertility management are rehashed as "goals" and metrics for women's reproductive agency. Bhatia et al. (2020) cites the global initiative called Family Planning 2020 or FP2020 (now 2030) as illustrative of this wider trend. FP2020 brought together multiple international development and humanitarian organizations and funding bodies such as the Bill and Melinda Gates Foundation, UK Aid, and USAID. Whereas the very reference to targets especially in relation to contraceptive use was opposed in the shift from population control to human rights discourse in the 1990s, Bhatia et al. (2020: 338) point out that the use of targets is now uncontested. Indeed, such a focus on discrete and measurable outcomes are mainstream to a neoliberal feminist agenda.

More recently, a report published by a similar global initiative, Women Deliver, compiles evidence on the linkages between SRHR and climate change. It aims to bridge SRHR programs with the growing normative acceptance of environmental sustainability and climate resilience. Among the key findings were the "quantifiable linkages between population growth and climate change" (Women Deliver 2021: ii). The report explains further that "voluntary efforts, rooted in a rights-based approach" to slow population growth could lead to reductions in GHG emissions but that such effects will only be reaped after several decades (2021: 16). Though the report stresses the importance of a "social justice framework" in framing family planning as a form of climate change action, the implications can be potentially dangerous. The underlying rationale remains that environmental degradation and GHG emissions are driven by population growth, which in turn is driven by *individual* women's lack of sexual and reproductive agency. Feminist critiques on the causal role of *macro-level structures and processes* of political economy tend to be silenced.

The danger lurking behind this "greening" of SRHR is that it resembles how neoliberal discourses of individual human rights, and of women's empowerment as "smart economics," have kept the depletive global economy intact. Such a neoliberal repackaging of women's bodily autonomy risks displacing attention away from eliminating logics of gendered and racialized control as well as systemic inequalities that underpin the Anthropocene. First, population myths serve to obscure how GHGs are overwhelmingly caused by excesses among affluent minorities in the developed world; moreover, that men from these countries produce more carbon emissions than other people in the world and especially those in countries dealing with the worst impacts of climate change. These myths are particularly effective because controlling women's bodies is seen as "smart economics" or indeed, as quoted in the Women Deliver report, a "cost-effective solution to reduce greenhouse gases" (2021: 16) compared to radically altering global patterns of consumption and production of resources. As pointed out by feminist scholars, this renewed concern with population growth tends to project gendered and racial anxieties because they rarely concern interventions on the bodies of White wealthy men (Sasser 2014; Hartmann 2016). Second, women's access to contraceptives is framed as a "win-win" solution to both gender inequality and environmental degradation through reinterpreting women's reproductive decision-making as "embodied environmental responsibility" or "sexual stewardship" (Sasser 2017; Bhatia et al. 2020).

Sasser uses the term sexual stewardship to denote how "women are expected to act as responsible environmental actors through managing their fertility and reproduction" (2017: 346). At the heart of sexual stewardship is the construction of an altruistic moral agent based on idealized gendered expectations such as women's own recognition that their childbearing (or the absence of it) has a positive effect on the environment, and as a responsible and ethical subject, her action is only constrained by issues of access to "Western" or medical forms of contraception (2017: 350). The gendered bias underpinning sexual stewardship is that its intended subject is women, rather than men, who will then bear the cost of environmental responsibility by sacrificing motherhood. Sasser's conceptualization of sexual stewardship aligns with the feminization of responsibility and strategic harnessing of female bodies to address crises, which I have discussed in the context of post-crisis

[164]   *Politics of Sexual & Reproductive Health*

and post-disaster settings. The same logic of depletion is manifesting in the instrumentalization of SRHR for climate change adaptation and mitigation.

What we might see is that these new formulations of "eco-smart" sexuality are popularized with the "aim to produce female subjects who empower themselves, promote economic development, and reduce environmental degradation by controlling their fertility" (Bhatia et al. 2020: 338). At the same time, these reformulations reflect an editing out of the more radical and far-reaching solutions implicit in taking sexual and reproductive health seriously from the perspectives developed with and by women from the Global South. There are indeed movements and organizations engaging with the global climate change agenda with SRHR and climate justice in mind, but these involve deliberately resisting individualizing solutions to both. The substantive concerns pushed by these movements highlight how the "material conjuncture of environmental and reproductive harms exceeds the sum of its parts" (Lappé, Hein, and Landecker 2019: 137). Bodily harms and deterioration of well-being for multiply marginalized groups are experienced collectively and form part of a larger collage of daily disruptions and historical violence that shape their lives.

SRHR movements, and specifically under the leadership of Black, indigenous and postcolonial feminists, stress the importance of *reproductive justice* (Ross et al. 2017). Reproductive justice signifies structural oppression as an embodied phenomenon and involves the pursuit of ending "injustices in all arenas: social, economic, gender, racial, environmental, financial, physical, sexual, environmental, disability and carceral" (2017: 14). Integral to the concept of reproductive justice is the ongoing collective resistance and building of social movements that see bodily autonomy as part of broader social justice and peace activism, including the creation of safe and healthy environments free from racial discrimination and environmental degradation (2017). Reproductive justice is neither individualistic nor individualizing. Instead, it demands systemic thinking and collective action. In comparison, climate change has been dominated by the language of "adaptation" or "mitigation," which translate to actions short of having to fundamentally re-orient people's material and ideological relationship with social reproduction and the environment. By contrast, regeneration constitutes explicit ethical goals of holistic, continuous, and relational flourishing for women, persecuted groups, and all life forms. Importantly, it encompasses a view that there are already losses and damages from climate change that need repair and reparations.

Combining the reproductive justice framework and critiques of Black, postcolonial, and Global South feminists, we learn that systems of oppression are interconnected and therefore the crises that emanate from these systems also need to be addressed in an integrated manner. For specific groups of people who have experienced historical violence and bodily harms due to symbolic associations with "nature," individual and collective survival and flourishing are deeply connected to resisting the erasure of their situated knowledges, to the return of stolen lands, and to a renewal of the environment. Indeed, as Lappé, Hein, and Landecker (2019: 137) point out, from this "environmental reproductive justice" lens, "reproduction of language and culture are as much concerns as are the physical reproduction of human beings." The distinction matters because these critical perspectives emphasize that power relations, not biology, shape how women relate to the environment. Women are connected to the environment because both have been on the receiving end of subjugation by means of extraction. The control of women's bodies—and particularly the depletion of their labor—reflects the interconnectedness of politics, economics, culture, and the environment.

Grounded as it is within these past and present feminist understandings of the nexus between bodily autonomy and environmental renewal, my conceptualization of regeneration differs in crucial ways from neoliberal interpretations of environmental sustainability, peacebuilding, and human capabilities. Regeneration does not regard non-human life as subordinate to human life and therefore that which can be utilized as a resource. It is distinctly non-instrumental, non-anthropocentric, and feminist. It implies active caring for the flourishing of non-human others as an extension of what it means for humans to exist. It underscores that a truly transformative solution to depletion is not bound by militarized, "states and markets" and "short-term" understanding of peace and security. Rather it traverses multiple scales of renewal from the self-determination of women and men to a planetary ecosystem that has a "right to regenerate" (Klein 2014).

In this respect, regeneration closely aligns with how the concept shas been articulated in peacebuilding literature. Pugh (2000: 2) describes regeneration as:

> a process of social, political and economic adjustment to, and underpinning of, conditions of relative peace in which the participants, not least those who have been disempowered and impoverished by violence, can begin to prioritise future goals beyond their immediate survival.

I develop regeneration further as a holistic analytical and normative lens, which suggests pathways for states, non-state actors, and the international community in circumventing the global logics of depletion by shining a light on how and why multiple political, economic, and ecological crises intersect. In the next section, I bring these insights together, to provide a preliminary illustration of how regeneration might occur in the context of post-conflict and post-disaster relief and recovery. The aftermaths of crisis can be fully realized as critical junctures along a continuum of peace by ethically orienting post-crisis approaches toward nurturing abundant lives. This involves actively assessing the ways in which material and ideological conditions before and

[166]   *Politics of Sexual & Reproductive Health*

after crises shape "why so much that is capable is not able to flourish, and how more flourishing might be made possible" (Cuomo 1998: 65).

REGENERATION IN PRACTICE

Regeneration engages with the strong consensus on the failure of neoliberal models of transitional justice, post-crisis reconstruction and peacebuilding in stemming the recurrence of conflict and instability (Brennan 2019). These mainstream interventions tend to be more "transitional" than "transformative" by prioritizing the re-institution of liberal democratic political and economic order, or formalized processes of national truth and reconciliation as templates for post-conflict reconstruction (Gready and Robins 2014). They lead to transitory changes because they involve the rolling out of default models of governance, which are typically gender blind. For example, research on three decades of peace processes worldwide shows that only 3% of peace agreements and 21% of peace processes include gender-specific transitional justice provisions. Overwhelmingly, these relate to a prioritization of women's subjectivity as victimhood (Jamar and Bell 2018; Political Settlements Research Programme 2019). Moreover, these models are assumed to be universally applicable or able to be exported from one crisis setting to another, thereby leaving unquestioned the complicity of global or international actors when domestic or localized processes fail.

Similar dynamics are evident in post-disaster reconstruction dominated by the prevailing framework of "resilience-building." Both domestic and external interventions are believed to be "crisis-proof" when they support "bottom-up" or participatory mechanisms and the everyday capacities of communities and individuals for "self-recovery." Yet, this has tended to absolve states and international actors from accountability and structural reform. Resilience, as a neoliberal and individualizing discourse, remains disconnected from critiques of disasters and disaster vulnerability as systemically rooted in global economy. In effect, both neoliberal versions of transitional justice or post-disaster resilience have tended to facilitate the re-arranging of a different but still unequal system of sharing power and resources in the aftermath of crisis. Examining post-crisis reconstructions from the foundational lens of bodily autonomy and especially women's health and well-being highlights how prevailing models and frameworks rarely involve the repair of care economies; and neither do they support "less visible," more diffused, and non-material conditions for the everyday reproduction of life.

So what difference does it make to begin taking regeneration seriously in the context of post-crisis recovery? I argue that it contributes to a fundamental re-orientation of peace and security in at least three main respects: (1) transforming economies to minimize ecological and bodily harms as well as promote material and ideological conditions for social reproduction; (2) addressing "invisible" markers of peace such as the importance of mental health and intangible cultural heritage; and finally, (3) broadening notions of, and mechanisms for, justice.

Rethinking Post-crisis Economic Transformation

Regeneration situates post-crisis reconstruction efforts within a continuum of economic processes.[9] As such, it both calls into question the economic impacts of post-crisis reconstruction and makes explicit the ethical goal that economies are (re)modeled to nurture the regenerative capacities of individuals, communities, societies, and the environment as a whole. That means scrutinizing where, which, and to whom resources are being mobilized before, during, and after crises, and the extent to which resource reallocations reflect a profound shift toward materially valuing care relations and the environment. Emerging research from feminist scholars working on post-conflict care economies have started drawing attention to why economic transitions in the aftermath of conflicts coincide with heightened gender inequalities, particularly as a result of gradual or immediate erosion of care institutions and services (Rai, True, and Tanyag 2019; Martin de Almagro and Ryan 2019; Bergeron, Cohn, and Duncanson 2017). Crucially, the post-conflict phase may bear witness to even harsher processes of depletion because this period may intensify the interrelated extraction of social reproductive labor and natural resources, which in turn further constrains the long-term ability of households and communities to maintain care provisioning effectively, let alone face an ecological crisis. This occurs under economic agendas that focus on post-conflict growth driven by industries around infrastructure construction and resource extraction, such as mining, to the exclusion of generating economic activities that support health and social welfare and land redistribution (Duncanson 2016; Ortiz 2016; Martin de Almagro and Ryan 2019; Ogden 2018). For instance, Maria Martin de Almagro and Caitlin Ryan (2019) caution that post-war women's economic empowerment agendas reproduce gendered divisions of labor and the artificial divide between formal and informal economies because they fail to account for women's multiple and diverse roles before, during, and after wars. In effect, post-conflict economic reform is about "simply the rebuilding of a patriarchal state in a neoliberal global order" (Martin de Almagro and Ryan 2019: 1066; Duncanson 2016). Whatever economic gains women in post-conflict sites may have, these will remain circumscribed by neoliberal logics of depletion unless post-conflict regeneration is envisioned to include the long-term transformation of the gendered and racialized devaluing of women's bodies and labor that characterizes relations within and between the Global North and Global South. Resourcing

[168] *Politics of Sexual & Reproductive Health*

institutions of care provisioning and health especially at household and community levels and in post-conflict transitions must be matched by broader shifts in improving overall labor conditions globally.

Feminist research has recently drawn attention to how neoliberal governance models actually harm women in the long-term because they involve accelerated large-scale extraction and export of natural resources to "fund" post-conflict economic growth (Cohn and Duncanson 2020; LSE Centre for Women, Peace and Security, Women International Peace Centre and Gender Action for Peace and Security 2021). Post-crisis recovery driven by a macroeconomic framework of establishing political order for the main purpose of facilitating global trade and investments is far from transformative when they come at the cost of depleting both the environment and women's bodies. As Cohn and Duncanson point out, post-war countries are attractive targets for extractive integration in the global economy because they represent landscapes yet to be exploited for natural resources. At the same time, these natural resources have typically fueled protracted conflicts and continue to reignite tensions in these countries (2020: 9). Moreover, extractive industries such as mining are shown to directly and indirectly impact women's health and physical security (Jenkins 2014; Cohn and Duncanson 2020). Yet, the harmful impacts of mining are often counted or assessed in terms of the environment, through pollution and degradation, and as a workplace for predominantly male miners. The unpaid care and social reproduction built around sustaining mines and the compounded costs women bear to mitigate both harms to environment and harms in their workplaces as women miners and to care for male miners are all rarely recognized or compensated (Goldblatt and Rai 2018; Lahiri-Dutt 2012). Most acutely, extractive industries have directly threatened ways of life and access to resources among indigenous peoples. They are implicated in violence, forced displacements, and extrajudicial killings (UN General Assembly 2016c). For example, the Philippines is reportedly among the deadliest countries for environmental and human rights defenders. Many indigenous or Lumad leaders have been targeted for violence because of their resistance against extractive industries to protect their ancestral lands and communities (Global Witness 2017; UN General Assembly 2016c; AWID 2017).

Regeneration prompts critical deliberations on the role of the state and non-state actors in ensuring that post-conflict or post-disaster recovery minimizes negative environmental impacts and progressively advances human stewardship of the environment. Recovery must also involve the natural environment and not just physical or man-made infrastructure since wars disrupt and damage other living ecosystems. There is an emerging research interest in the concept of "environmental peacebuilding," which Dresse et al. (2019: 104) define as "the process through which environmental challenges shared by the (former) parties to a violent conflict are turned into opportunities to build lasting cooperation and peace." As an emerging framework, they argue that environmental peacebuilding aims to integrate the resolution of conflicts with mechanisms that alleviate resource scarcity and promote dialogue and sustainable development. Its core premise is that "trans-boundary environmental issues represent an opportunity to move from rivalry to partnership by switching from administrative, politico-territorial borders to ecosystem borders" (2019: 103). This concept therefore resonates with regeneration in that environmental peacebuilding aims to harness crisis transitions to attend to the indivisibility of political, economic, and environmental insecurities, and to recognize that the health and flourishing of the environment goes hand in hand with the health and flourishing of people (Robinson 2011: 144). However, environmental peacebuilding has yet to be in dialogue with the rich feminist scholarship on gender and the environment, and vice versa. Taking feminist regeneration and environmental peacebuilding together offers one pathway for making visible the continuities of women's social reproductive roles in sustaining conflicts and peacebuilding, and how these are materially tied with their access, or lack thereof, to land and water resources (see Chandra et al. 2017). Removing barriers to women's access to sexual and reproductive health is part of environmental peacebuilding.

Finally, regeneration through environmental peacebuilding can be extended further by drawing the linkages between climate change and the gendered, racialized, and environmentally extractive material structures that organize social reproduction globally (Robinson 2016). Regeneration challenges the relationship between the continued increase in global military expenditure, especially nuclear proliferation, and climate change, because of how it will profoundly undermine possibilities for both human and environmental flourishing. State and non-state actors bear equal responsibility to protect the most climate risk-affected populations, such as women, and to respond to how environmental crises increasingly reverse the gains of peace, which includes the attainment of gender equality.

"Invisible" and Slow Peace

Post-crisis transitions can provide opportunities to pay equal attention to how peace constitutes invisible and slow dimensions. Regeneration means recognizing that material or physical reconstructions are interconnected with non-material or invisible markers of peace, such as the mental or spiritual well-being that comes when people's cultural heritage, rituals, and practices are protected and promoted. Enabling regeneration will require re-examining how prevailing approaches to post-conflict and post-disaster reconstruction obscure social reproduction and the long process of restoring individual and community well-being after suffering the loss of material and non-material

[170]   *Politics of Sexual & Reproductive Health*

aspects of their cultural identity. For example, the protection of cultural and natural heritage was established as early as 1972 in existing international legal frameworks particularly under the UN Educational, Scientific and Cultural Organisation (UNESCO 1972). In 2017, the UN Security Council passed Resolution 2347, which tackled the unlawful destruction of cultural heritage and the looting and smuggling of cultural property in armed conflicts and set an important precedent, that damages to sacred and historical sites may amount to war crimes. It is instructive of implementing peace in multidimensional ways based on valuing the promotion of culture as key to fostering reconciliation and dialogue.

Resolution 2347, however, emerged largely in response to terrorist activities conducted by non-state actors, specifically Islamic State in Iraq and the Levant and Al-Qaeda. While it mentions armed conflicts, it does not discuss state-led atrocities such as those targeted at minorities and indigenous peoples. The protection of tangible and intangible heritage must be part of a broader suite of reforms and interventions in post-conflict settings. This is important because the daily reproduction and protection of culture occurs in less visible ways, in part when this is treated as feminized labor—i.e., women's cultural contributions are expected or excluded and thus taken for granted (Nakashima, Krupnik, and Rubis 2018: 3). Many cultural resources tend to be economically devalued except in cases where cultural property and artifacts have direct or immediate financial value. The regeneration of aspects of cultural heritage that cannot be adequately valued in monetary terms, such as traditional knowledge, spiritual beliefs, and practices, is typically absent from post-crisis reconstruction efforts. The level of their disruption and scale of loss due to conflicts and disasters remain poorly understood or underexamined. If the profound and lasting emotional harm of conflicts and crises, such as trauma, is to be healed, these invisible aspects of peace should be treated as equally important for regenerating societies holistically.

What might a post-crisis response look like when it values social and cultural restoration equally alongside the rebuilding of physical infrastructures and the formal economy, for example in replenishing social reproduction through material inflows that prioritize health in post-crisis reconstruction? More attention is now being given to promoting peace through health, such as using the concept of "biopolitical peacebuilding" which, Seán Brennan (2019) argues, reflects a shift from prioritizing state-building to the delivery of basic human needs and facilitating conditions for radically transforming life conditions. It focuses on modeling post-conflict (as well as post-disaster) transformation in pursuit of "quality of life" goals. This approach aims to:

> not only heal the body (and mind) of the individual but also the body politic of a global community currently struggling with the growing challenge of Mutually Assured Destruction through the termination of Life as species, in all its

> human, animal, and ecological manifestations, from climate change. (Brennan 2019: 140)

It is the people collectively, and individual healthy bodies, that enable the restoration of visible and invisible peace.

Brennan's concept underscores a broader understanding of positive peacebuilding and one that is strongly informed by the pioneering work of Johann Galtung in the peace studies literature. The key thesis in biopolitical peacebuilding aligns with the conceptualization of regeneration I advance in that both consider deliberate efforts to prioritize health and well-being in post-crisis responses as critical for fully utilizing the windows of opportunity often present in transitioning societies. In addition, both represent attempts to situate post-crisis reconstruction within the intersections of political economy and ecology through an integrated analyses of how the (re)organization of care institutions and practices in post-conflict or post-disaster societies "benefits the individual, community, biosphere, and planetary environment" (Brennan 2019: 145). However, unlike this initial definition of biopolitical peacebuilding, regeneration takes an explicit feminist starting point by making visible the role of gendered assumptions and expectations in shaping post-crisis reconstruction. It situates peacebuilding models squarely within the global politics of bodily autonomy.

Lastly, transformative peace takes time. Regeneration attends to the longue durée realities of rebuilding life in the aftermath of crises and considers the ways in which post-crisis transitions are part of a long continuum of peace. This aspect of regeneration engages with Rob Nixon's (2011) concept of "slow violence," which draws attention to forms of violence that are not immediate or visually arresting. Slow violence, as Nixon (2011: 201) argues, is typically uncounted and underestimated, as is evident in the case of militarism. The aftermath of conflicts leaves human and environmental harms that are long-enduring and intergenerational. These are "the wounds that remain" and feed into other forms of violence and predispose societies to war (Cockburn 2004: 39, 2010). For example, the toxicity of warfare and increasingly militarized disaster responses lies not just in psychosocial trauma, but also in environmental and biological reproductive residues, from landmines to chemicals weapons. Consequently, the concept of slow violence implies a process of "slow peace"—demanding that post-crisis transitions place on the balance the hidden, ecological, and laborious costs to achieving peace.

Slow peace attends to the continuum of peace, which the inverse of a "continuum of violence" implies (see Chapter 1). Cynthia Cockburn's concept of a continuum of violence has drawn attention to the persistence of gendered violence and inequalities across phases of conflict and post-conflict, crisis and post-crisis. It alerts us to the continuity of war across scales from individual everyday life encounters to global financial institutions. Therefore, as

Politics of Sexual & Reproductive Health

other feminists have argued, peace is not simply the absence of war but the progressive transformation across scales, phases, and bodies where violence operates. Regeneration is the end goal in a continuum of peace, such that the renewal of women's bodies is mutually constitutive of, and has cascading effects for, renewing societies, economies, and ecosystems alike. Politically, a continuum of peace includes as a core component the slow process of solidarity building and consciousness-raising that activists, especially women from the Global South, have long used in their resistance repertoire (hooks 1984). Regeneration therefore challenges the efficacy of post-crisis transition that obscures slow peace, instead highlighting that peace requires sustained resources including time, political commitment, and physical well-being for the hard work of building alliances "capable of acting in many places, at many levels, and on many problems simultaneously (Cockburn 2004: 44).

Regeneration as Justice

Regeneration can deepen and broaden definitions of justice in the aftermath of crises. Here I specifically develop *regenerative justice* based on a synthesis of two interrelated concepts: reproductive justice and environmental justice. Social movements largely led by indigenous women and women of color have developed these ideas through strategic coalitions and political alliances (Di Chiro 2008; de Onis 2012; SisterSong 2012; Jimenez, Johnson, and Page 2017; Ross et al. 2017). There are strong overlaps between the struggle for reproductive justice and environmental justice. For instance, in her analysis of the US-based international non-governmental organization Asian Communities for Reproductive Justice, De Onis (2012) cites their usage of "looking both ways" as a metaphor to advance an epistemology that addresses the simultaneous and interrelated bodily and ecological injustices experienced by marginalized women and groups. The discursive framing of "looking both ways" facilitates wider alliances among those whose politics reside at the crossroads of ensuring human and planetary survival amid the threats of climate change. Regenerative justice draws on this synergy to locate, as part of post-conflict and post-disaster transformations, the global structures and processes that determine which individuals, groups of people, and life forms are worthy of existence and flourishing. This translates to exposing the racist, classist, and neo-eugenicist underpinnings of maneuvers to promote population control as a response to climate change, and consequently to ensure that bodily autonomy and well-being are considered central rather than auxiliary to the climate change agenda. As reproductive justice movements point out, there is a clear danger that the neo-Malthusian logic of limiting population growth is deliberately used not only to distract from profound environmental inequalities that render specific bodies dispensable, but also to embed the traditional state-centric and militarized security that continues to benefit some at the expense of others (Ojeda, Sasser, and Lunstrum 2020: 321). Justice as regeneration, therefore, lies in the mutually reinforcing agendas of sexual and reproductive freedoms and the right to a healthy environment.

Regenerative justice can be applied in the narrow context of transitional justice mechanisms. Regeneration places in sharper focus the embodiments of, and bodily requirements for, societies to have a just transition in the aftermath of conflicts. Transitional justice, according to the UN definition, refers to:

> the full range of processes and mechanisms associated with a society's attempts to come to terms with a legacy of large-scale past abuses, in order to ensure accountability, serve justice and achieve reconciliation. These may include both judicial and non-judicial mechanisms, with differing levels of international involvement (or none at all) and individual prosecutions, reparations, truth-seeking, institutional reform, vetting and dismissals, or a combination thereof. (UN Security Council 2004: 4)

Feminist scholars, however, have critiqued the frequent exclusion of women, sexual minorities, and gender issues in transitional justice processes (for examples, see Ashe 2019; O'Rourke 2013; Ní Aoláin 2009). Gender analysis in transitional justice scholarship is now established in international security agendas, notably the Women, Peace and Security agenda. However, in practice, gender-sensitive reforms continue to remain at the margins. Transitional justice has been limited to the prioritization of civic and political institution-building; and limiting in that it stops short of challenging the dominant "liberal peace" model that tends to reproduce elite and market-driven transitions (Gready and Robins 2014: 341-342).[10] As such, many forms of multiple and intersectional harms distinctly experienced by women are rendered invisible due to a lack of understanding within transitional justice of the global political economic drivers of gendered experiences in armed conflicts (Sifris and Tanyag 2019).

In Rai, True, and Tanyag (2019), we proposed that regeneration can begin addressing the root causes of women's post-conflict depletion through specific policies that ensure the rebuilding of social infrastructures, participatory policy-making, and the creation of accountability mechanisms. In addition to the transformation in formal institutions that we first envisioned, I argue that transitional justice anchored upon the ethical goals of regeneration represents a strong guarantee of non-recurrence of violence and an end to cycles of displacements precisely because it attends to environmental conditions of depletion. This is because regeneration takes as a starting point the re-organization of political, economic, and social institutions based on who gets to replenish and renew—when, where, and how—as matters of justice. It entails asking,

[174]   *Politics of Sexual & Reproductive Health*

for example, what it means for post-conflict reparations to reflect not just a broadening of procedural considerations to include women's distinct experiences of sexual and reproductive violence, such as forced sterilization and criminalization of abortion within transitional justice programs (UN General Assembly 2010a; see also Sifris 2014). Importantly, these reparations embody wider aspirations of ending the multiple structures of inequality that limit women's life chances before, during, and after conflicts. Therefore, transitional justice mechanisms represent an important juncture to experiment with mechanisms for renewing social reproduction and specifically women's care labor, in conjunction with challenging global resistance to both bodily autonomy and ecological health.

Regeneration can inform deliberations of what constitutes justice for global politics in dystopic times. How might the rapidly changing security context posed by climate change–induced crises reshape the boundaries of political claims-making and responsibility? Justice, according to feminist political theorist Nancy Fraser (2013: 193), is expressed as a "parity of participation." Consequently, "justice requires social arrangements that permit all to participate as peers in social life." A transformative feminist politics in the age of globalization and neoliberal crisis requires a multi-dimensional theory of justice.[11] Fraser's theory incorporates three dimensions on recognition, redistribution, and representation, and represents the complexity to key feminist struggles of our time. As she explains, participatory parity, especially for women and marginalized groups, are impeded on the one hand by economic structures that define how resources are allocated (redistribution) and on the other by cultural or status hierarchies that systematically depreciate specific groups of people and attributes (recognition). Increasingly, the economic and cultural dimensions of injustice are mediated by a third pillar: political representation. This dimension of justice relates to the ways in which the parameters for belonging are established and whether "the boundaries of the political community wrongly exclude some who are actually entitled to representation" (Fraser 2013: 195). For women and marginalized groups, equal participation in society cannot be fully realized without the requisite access to material resources and the scaffolding provided by gender-equal cultural values and political decision-making. All three dimensions of justice are therefore indivisible from one another, in "mutual entwinement and reciprocal influence" (Fraser 2013: 199).

Fraser's three-dimensional justice, however, is no longer sufficient to encompass the range of injustices at the nexus of bodily and environmental depletion. I argue that justice requires a fourth dimension: regeneration. Regeneration offers a way of revealing another interrelated aspect of justice/injustice in global politics—whose bodies and ways of being have a right to regenerate and flourish. As I have shown in this book, transformative feminist politics must be informed by an understanding of justice that is responsive to how parity of participation is being redefined under a neoliberal logic of depletion. The pursuit of a good life can no longer persist without reckoning with the interdependence of humans and the environment, and the distinct bodily depletion experienced by women situated within multiple forms of crisis. Participation in the face of our contemporary ecological crisis is ultimately about *existence*. Regeneration thus makes visible the profound interconnectedness of justice and care (see Robinson 2011, 2016; Deveaux 1995: 117). There can be no politics of recognition, redistribution, and representation without regeneration.

CONCLUSION

This chapter offered a vision of a feminist global agenda on bodily autonomy beginning with a cartography of struggles toward flourishing. It is insufficient to account for and explain restrictions to sexual and reproductive health alone—the point is to change these restrictions and show what this change could look like. Synthesizing disparate bodies of feminist scholarship across ecofeminism, "Third World"/postcolonialism, care ethics, and justice, I advanced the concept of regeneration as a model for transforming the material and ideological roots that underpin global neoliberal processes of depletion. Regeneration attends to the systemic interlinkages of political, economic, and environmental crises and to the nexus between sexual and reproductive freedoms and sustaining our environment. It therefore explicitly contributes a normative perspective of interdependent flourishing. If we understand gendered crises as interlinked, then we must find ways to overcome their root causes simultaneously.

Regeneration cannot occur in political-economic-environmental siloes. It takes as a necessary feminist starting point sustaining men's and women's bodies and social reproduction in general, for these ensure the continuity of life in all dimensions and scales. Regeneration understands that crises are critical junctures not only for reversing the simultaneous and interlinked depletion of women's bodies and environment. They also represent opportunities for realizing the radical and revolutionary vision for peace and security promoted by transnational reproductive and environmental justice movements.

First, a shift toward regeneration as the organizing principle for post-conflict and post-disaster recovery emphasizes human and environmental flourishing, and not just survival or "building back better" on the backs of gendered invisible labor. Instead, regeneration rethinks post-crisis economic reforms to consist of rebuilding social welfare and care institutions as a priority. It cultivates alternative economic models to extraction and attends to the ways in which climate change can and already does undermine the gains of post-crisis recovery. Second, regeneration places post-crisis transitions

[176]   *Politics of Sexual & Reproductive Health*

within a long continuum of peace. Feminist solidarity, consciousness-raising, and healing are intergenerational and therefore take time and resources. Yet, because these often represent invisible and slow forms of peace, they continue to be neglected and feminized especially in post-crisis responses, thereby enabling the recurrence of violence and displacement. Finally, regeneration helps deepen what justice means for a world beset by multiple crises. I raised preliminary reflections on how and why enabling the flourishing of women's health and well-being—as a foundational pillar of justice—contributes to overall welfare at community, societal, and global levels. Bodily autonomy, especially for women and girls in crisis situations, is both an outcome of addressing pre-existing gendered violence and an urgent precondition for meaningful political, economic, and socio-cultural participation in response to future crises.

In conclusion, I am reminded of the experiences of women who, despite enduring cycles of loss and displacement, carry within them a deep source of human flourishing and a vitality of life. Even in situations of dire crisis, individuals do not cease to be bodies that experience pleasure, beauty, and desire. Neither do individuals exist separate from the human and non-human relationships they inhabit. Asking what makes a good life is perhaps precisely what we need in times of ruptures and repair. We need an understanding of peace that involves allowing bodies, both human and environmental, to regenerate. This peace is radically opposed to modernist and anthropocentric accounts of linear progress and of growth underpinned by individualism and extraction. Embracing a feminist and ecological conceptualization of peace—which regeneration entails—opens peace processes, disaster resilience, and climate change responses to truly transformative and integrated reforms that mutually enable women's sexual and reproductive freedoms and environmental renewal.

Conclusion

In 2012, at the height of the national debates over the Reproductive Health (RH) Bill in the Philippines, among the controversial issues was whether the proposed legislation should include the phrase "safe and satisfying sex life" in its definition of sexual and reproductive health. Conservative male legislators challenged the propriety of the phrase and objected to what this move represented politically for the country. Can and should the idea of pleasure be enshrined in law? Among these conservative male legislators was Senator Vicente Sotto III who proposed that these portions be removed because they are incompatible with "Filipino culture." He argued that:

> The reason why I wanted to remove the whole phrase originally is that I believe Reproductive Health in the context of a *true Filipina* does not pertain to safe and satisfying sex. When a *true Filipina* speaks of reproductive health, she means family, marriage, responsible parenthood, nurturing and rearing her children and the mother.[1]

He further stated, "Isn't that happening anyway? We can decide if, when, and how to do so. Why do we need to put that in the law? *Ang sagwa*. I will not be a part of that."[2] The opposition against these phrases was echoed outside the chamber of Congress with pro-life groups calling out the language as obscene. In response, two women proponents of the RH Bill—Senators Pia Cayetano and Miriam Defensor-Santiago—defended the use of the phrase and insisted that it cannot be removed to "protect the essence of the RH Bill." Defensor-Santiago added further that the phrase is a global standard and is "used in the final act of the International Conference on Population and Development" (quoted in Bordadora 2012). In the

---

The Global Politics of Sexual and Reproductive Health. Maria Tanyag, Oxford University Press.
© Oxford University Press 2024. DOI: 10.1093/oso/9780197676332.003.0008

end, the RH Bill had enough votes from supportive legislators to be enacted and the phrase was, in the end, retained. However, "Responsible Parenthood" was added into the official title of the legislation in a bid to modulate what could otherwise have been a law too transgressive of Filipino culture.

In another part of the world and from a different time, Black feminists who formed the Combahee River Collective authored a Statement which raised the importance of self-care not as an individualizing project but rather as pre-requisite for collectively fighting racist and sexist oppression: "Our politics evolve from a healthy love for ourselves, our sisters, and our community, which allows us to continue our struggle and work" (Combahee River Collective 1978/2014: 273). These ideas still resonate today as Black women continue to face the highest rates of maternal mortality in the United States. Together with Native American women, they are two to three times more likely to die from pregnancy-related causes than White women (Centers for Disease Control and Prevention 2019; Petersen et al. 2019). From Black feminist perspectives, when prevailing systems and structures of oppression are built to deplete women, existence itself becomes a form of resistance. Indeed, Audre Lorde wrote in *A Burst of Light* about the devastating effects of "overextension" based on her experiences as a Black woman diagnosed with cancer. There she reflected on a realization that resonates with the lives of many women facing depletion on a daily basis: "Caring for myself is not self-indulgence, it is self-preservation, and that is an act of political warfare" (1988: 140).

Despite the vast geographic and historical contexts that may appear to separate Filipino women's ongoing struggles to expand sexual and reproductive freedoms in the Philippines from that of indigenous women, Black women and other women of color worldwide, their experiences are connected. Their lives evoke the highest of stakes in defending bodily health and well-being. Recognizing one's pleasure as an entitlement constitutes a form of "political warfare," as Lorde puts it, because the very idea rebels against overlapping structures of power that are built upon the sustained depletion of women's bodies. This is why self-care cannot simply be about individual women and girls recognizing the importance of their bodily autonomy. Similarly, the deterioration of sexual and reproductive freedoms cannot be reduced to individual perpetrators of violence, or to pre-existing harmful laws, cultural practices, or beliefs alone. Self-care must be global, for it requires the presence of enabling political, legal, economic, and socio-cultural conditions for all individuals to be able to survive and have flourishing lives.

EMBODIMENTS OF CRISIS

When I began researching the politics of bodily autonomy, I was interested in understanding what is so radical about sexual and reproductive freedoms that

CONCLUSION [179]

they remain the most intractable and deeply contested of all gender equality issues? At a time when women are regarded as central to global agendas, what explains pervasive inequalities in sexual and reproductive health and rights (SRHR) and the failure to address them, especially in crisis settings? To find answers, this research has led me to re-examine my own life and relationships, to draw on the insights and experiences of the women and men I met while doing field work, and to situate the particular lives of Filipino women within global political, economic, and security processes. This approach allowed me to develop a multi-layered and contextualized analysis of SRHR as associated with "occupational hazards" of doing social reproductive labor at the household level, the economic devaluing of global care workers, and the tremendous sacrifices and compounded security risks women take on as frontline responders in crisis settings. What I found is that examining the case of SRHR in the Philippines revealed a more global paradox whereby women's bodies and social reproductive labor are clearly central for the production and reproduction of human life yet are also routinely depleted and violated in the service of broader political projects.

The account presented in this book differs from both biomedical explanations, which seek to examine unequal SRHR outcomes in terms of individual bodies, and public health and legal approaches which attribute inequalities as problems of local culture, infrastructural accessibility of family planning services and supplies, and household dynamics and behavioral factors. These perspectives are important in exposing micro-level dimensions to sexual and reproductive freedoms. What this book does, in addition, is to draw their connections to macro-level issues and to incorporate critiques of women's status in the global order. Here I make explicit that persistent and pervasive inequalities in SRHR are internal contradictions to a neoliberal global economy. They constitute a symptom of a global crisis in social reproduction, which in turn results from the relentless demands on women's bodies and labor while inflows to ensure their sustainability are misvalued in both economic and security terms. States and markets function through decade's worth of care deficits matched by the constant supply of altruism and self-sacrifice reproduced across household, community, state, and global levels. In the everyday and during times of crisis, restrictions to bodily autonomy are not incidental to the neoliberal global economy and security but rather integral to their very reproduction. They persist because they are consistent with prevailing logics of power.

Mapping the global politics of SRHR highlighted that there are varieties of political dynamics for different gender equality issues (Htun and Weldon 2018). For example, the need to broaden women's participation and leadership in peace processes, conflict prevention, post-disaster reconstruction, and climate change adaptation has been far more globally accepted than the right of women to freely make sexual and reproductive

[180]   *Politics of Sexual & Reproductive Health*

decisions. SRHR reveals the consequences of a double fragmentation in feminist analyses and feminist agendas to women's capacity for self-determination. First, while feminist International Relations (IR) research has been pivotal in drawing attention to the *continuums* of violence between sexual and gender-based violence and crises such wars and disasters, less attention has been given to explaining growing *contradictions* in the selective incorporation in global agendas of different women's rights, and what this selectivity means for advancing feminism more broadly. These contradictions, as evidenced by the uneven implementation of gender equality reforms, have been underexamined as a result of what scholars point out as the siloing of feminist IR scholarship between two key strands of political economy and security studies and between materialist and discursive/cultural-based critiques.[3] For instance, the mutual neglect of political economy in feminist security studies, and of violence in feminist political economy research, has come at the expense of making the links visible between crisis-specific sexual and gender-based violence and ongoing and long-term harms due to structural and symbolic violence embodied by health inequalities and racialized labor migration in the global economy. This book demonstrates why it is necessary to bridge all forms of analytical siloes to make sense of persistent and prevalent inequalities in SRHR in the context of broad-based support for gender equality, and given the extent to which feminist perspectives in security and development agendas have been well-established.

Second, the bifurcation of feminist IR scholarship has coincided with the piece-meal implementation of gender equality and the specific "bracketing off" of sexual and reproductive health in global agendas. This other fragmentation has been primarily attributed to the funneling of feminist activisms and co-optation of feminist discourses under neoliberal economic governance (Fraser 2013). Feminist scholars have argued that the mainstreaming of feminist perspectives in global agendas has unintentionally led to depoliticization of gender equality and ambivalences in the everyday lives of women and men. This fragmentation is rarely causally linked with the global influence of conservative and anti-feminist resistances that do not challenge women's economic and political participation per se but instead seek to subordinate it in the service of reproducing tradition, nation, or family. It remains unmoored from analysis of who enacts (in)security and how in crisis settings. Yet, as illustrated by the case of Catholic fundamentalist actors in the Philippines, their capacity to directly restrict sexual and reproductive health was broadened around the same time crucial restructurings over state provision of health care were occurring. This has since been carried over in crisis settings where faith-based groups have increasingly taken up spaces opened by gaps in emergency responses, relief, and reconstruction efforts to actively promote a pro-life/"pro-mother" agenda.

CONCLUSION   [181]

As I have shown in this book, there are structural connections between the implementation of global agendas that address women as individuals, the intensification of women's unpaid or poorly paid social reproductive labor in order to mitigate demands for survival, and the absence of necessary inflows to replenish their labor. The disproportionate focus on individualizing women (as victims of sexual and gender-based violence, as resilient or "self-helping" heroes of post-disaster recovery, or as "eco-smart" sexual agents in the Anthropocene) dangerously divests responsibility and accountability from the state and international actors in addressing collective harms and material inequalities rooted in political economy. I extended my analysis further to show why the proliferation of social reproductive crises is interconnected with the growing global influence of religious fundamentalisms manifested in the repurposing of feminist discourses, particularly the mobilization of valorized feminine and masculine identities, for anti-feminist gains. When feminist analysis and politics are fragmented, we will continue to not only miss the broader workings of patriarchy but also run the risk of legitimizing it.

Based on the findings of this book, it is therefore important that we *analytically* disaggregate gender equality issues to account for the distinct politics activated by sexual and reproductive freedoms. Disaggregated analysis is of course not the same as truncated analysis. Recognizing and responding to these multiple gendered politics actually demands eclecticism and pluralism in our theoretical frameworks. It requires synthesizing a range of concepts, methodologies, and analytical tools that allow us to put the perspectives of those in the margins at the center of re-interpreting and re-making global peace and security. This has clear implications in the area of global health. Why do everyday forms of health inequalities routinely go "under the radar" and how might this neglect exacerbate vulnerabilities in times of crisis especially for women, girls, and sexual minorities? Understanding why, for instance, maternal mortality rates count as "non-crises" even when these are situated in conflicts and disaster settings requires examining both material distributions of resources and authority and the range of complementary ideologies that naturalize these allocations. However, research on global health security has thus far disproportionately focused on "spectacular" or "alarming" cases where there is direct or immediate threat to state security. Analyses of health-related crises and emergencies and of routine challenges to health care provisioning have been separate. Such gaps in knowledge contribute to the invisibility of gendered dynamics to global health. These include how the impacts of privatization and austerity measures are continuously mitigated by the periodic intensification of women's social reproductive or care burdens; how crisis-affected societies survive because of health systems that rely on a largely female workforce who are unpaid or underpaid all while women continue to be underrepresented in health decision-making across global and national levels; and how the growing influence of religious fundamentalist

[182]   *Politics of Sexual & Reproductive Health*

actors in crisis response and recovery can further shrink spaces for feminist activism. We need a broad range of perspectives to lay bare the gendered and global political economy dynamics surrounding the stratification of various health issues, which are made to compete for resources and political attention under the rubric of crisis.

Politically, dissociating SRHR from feminist and gender equality agendas in order to supposedly achieve pragmatic and incremental gains is no longer tenable. Past and present strategies that view gender transformations as achievable despite negotiated outcomes that "soften" or exclude references to SRHR serve to undermine feminist political projects as a whole. Feminist peace and security cannot be realized when the right to bodily autonomy continues to be treated as a collateral issue. Restrictions to bodily autonomy occur at various levels, from "high-level" contestations over the inclusion of language relating to SRHR at UN conferences and Security Council outcome documents to more "grounded," everyday, and internalized barriers such as the instrumentalization of women's self-sacrificing practices for household or community crisis coping mechanisms. As I have shown in this book, interrelated restrictions to SRHR in the household (Chapter 2), community (Chapter 3), nation (Chapter 4), and globally (Chapter 5) serve to embed a neoliberal economic logic of depletion. This logic conditions a feminization of survival while keeping the costs and benefits of survival profoundly unequal. Crucially, what has made depletion acceptable or normal especially in times of crisis is the complementary role of religious fundamentalisms in valorizing female altruism and self-sacrifice as ideal femininity. Feminist political strategies and women themselves become complicit in reproducing this logic of depletion through "patriarchal bargains" in the form of concessions made regarding SRHR in everyday life and during times of crisis. Indeed, this is demonstrated even in the case of a widely celebrated and "world-leading" model nation such as the Philippines, which has successfully developed gender-responsive laws and achieved milestones in women's political and economic participation. National peace processes, disaster resilience, and climate change adaptation will ultimately remain partial and elusive of gender justice when they neglect, or come at the cost of undermining, sexual and reproductive freedoms. Worse, these efforts may even exacerbate pre-existing inequalities that render transitions from crisis profoundly uneven and fragile.

As the fullest embodiments of crisis, the depletion of women's bodies can reveal underlying relationships, sites, and configurations of power, violence, and resistance that are often kept hidden or silenced as part of crisis signification. During and after crises like conflicts and disasters, this depletion is even more likely to intensify due to the confluence of material and ideological factors that normalize the lack of inflows to sustain women's health and well-being at the household, community, state, and global levels. It is precisely at critical junctures when the need for care intensifies that we also witness the severity of authoritative struggles over how society and the roles and relationships within it ought to be, as well as how costly these are for women's bodily autonomy. Thus, sexual and reproductive health is an indispensable prerequisite for gender equality in conflict and disaster response, and a marker of inclusive long-term adaptation and post-crisis recovery of societies.

EMBODYING FEMINIST FUTURES

Why does it matter that we recognize the revolutionary potential of bodily autonomy now? How does it contribute to our ability to navigate a time of profound uncertainty posed by the climate crisis and all the compounded consequences it brings to the vast majority of peoples, particularly women, who are in the margins of society? In seeing how crises are embodied through the deterioration of sexual and reproductive freedoms, how might we be able to begin embodying feminist futures with bodily autonomy as our starting point? This book seeks to open new lines of inquiry on how the global politics of bodily autonomy might offer us alternative visions and inspire new modes of activism at a time when multiple forms of crisis are prevailing upon us. Going back again to the quote from Audre Lorde, we can start by reframing discussions of bodily autonomy beyond the limited but necessary starting point of "warfare." After all, when we say SRHR, we are talking about much more than the absence of violence. Bodily autonomy relates to the openness of the body to desire and pleasure too. The concept is ultimately life-affirming, for it embodies how everyone can have a chance at enjoying safe and satisfying sexual lives—if, when, and however one chooses.

My intention in developing this book is to contribute to gradually shifting focus toward a balanced recognition of experiences of sexual violence and victimhood in crisis settings, and sex and sexuality as positive forces for women's individual agency as well as for collective and global well-being. Examining women's lives from the vantage point of sexual and reproductive health matters because it opens us to subjectivities and relationships that spring from love, joy, and care. It instantly affirms a different ontology, that of interdependence and relationality, as core to global politics. People's lives in armed conflicts, disasters, and other crises are not monopolized by strife and suffering even as research and policies tend to overrepresent them as such. According to Cornwall (2006: 275), "sex has been treated as a problem, rather than as a source of happiness, intimacy, fulfillment and pleasure. Words like 'love' or 'desire' are not part of the development lexicon." I argue that there are similarities in peacebuilding and crisis response, when positive forms of sexuality are obscured or considered irrelevant through an overemphasis on protection and prevention of violence. As Jolly (2010: 34) points out, "negative approaches to sexuality risk being disempowering, reinforcing gender

[184] *Politics of Sexual & Reproductive Health*

stereotypes, crushing space for discussion of women's pleasure, and converging with right-wing discourses around sexual morality." Ideas that narrowly frame women's relationship with sex in terms of victimhood and sexual passivity merely reinforce the very sexual codes and morals that make women insecure in the first place. These are also damaging to men and sexual minorities in that they limit representation of men's sexual experiences as intimately tied to violence and necessarily exploitative of (heterosexual) women. Feminist analysis must involve questioning and revealing the vested material interests at play in keeping sexual violence as the only intelligible form of sex in times of crisis.

A feminist future inspired by SRHR involves a more inclusive peacebuilding agenda that acknowledges not just protection from violence but also the active nurturing of caring and loving relationships in the aftermath of crises. It represents an openness to understanding and amplifying diverse notions and capabilities of pursuing pleasure—beyond maternalist and heteronormative frames. Moreover, feminist peacebuilding anchored on regenerating women's bodies expands our analytical lenses and political actions in order to be more pro-active in pursuing alternative models to post-crisis reconstruction. However, the promotion of bodily autonomy as a feminist form of peace building does not mean that we arrive at easy or coherent categories of "good" versus "bad" bodily autonomy (Petchesky 2005). We have seen, for example how globally, individuals can weaponize their own bodies in pursuit of terror or in response to fear (Wilcox 2015; Fierke 2012). In this context, the right to bodily autonomy becomes perverse or disruptive thereby evoking dangers in the liberal misuse of individualizing narratives such as "my body, my choice." It is important to stress that, based on the long history of activism and genealogy of SRHR, bodily autonomy must be explicitly aligned with the normative goal of reproductive justice.

SRHR movements and specifically Black, Global South, and postcolonial feminist frameworks stress the importance of promoting bodily autonomy so that the allocation of power and resources—as well as cultures—is radically transformed to enable healthy and fulfilling lives for all (Ross et al., 2017; Petchesky 2003; Corrêa 1994; Sen and Grown 1987). We must not forget the ongoing struggle to dismantle overlapping structural oppressions for the pursuit of sexual and reproductive health (Ross et al. 2017: 14). Integral to the concept of reproductive justice is collective resistance and the building of expansive social movements that see bodily autonomy as part of social justice and peace activism, including the creation of safe and healthy environments free from racial discrimination and environmental degradation (Ross et al. 2017).

bell hooks, in her book *From Margins to Center*, discusses how sexual freedom is neither a placeholder nor a substitute for a larger multi-issue feminist revolution. The goal has not been to privilege sexual freedom above, or to detach it from, the broader goal of transforming society. Bodily autonomy must be conceived of as both a starting point and an outcome of feminist transformative change. In the words of hooks, "it has been a far more difficult task for women to envision new sexual paradigms, [and] to change the norms of sexuality. The inspiration for such work can only emerge in an environment where sexual well-being is valued" (1984: 148). By examining the global politics of SRHR, this book brings to IR a new research agenda that hopefully will contribute to a radical feminist re-imagination of a global order underpinned not by depletion but by regeneration.

In Chapter 6, I provided a preliminary attempt at charting how a different logic of regeneration might make possible other ways of knowing, doing, and being for global peace and security. I conceptualized regeneration by synthesizing early "Third World" or Global South feminist scholarship with emerging discussions on the need to ensure that economic transformations are central if we are to achieve lasting peace informed by the ontological interdependence of people and planet. Regeneration builds on existing work on care ethics, gendered crises, and social reproduction to theorize how restrictions to bodily autonomy constitute *the* underlying and ongoing crisis that allows us to "draw lines of connection among apparently diverse international issues: global health crises and pandemics; 'refugee crises'; humanitarian emergencies; 'failed' states; peacebuilding; environmental security" (Robinson 2010: 142–143). What has been referred to as "reproduction failures" (Sen and Grown 1987) and as "crisis of/in social reproduction" (Bujra 2004; Kunz 2010; Elson 2012) signals the systemic and structural problem of how care is (mal)organized in the household, community, and state as well as globally. The prevailing global order not only takes for granted but actually actively depletes women's bodies and labor despite how they constitute "the permanent background of giving and receiving care that is central to preventing crises, and responding to crises when they do occur" (Robinson 2010: 142). Consequently, we can expect the recurrence of different and overlapping crises because we have not transformed the material and ideological drivers that deprive people and planet of opportunities to regenerate.

Important pathways are being opened by emerging feminist research that centralizes rebuilding care economies globally and rethinking established notions of "economic empowerment" in post-crisis societal restoration and in the face of climate change (Cohn and Duncanson 2020; Rai, True and Tanyag 2019; Martin de Almagro and Ryan 2019; Duncanson 2016). This promising body of work re-imagines security not as "fire-fighting" from one crisis to another but as the refocusing of resources and political leadership toward planetary health and more expansive, ecological understandings of security. It will yield fruitful discussions on post-conflict or post-disaster transitions that go beyond mitigating or replenishing the same global order that enables depletion. Here I make my own crucial distinction in that regeneration is not possible without sexual and reproductive freedoms. As I have analyzed in this book, care has been so profoundly feminized and typically understood to entail effacing women's own needs for care. We can expect conservative and religious fundamentalist forces to equally champion the idea of regeneration but to do so by further embedding women's bodies in biological essentialism and by "bracketing off" any reference to pleasure or sexuality. Regeneration is politically and normatively committed to SRHR. The re-organization of care and social reproduction ought to proceed in ways that also force us to rethink the limitations of current political strategies that take pragmatic and incremental gains as well as fragmented agendas as feminism *de rigueur*. To regenerate feminist revolutionary imaginaries, we must be willing to also regenerate our activisms and begin anew.

A new feminism strongly anchored upon bodily autonomy progressively breaks down polarities, analytically and politically. To regenerate feminism by starting with SRHR is to directly address the current climate of divisive politics. Anti-feminist backlash and hatred have created a political environment that routinely weaponizes differences to sow division. Yet, it is in fact our diversity—through the multiple situatedness of our knowledges—that offers us an important lens to understand the total workings of White supremacist and sexist oppression. The way to fight domination is through dialogue. A feminism animated by sexual and reproductive freedoms extends the idea that all human beings share in joy, love, and kindness, even to those who oppose it for others. Here I return once more to bell hooks who argued for the need to "restore the revolutionary life force to feminist movement," by struggling for cultural transformations, and for radically altering "the world we have most intimately known, the world in which we feel "safe" (even if such feelings are based on illusions) (1984: 163). Might it be time to rethink feminism precisely at this juncture when seemingly all signs point to a dystopic future? Whose knowledge and what experiences ought to inform new theories and practices of feminism?

Finally, in this book I have placed emphasis on bodily autonomy and rendering visible the embodiments of crisis. I have sought answers to why certain bodies are considered disposable, why particular forms of labor are valued less than others, and what the consequences of these are for women's wellbeing and durable peace. In drawing the connections between the depletion of Filipino women's bodies and labor and the multiplicity of crises occurring in the Philippines, I have also come to ask new questions: How does situatedness to overlapping forms of crises imbue one with perspectives and starting points for re-imagining alternatives to our current politics? As crisis becomes more mundane, how might the lives of different groups of women and girls—especially the indigenous and internally displaced who have historically been subjected to multiple oppressions—help fundamentally shift global politics? Indigenous peoples and minority groups worldwide have long faced existential

CONCLUSION [187]

threats, from colonialism to climate change. They have resisted violent incursions into their daily lives and have committed to flourishing regardless. How can we better value and learn from their "epistemes of crisis" as part of (re)configuring social reproduction, as well as pursuing justice in an increasingly fragile world?

Feminist epistemologies that understand knowledge as embodied and situated can help draw the connections between bodily autonomy and the global politics of expertise and authority over competing interpretations of crisis and security. There are now stronger and wider debates on the need to decolonize universities, research practices, and academic knowledge production. Part of this effort involves examining how the discipline of IR itself is most directly implicated in producing and reproducing a specific type of international order characterized by extraction and depletion. These critical debates must engage with the work of feminist and postcolonial scholars and activists who have long argued that mainstream IR is complicit in the silencing and erasure of alternatives to state-centric, militaristic, and marketized crisis responses. The silencing of alternative perspectives is of course tied to the marginalization of specific bodies and embodiments in IR. Thus, we cannot envision a feminist future without decolonizing our own disciplinary canons on peace, security, and "crisis." This grand challenge must grapple with yet unknown epistemic barriers in tracing uncharted bodies, situated knowledges, and embodied experiences. Borrowing Federici's (2012) words, our "revolution at point zero" truly rests in the struggle for bodily autonomy. The right of all women and men to self-determination is essential for developing global solutions that attend to the paramount imperative of flourishing in the increasingly crisis-prone world we live in today.

[188]   *Politics of Sexual & Reproductive Health*

NOTES

INTRODUCTION

1. According to the World Health Organization (WHO), the official definition of maternal deaths is "The annual number of female deaths from any cause related to or aggravated by pregnancy or its management (excluding accidental or incidental causes) during pregnancy and childbirth or within 42 days of termination of pregnancy, irrespective of the duration and site of the pregnancy." https://www.who.int/data/gho/indicator-metadata-registry/imr-details/4622

2. It is also measured in terms of maternal mortality ratio (MMR) expressed in the equation: MMR = (Number of maternal deaths/Number of live births) × 100,000. However, there are ongoing problems with data collection including under-reporting of maternal deaths, inconsistencies or misclassifications in recording cause of death, and lack of or poor health systems for recording data.

3. Some of the earlier legal references for SRHR include the Universal Declaration of Human Rights (UN General Assembly 1948) Article 25, which states that "everyone has the right to a standard of living adequate for the health and well-being of himself and his family"; and Article 23(2) of the International Covenant on Civil and Political Rights (UN General Assembly 1966), which provides that "the right of men and women of marriageable age to marry and to found a family shall be recognized."

4. See the Preamble and Articles 5, 12, and 16 (UN General Assembly 1979). The Philippines is among the first countries to have ratified CEDAW, having done so in 1981.

5. As I discuss further in this book, the definition itself is the subject of political contestations and debate. Here I explicitly use the term sexual and reproductive health rather than simply reproductive health to render visible the equal importance and interdependence of these two dimensions for bodily autonomy. In subsequent discussions, I refer to sexual and reproductive health and rights (SRHR) noting the differences between sexual health and reproductive health. The distinction does not imply a hierarchy between the two dimensions of health. SRHR is consistent with the subsequent development of the concept in academic, activist and human rights literature (see for examples UN General Assembly 2013; PAI 2015; OURs 2017; UNFPA 2021).

6. See for key examples Mies (1982/2012); Marchand and Runyan (2010); Enloe (2000, 2004, 2013); Rai, Hoskyns, and Thomas (2014); and True (2012).

7. This exclusion was a deliberate decision based on a number of reasons. First, because while I was in the field, my informants made me increasingly aware that numerous interviews had already been conducted with internally displaced persons

prior to my first trip in 2015. Had I conducted more "grassroots" interviews, there was a risk of encountering rehearsed performances. Second, given my relatively short time in the field, I did not feel it was appropriate to expose potential participants to unnecessary harms. Nor did I want to be perceived as another spectator in their fragile lives. Finally, I was also mindful of my broader ethics, given the fact the crisis spaces I was working in were also places where research and development practices were beginning to be criticized as "extractive" (for related discussions see Gaillard and Gomez 2015; and Wibben 2016).

8. In total, there were 44 key-informants divided between 34 females and 10 males. According to affiliation, 9 were from different national bodies including a women's political party, a youth branch of a political party, and the national commission on human rights; 13 from international humanitarian and development NGOs; 3 from international organizations; 14 from local NGOs; and finally 5 academic experts.

9. At the time, the security risks in the most conflict-prone region of Philippines, the Autonomous Region in Muslim Mindanao (ARMM), prevented me from designing a project that allowed field work. However, two representatives from one of the international development organizations I interviewed recommended that I meet representatives of local NGOs from the ARMM that they were in partnership with for a specific development program that they were about to implement at the time (March–April 2015). Hence, even if I did not travel directly to ARMM, I was able to recruit interview participants from NGOs based there.

10. Participants were then recruited using publicly available information from these organizations, while subsequent participants were identified through purposive snowball sampling. This recruitment process involved asking a research participant if he or she was willing to pass on my details to relevant persons or organizations related to my topic. In some cases, research participants facilitated the introduction to potential recruits directly.

CHAPTER 1

1. For extensive documentation of gaps and funding challenges in humanitarian crises and emergencies, see Reproductive Health Matters 2017; Askew et al. 2016; UNFPA 2015; Tanabe et. al 2015; Patel et al. 2009; Reproductive Health Matters 2008.

CHAPTER 2

1. The UCDP identifies and categorizes three main forms of conflict. First, *interstate* conflict refers to conflict between two or more governments or states. Second, *intra-state* refers to a conflict between a state and a non-state actor with no interference from other countries. Third, *one-sided violence* occurs when the state or a non-state actor targets civilians. The UCDP distinguishes intensity levels according to *minor conflict* constituting at least 25 but less than 1,000 battle-related deaths in one calendar year; and *war* with at least 1,000 battle-related deaths in one calendar year. For full details, see Uppsala Conflict Data Program (2017).

2. Clan feud or *rido* as it is termed in Moro culture is typical of "small-scale societies where family and kinship ties are the main sources of authority and where there is a lack of effective state control and authority" (Torres 2014: 8).

3. Personal interview, female representative of non-governmental organization (NGO), Quezon City, February 18, 2015.

4. Personal interview, male representative of NGO, Quezon City, March 25, 2015.

5. Personal interview, Moro female representative of NGO based in the ARMM, Quezon City, March 18, 2015.
6. Personal interview, female representative of international NGO, Davao City, March 10, 2015.
7. Personal interview, Moro female representative of NGO based in the ARMM, Quezon City, March 18, 2015.
8. Personal interview, female, Tacloban City, 23 February 2015.
9. Personal interview, male representative of NGO, Quezon City, March 25, 2015.
10. Personal interviews with female representative of NGO, Quezon City, February 18, 2015; male representative of NGO, Quezon City, March 25, 2015; and female representative of international NGO, Davao City, March 10, 2015.
11. Personal interview, male country representative for international organization, Makati City, April 18, 2016.
12. Personal interview, male representative of international NGO, Tacloban City, February 26, 2015.
13. Personal interview, female, Tacloban City, February 23, 2015.
14. Personal interview, Tacloban City, February 26, 2015.
15. Personal interview, female representative of government organization, Tacloban City, February 25, 2015.
16. Personal interview, male representative of international NGO, Tacloban City, February 26, 2015.
17. Personal interview, Tacloban City, February 24, 2015.
18. Personal interview, Tacloban City, February 26, 2015.
19. Personal interview, female representative of NGO, Tacloban City, February 24, 2015.
20. Personal interview, female representative of NGO, Quezon City, April 15, 2016.
21. Ibid.
22. Personal interview, female representative of international NGO, Guiuan, Samar, February 24, 2015.

CHAPTER 3

1. Personal interview, female activist and non-governmental organization (NGO) representative, Quezon City, April 11, 2016.
2. Guijt and Shah (1998: 4–5) point out that the interest in the "community" is not new and can be traced back to earlier phases of nation-building toward devolved governance, poverty alleviation, and social transformation, particularly of rural and remote areas that would give "voice to the voiceless" around the 1950s and 1960s. This was followed by a phase in the 1980s of growth in NGOs and grass-roots activism that further carried on the participatory ethos.
3. A "gender-lite" approach is different from "gender-blind" in that there are steps taken to promote "gender" via community participation, but this is done in ways that depoliticize gender issues as a matter of bureaucratic "tick box" or procedural conformity (Bracke 2014).
4. Personal interviews, female representative of international non-governmental organization (INGO), Guiuan, Samar, February 24, 2015; male academic, Quezon City, February 3, 2015.
5. This refers to disbursing resources based on whoever has the strongest relations or bond with a patron (i.e., *malakas* meaning strong).
6. Personal interview, female NGO representative, Quezon City, March 18, 2015.
7. Personal interview, female NGO representative, Quezon City, March 18, 2015.

Notes [191]

8. Personal interview, female INGO representative, Quezon City, February 18, 2015.
9. Tacloban City, February 24, 2015.
10. Personal interview, female city social welfare officer, Tacloban City, February 26, 2015.
11. Personal interview, male representative of INGO, Tacloban City, February 26, 2015.
12. Personal interview, male representative of an INGO, Makati City, April 18, 2016.
13. From the root word *bayan* or nation. The concept denotes a sense of collective action and cooperation to meet shared goals. *Kapwa tao* or *pakikipag-kapwa tao* means fellowship or to be part of the community. Literally, this means the self in community.
14. For example, throughout Cooper's Haiyan coverage, he often remarked that "the strength of [Filipino] people is just extraordinary" (quoted in Macaraig 2013).
15. Personal interview, Tacloban City, February 26, 2015.
16. Personal interview, female representative of INGO, Guiuan, Samar, February 24, 2015.
17. Personal interview, female representative of government organization, Tacloban City, February 25, 2015.
18. Personal interview, male country representative of international organization, Makati City, March 4, 2015.
19. Personal interview, Makati City, April 18, 2016.
20. Ibid.
21. Personal interview, female representative of NGO, Quezon City, April 15, 2016.
22. Personal interview, male country representative of international organization, Makati City, March 4, 2015.
23. Personal interview, Tacloban City, February 25, 2015.
24. Republic Act 9262 also known as Anti-Violence Against Women and Their Children Act of 2004. The full text of the law is available at http://www.lawphil. net/statutes/repacts/ra2004/ra_9262_2004.html.
25. Personal interview, female representative of NGO, Quezon City, April 15, 2016.
26. Personal interview, female representative of government organization, Tacloban City, February 25, 2015.
27. Personal group interview, Quezon City, February 18, 2015.

CHAPTER 4

1. The peace process between the MNLF and government has not progressed since 1996 (HD Centre 2011: 46).
2. The alternative spelling for Maranao is Meranao.
3. Personal interview, male academic, Quezon City, February 4, 2015.
4. According to surveys, national-level support or approval of the peace talks and the Bangsamoro Basic Law were negatively affected by a violent episode in January 2015 popularly called the "Mamasapano Incident." It involved the Bangsamoro Islamic Freedom Fighters, which is an extremist, splinter group from the MILF, and unnamed private armed groups that were implicated in the deaths of Philippine National Police Special Action Force troopers in Mamasapano, a municipality in conflict-ridden Maguindanao, Mindanao. National public opinion surveys recorded that 48% of Filipinos disapproved of Bangsamoro autonomy after the incident and despite previous high levels of support. While the dissatisfaction of fringe Moro groups threatened to undermine the peace process, Bangsamoro communities still supported the law. Peaceful resolution to armed conflicts was

still viewed as the most effective and legitimate way to move forward by many Filipinos (also at 48%) (Social Weather Stations 2013, 2015).

5. The full text is available at http://www.ifrc.org/docs/IDRL/RA209729.pdf.

6. The full text is available at http://www.ndrrmc.gov.ph/attachments/045_RA%2010121.pdf.

7. The full text is available at http://pcw.gov.ph/law/republic-act-9710.

8. A series of crucial actions required to respond to reproductive health needs at the onset of every humanitarian crisis (see Inter-Agency Working Group on Reproductive Health in Crises 2010; UN Women 2015).

9. The full text is available at https://pcw.gov.ph/republic-act-10354/.

10. Personal interview, Manila City, April 19, 2016.

11. Nisa Ul Haqq Fi Bangsamoro was a key Moro women's NGO that participated in the peace consultations.

12. Personal interview, female INGO representative, Davao City, March 10, 2015.

13. Personal interview, female representative of NGO, Quezon City, April 15, 2016.

14. Personal interview, female representative of international organization, Quezon City, April 19, 2016.

15. From the 1930s to 2005, 1,266 cases of *rido* were documented, 64% of which remain unresolved (Torres 2014). Approximately half of the *rido* incidences recorded by the Bangsamoro Conflict Monitoring System occurred between 2000 and 2004, averaging around 127 new cases per year (see also Hilsdon 2009).

16. Personal interview, female academic, Quezon City, February 3, 2015.

17. Indeed, Article XV of the 1987 Philippine Constitution explicitly states the importance of the family for nation-building. See http://www.officialgazette.gov.ph/constitutions/1987-constitution/; also Hudson, Bowen, and Nielsen 2015.

18. The human rights violations perpetrated by the Ampatuans have been reported by Human Rights Watch (2010) including clan members' tendency to kill female victims after raping them. This crucial information strengthens the links between sexual violence, the documented prevalence of extrajudicial killings and forced disappearances in Mindanao primarily perpetrated by armed state actors, and the use of state forces by clans such as Ampatuans as their de facto personal army (Human Rights Watch 2010; Amnesty International 2011).

19. Personal interview, male representative from a government organization, Davao City, March 13, 2015.

20. Personal interview, female academic, Quezon City, February 3, 2015.

21. Personal interview, female representative of international organization, Quezon City, April 19, 2016.

22. Personal interview, Moro female representative of NGO, Quezon City, March 18, 2015.

23. Personal interview, female academic, Quezon City, February 3, 2015.

24. Personal interview, female representative of INGO, Davao City, March 10, 2015.

25. Personal interview, female academic, Tacloban City, February 23, 2015.

26. Ibid.

27. Personal interview, male representative of INGO, Tacloban City, February 26, 2015.

28. Personal interview, female representative of INGO, Tacloban City, February 25, 2015.

29. Personal interview, female representative of INGO, Guiuan, Samar, February 24, 2015.

30. Personal interview, female, Tacloban City, February 23, 2015.

31. Personal interview, female representative of government organization, Tacloban City, February 26, 2015.
32. Personal interview, female representative of INGO, Tacloban City, February 25, 2015.
33. *Pikat* in Waray means *malandi* in Tagalog/Filipino and "sexually promiscuous" in English.
34. Personal interview, male representative of INGO, Tacloban City, February 26, 2015. Another female informant from an INGO shared similar anecdotes in a personal interview, February 26, 2015.
35. Personal interview, male academic and specialist in disaster research, Quezon City, February 3, 2015.
36. Personal interview, female representative of INGO, Guinan, Samar, February 24, 2015.
37. Personal interview, female representative of INGO, Tacloban City, February 25, 2015.
38. Ibid.
39. Personal interview, male representative of NGO, Quezon City, March 25, 2015.
40. Personal interview, male country representative of international organization, Makati City, March 4, 2015.
41. Ibid.
42. Ibid.
43. Field notes, April 25, 2016, Hotel Alejandro, Tacloban, Philippines.
44. Personal interview, female representative of INGO, Guiuan, Samar, February 24, 2015.

CHAPTER 5

1. The countries composing the UN Security Council at the time were: the permanent five namely China, France, Russia, the United Kingdom, and the United States; and non-permanent members consisting of Cote d'Ivoire, Equatorial Guinea, Kuwait, Peru, Poland, Belgium, Dominican Republic, Germany, Indonesia, and South Africa. See UN Security Council (2019a, 2019b). See also https://www.un.org/press/en/2019/sc13790.doc.htm.
2. Prior to CEDAW, the Declaration on the Elimination of Discrimination against Women was adopted by the UN General Assembly on November 7, 1967.
3. Keller (2014: 311) notes that this contentious status is debatable given that other scholars point out how the Convention on the Rights of the Child (CRC) has more substantive reservations than CEDAW. In addition, many of the initial CEDAW reservations have been withdrawn or amended. Even the reservations to CRC, however, are interrelated with CEDAW because they also reflect ideological contestations over the family and women's status.
4. See "Reservations to CEDAW," https://www.un.org/womenwatch/daw/cedaw/reservations.htm; and UN General Assembly 1998: 47–49.
5. In International Law, a State Party has the following options regarding treaty reservations: (1) maintain its reservation even after examining in good faith a basis for removal; (2) withdraw the reservation; (3) replace the impermissible reservation with a permissible one; and finally, (4) renounce being a party to the treaty.
6. As of January 28, 2020, there have been a total of 155 registered communications by country only 37 of which progressed to a decision; 46 are pending cases; and 72 are either inadmissible or discontinued. In the 37 cases that progressed to a

[194]   *Notes*

decision, 35 were found by the CEDAW Committee to have constituted human rights violations (see OHCHR 2020).

7. The group consists of five independent experts drawn from balanced geographical representation. See UN General Assembly 2010b.

8. In addition to women's rights, there were other thematic UN conferences on environment, population, social development, habitat, children, HIV/AIDS, small island states, food security, and racism, which made for a period marked by optimism and transnational network-building (Sen 2005).

9. These include countries such as Egypt, Libya, Morocco, Malaysia and Pakistan.

10. Mirroring these definitional debates, the journal has changed its name to *Sexual and Reproductive Health Matters* in 2019. The very first issue of the journal that year discusses how "sexual" was dropped out because of fierce negotiations in Cairo. For too long, "sexual" was "carefully wrapped historically, so as not to be too visible, in order not to offend" (Cottingham, Kismödi, and Hussein 2019: 2). Headlining "sexual" in the journal's name constitutes a deliberate political act to affirm the equal and interlinked importance of sexual rights with reproductive rights.

11. The banning of the EC pill in the Philippines was viewed as a "pro-life victory" by the US conservative media, *CNSNews* (Goodenough 2008). This example demonstrates the transnational dimension of restrictions to SRHR and the importance of the Philippines to the global pro-life movement as the "only Catholic country" in Asia (see Tan 2004).

12. Office of the Press Secretary, "President Bush Signs Unborn Victims of Violence Act of 2004," April 1, 2004. https://georgewbush-whitehouse.archives.gov/news/releases/2004/04/20040401-3.html.

13. The special session was called Religious Engagement: The Contributions of Faith Communities to our Shared Humanity. See World Humanitarian Summit and Agenda for Humanity (2016) for a summary of the session.

14. Personal interview, Quezon City, April 10, 2016.

15. Personal interview, female representative of non-governmental organization (NGO), Quezon City, April 29, 2016.

16. Personal interview, male representative of NGO, Manila City, April 18, 2016.

17. Personal interview, female representative of international non-governmental organization (INGO), Quezon City, April 14, 2016.

18. Personal interview, female representative of NGO, Quezon City, April 15, 2016.

19. Field notes, April 25, 2016, Hotel Alejandro, Tacloban, Philippines. See Commission on Human Rights Philippines 2016 for full details.

20. Personal interview, female representative of NGO, Quezon City, April 15, 2016.

21. Personal interview, female representative of NGO, Quezon City, April 29, 2016.

22. Personal interview, female representative of INGO, Quezon City, April 14, 2016.

23. Personal interview, Makati City, March 4, 2015.

24. For cultural and material explanations on how crises may intensify feelings of being "obliged to be grateful" in the Philippines see Su and Tanyag 2019; Ong, Flores, and Combinido 2015; and Sherwood et al. 2015.

25. Personal interview, Manila City, April 18, 2016.

26. The US Global Population Strategy in the 1970s stressed the need to control population in developing countries to secure "US security and overseas interests" (US Department of State 1975). See Chapter 6 for further discussion on this point.

27. The Second Vatican Council or Vatican II (1962–1965) refers to the religious council gathering that deliberated on church doctrinal teachings in response to

Notes [195]

then ongoing critique from within and outside of Catholicism. It led to a push for the Church's greater social relevance especially to the poor by shifting from an exclusive focus on doctrinal and spiritual teachings into one that also responds to unequal social, political and economic conditions.

28. Personal interview, female representative of NGO, Quezon City, April 27, 2016. See also Holden and Nadeau 2010.

29. Personal interview April 29, 2016. Cardinal Sin was a prominent Catholic bishop in the anti-Marcos dictatorship movement.

30. Personal interview, female representative of NGO, Quezon City, April 29, 2016.

31. Personal interview, Quezon City, April 29, 2016.

32. See for example the full Special Issue on the GGR in *Sexual and Reproductive Health Matters* (formerly *Reproductive Health Matters* 2020).

33. According to Crane and Dusenberry, "throughout its history, the politics of the Gag Rule have been rooted in domestic political struggles over abortion, played out between anti-abortion and pro-choice factions of the Republican Party, between Republicans and Democrats, and between the Executive branch and Congress" (2004: 129). Indeed, prior to the creation of the GGR, abortion-related legal restrictions on the use of US aid had already been in place, such as the 1973 Helms Amendment to the Foreign Assistance Act (see Crane and Dusenberry 2004; Gezinski 2012).

CHAPTER 6

1. By ecofeminism, I narrowly refer to critical strands of movements and theoretical approaches that challenge neoliberal feminism and environmentalism for leaving contemporary political and economic structures intact instead of calling for revolutionary and transformative ways.

2. Not unproblematically, usual examples cite how this created empowered roles for women on the basis that they are "closer to nature" than men, holding distinct knowledge as traditional healers, gifted in accessing spiritual worlds, and matriarchs. But the same women-nature associations have also been legitimized to inflict violence against women as witches or to maintain gender-segregated governance structures and exclude women from positions of power (see Federici 2014).

3. Personal interview, Quezon City, March 16, 2015.

4. *Malong* is a multi-tasking length of fabric that can be used as a wrap-around dress or skirt, a blanket, or a curtain used as make-shift dressing room.

5. See for example the debate on "Planet Politics" among Burke et al. 2016; Chandler et al. 2018; Fishel et al. 2018.

6. See Moore 2017, 2018; and Haraway 2016.

7. For further discussions on Malthus and the ideologies that drive population control see Hartmann 2016 and Yuval-Davis 1997.

8. The original memorandum can be accessed via https://static.history.state.gov/frus/frus1969-76ve14p1/pdf/d121.pdf.

9. See Pugh, Cooper, and Turner (2008) on the political economy of peacebuilding and for an explanation of how economics function to enable both war-making and peace building.

10. Transitional justice traditionally relates to post-conflict transitions whereas by invoking regeneration, I refer to diverse forms of crisis transitions such as in the aftermath of conflicts, disasters, and their increasing overlaps. As I have shown in Chapters 2 and 3, disasters are sites where multiple forms of sexual and

gender-based violence also occur, and there is a need to enact similar measures for accountability, reconciliation, truth, and healing.

11. Fraser initially argued for two dimensions—recognition and redistribution—which responded to cultural and economic struggles for justice respectively. Subsequently, she revised her theory of justice in response to what she then observed as contemporary challenges of globalization to add a third dimension to capture the competing accounts of representation in justice (see Fraser 2005).

CONCLUSION

1. David Dizon, "Sotto: I give my wife 'safe, satisfying sex,'" *ABS-CBNnews.com*, December 17, 2012, http://www.abs-cbnnews.com/nation/12/17/12/sotto-i-give-my-wife-safe-satisfying-sex (italics mine); Kimberly Jane Tan, "Senate keeps 'safe and satisfying sex life' in definition of reproductive health," *GMA News*, December 4, 2012, http://www.gmanetwork.com/news/story/284978/news/nation/senate-keeps-safe-and-satisfying-sex-life-in-definition-of-reproductive-health. I watched the session via live video streaming from www.senate.gov.ph.

2. See Tan, "Senate keeps 'safe and satisfying sex life' in definition of reproductive health." The Tagalog *Ang sagwa* roughly translates to that/it is vulgar, obscene, or indecent.

3. See *Politics & Gender* 2015, 2017, 2020.

REFERENCES

Abinales, Patricio N., and Donna J. Amoroso. 2005. *State and society in the Philippines*. Lanham, MD: Rowman & Littlefield.

Ackerly, Brooke, and Jacqui True. 2010. *Doing feminist research in political and social science*. Basingstoke, UK: Palgrave Macmillan.

ActionAid International. 2016. *On the frontline: Catalysing women's leadership in humanitarian action*. Johannesburg: ActionAid.

Allen, Louise, and Laura Shepherd. 2019."In pursuing a new resolution on sexual violence Security Council significantly undermines women's reproductive rights." *LSE Blogs*, April 25. https://blogs.lse.ac.uk/wps/2019/04/25/in-pursuing-a-new-resolution-on-sexual-violence-security-council-significantly-undermines-womens-reproductive-rights/.

Alston, Margaret, Kerri Whittenbury, Alex Haynes, and Naomi Godden. 2014. "Are climate challenges reinforcing child and forced marriage and dowry as adaptation strategies in the context of Bangladesh?" *Women's Studies International Forum* 47: 137–144.

Amnesty International. 2011. "Philippines: Impunity for torture, unlawful killings and enforced disappearances: Amnesty International Submission to the UN Universal Periodic Review, May–June 2012." ASA 35/007/2011, November 28.

Amoyen, Napoleon, and Christine Diaz. 2010. *Experiences of violence against women among upland women in NPA-transit community*. Davao City, Philippines: Mindanao Working Group.

Ang, Getrudes R. 1979. "The Bayanihan spirit: Dead or alive?" *Philippine Quarterly of Culture and Society* 7(1/2): 91–93.

Angeles, Leonora. 2020. "Only in the Philippines? Postcolonial exceptionalisms and Filipina feminisms." *Critical Asian Studies* 52(2): 226–247.

Arnado, Mary Ann M. 2012. "Women's involvement in conflict early warning systems: Moving from rhetoric to reality in Mindanao." Opinion. Geneva: Centre for Humanitarian Dialogue.

Arora-Jonsson, Seema. 2011. "Virtue and vulnerability: Discourses on women, gender and climate change." *Global Environmental Change* 21(2): 744–751.

Arora-Jonsson, Seema. 2014. "Forty years of gender research and environmental policy: Where do we stand?" *Women's Studies International Forum* 47: 295–308.

Ashe, Fiedelma. 2019. "Sexuality and gender identity in transitional societies: Peacebuilding and counterhegemonic politics." *International Journal of Transitional Justice* 13(3): 435–457.

Askew, Ian, Rajat Khsola, Ugochi Daniels, Sandra Krause, Clare Lofthouse, Lale Say, Kate Gilmore, and Sarah Zeid. 2016. "Sexual and reproductive health and rights in emergencies." *Bulletin of the World Health Organization* 94(5): 311.

ARROW (Asian-Pacific Resource and Research Centre for Women). 2014. "Identifying opportunities for action on climate change and sexual and reproductive health and rights in Bangladesh, Indonesia, and the Philippines." ARROW Working Paper. Kuala Lumpur, Malaysia: ARROW.

Asian Institute of Journalism and Communication. 2015. "Zamboanga learning review on post-conflict community engagement." January 14. Zamboanga: Asian Institute of Journalism and Communication. https://www.humanitarianrespo nse.info/sites/www.humanitarianresponse.info/files/documents/files/zambo-anga_learning_report_final_14_january_2015.pdf.

Atienza, Maria Ela L. 2004. "The politics of health devolution in the Philippines: Experiences of municipalities in a devolved set-up." *Philippine Political Science Journal* 25(48): 25–54.

Atienza, Maria Ela L. 2006. "Local governments and devolution in the Philippines." In *Philippine politics and governance: An introduction*, edited by Noel M. Morada and Teresa S. Encarnacion Tadem, 415–439. Quezon City: University of the Philippines.

AWID (Association for Women's Rights in Development). 2008a. "Religious fundamentalisms on the rise: A case for action." AWID Case Studies Report. November 1. Toronto: AWID. https://www.awid.org/publications/religious-fundamentali sms-rise-case-action.

AWID (Association for Women's Rights in Development). 2008b. "Shared insights: Women's rights activists define religious fundamentalisms." AWID Research Reports. Toronto: AWID. https://www.awid.org/publications/shared-insights-womens-rights-activists-define-religious-fundamentalisms.

AWID (Association for Women's Rights in Development). 2011. *Towards a future without fundamentalisms: Analyzing religious fundamentalist strategies and feminist responses.* Toronto: AWID. https://www.awid.org/sites/default/files/atoms/files/towards_a_future_2012.pdf.

AWID (Association for Women's Rights in Development). 2016. *The devil is in the details: At the nexus of development, women's rights, and religious fundamentalisms.* Toronto: AWID. https://www.awid.org/sites/default/files/atoms/files/final_web_the_devil_is_in_the_details.pdf.

AWID (Association for Women's Rights in Development). 2017. *Women human rights defenders confronting extractive industries.* AWID and WHRDIC. https://www.awid.org/sites/default/files/atoms/files/whrds-confronting_extractive_indust ries_report-eng.pdf.

Bakker, Isabella. 2007. "Social reproduction and the constitution of a gendered political economy." *New Political Economy* 12(4): 541–556.

Bakker, Isabella, and Stephen Gill (eds). 2003. *Power, production and social reproduction: Human in/security in the Global Political Economy.* Basingstoke, UK: Palgrave Macmillan.

Bakker, Isabella, and Stephen Gill. 2011. "Towards a new common sense: The need for new paradigms of global health." In *Global health and global health ethics*, edited by Solomon Benatar and Gillian Brock, 329–332. Cambridge: Cambridge University Press.

Ball, Rochelle E. 2004. "Divergent development, racialised rights: Globalised labour markets and the trade of nurses—the case of the Philippines." *Women's Studies International Forum* 27(2): 119–133.

Bankoff, Greg. 2003. *Cultures of disaster: Society and natural hazard in the Philippines*. London: Routledge Curzon.

Bankoff, Greg. 2007. "Living with risk; Coping with disasters: Hazard as a frequent life experience in the Philippines." *Education about Asia* 12(2): 26–29.

Bankoff, Greg. 2015. "'Lahat para sa lahat' (everything to everybody): Consensual leadership, social capital and disaster risk reduction in a Filipino community." *Disaster Prevention and Management* 24(4): 430–447.

Barber, Pauline Gardiner. 2011. "Women's work unbound: Philippine development and global restructuring." In *Gender and global restructuring: Sightings, sites and resistances*, 2nd ed., edited by Marianne H. Marchand and Anne Runyan, 143-162. Abingdon, UK: Routledge.

Basham, Victoria M., and Sergio Catignani. 2018. "War is where the hearth is: Gendered labor and the everyday reproduction of the geopolitical in the army reserves." *International Feminist Journal of Politics* 20(2): 153–171.

Bayangos, Veronica B. 2012. "Going with remittances: The case of the Philippines." BSP Working Paper Series No. 2012-01. Quezon City: Bangko Central ng Pilipinas [Central Bank of the Philippines].

Bedford, Kate, and Shirin M. Rai. 2010. "Feminists theorize international political economy." *Signs* 36(1): 1–18.

Bell, Christine, and Kevin McNicholl. 2019. "Principled pragmatism and the 'inclusion project': Implementing a gender perspective in peace agreements." *feminists@law* 9(1): 1–51.

Bello, Walden. 1998. "The Asian economic implosion: Causes, dynamics, prospects." *Race and Class* 40(2/3): 133–143.

Bello, Walden. 1999. "The Asian financial crisis: Causes, dynamics, prospects." *Journal of the Asia Pacific Economy* 4(1): 33–55.

Benatar, Solomon R., Stephen Gill, and Isabella Bakker. 2011. "Global health and the global economic crisis." *American Journal of Public Health* 101(4): 646-653.

Berer, Marge. 2011. "Repoliticising sexual and reproductive health and rights." *Reproductive Health Matters* 19(38): 4–10.

Berer, Marge, and Sundari Ravindran. 1996. "Fundamentalism, women's empowerment and reproductive rights." *Reproductive Health Matters* 4(8): 7–10.

Bergeron, Suzanne, Carol Cohn, and Claire Duncanson. 2017. "Rebuilding bridges: Toward a feminist research agenda for postwar reconstruction." *Politics and Gender* 13(4): 715–721.

Berowa, Alma. 2006. *Armed conflict in Lanao del Sur: Experiences and coping strategies of Maranao grassroots women*. Davao City, Philippines: Mindanao Working Group.

Beyani, Chaloka. 2015. "Statement of the United Nations Special Rapporteur on the human rights of internally displaced persons, Chaloka Beyani, on the conclusion of his official visit to the Philippines, 21 to 31 July 2015." July 31. http://www.ohchr.org/en/NewsEvents/Pages/DisplayNews.aspx?NewsID=16280&LangID=E.

Bhatia, Rajani, Jade S. Sasser, Diana Ojeda, Anne Hendrixson, Sarojini Nadimpally, and Ellen E. Foley. 2020. "A feminist exploration of 'populationism': Engaging contemporary forms of population control." *Gender, Place & Culture* 27(3): 333–350.

Bjorkdahl, Annika, Martin Hall, and Ted Svensson. 2019. "Everyday International Relations: Editor's introduction." *Cooperation and Conflict* 54(2): 123–130.

Bordadora, Norman. 2012. "Senate's RH bill retains clause on 'safe, satisfying sex.'" *The Inquirer*, December 5. https://newsinfo.inquirer.net/319077/senates-rh-bill-retains-clause-on-safe-satisfying-sex#ixzz6lYAzGP8k.

References [201]

Bosmans, Marleen, Dina Nasser, Umaiyeh Khammash, Patricia Claeys, and Marleen Temmerman. 2008. "Palestinian women's sexual and reproductive health rights in a longstanding humanitarian crisis." *Reproductive Health Matters* 16(31): 103–111.

Bracke, Sarah. 2014. "The unbearable lightness of 'gender and diversity.'" *DiGeSt: Journal of Diversity and Gender Studies* 1(1): 41–50.

Bradshaw, Sarah. 2014. "Engendering development and disasters." *Disasters* 39(S1): S54–S75.

Brennan, Seán. 2019. "Biopolitical peacebuilding—peace through health." *Peace Review* 31(2): 139–147.

Brickell, Katherine. 2012. "Geopolitics of home." *Geography Compass* 6(10): 575–588.

Brickell, Katherine, and Sylvia Chant. 2010. "'The unbearable heaviness of being': Reflections on female altruism in Cambodia, Philippines, The Gambia and Costa Rica." *Progress in Development Studies* 10(2): 145–159.

Brune, Nancy E. 2005. "Comparative study of contraceptive self-reliance (CSR) around the world: Lessons for the Philippines." October. Boston, MA: International Health Systems Program, School of Health, Harvard University.

Bujra, Janet. 2004. "AIDS as a crisis in social reproduction." *Review of African Political Economy* 31(102): 631–638.

Burke, Anthony, Stefanie Fishel, Audra Mitchell, Simon Dalby, and Daniel J. Levine. 2016. "Planet politics: A manifesto from the end of IR." *Millennium* 44(3): 499–523.

Busran-Lao, Yasmin. 2005. "Human development, economic and social costs, and spillovers of conflict: The case of the province of Lanao del Sur." Background paper. Quezon City: Human Development Network Foundation, Inc.

Cabaraban, Magdalena. 2006. *Conflict situations: Their consequences on reproductive health and reproductive rights*. Davao City, Philippines: Mindanao Working Group.

Cabato, Regine. 2016. "DOH secretary: Philippines lacks 15,000 doctors." *CNN Philippines*, October 13. http://cnnphilippines.com/news/2016/10/13/department-of-health-lack-of-doctors.html.

Cabusao, Amalia Bandiola. 2019. "Women commanders speak: 'How do you suppose the battle raged on for days and weeks if there was no BIWAB to support the men fighting?'" *Minda News*, March 27. https://www.mindanews.com/peace-process/2019/03/women-commanders-speak-how-do-you-suppose-the-battle-raged-on-for-days-and-weeks-if-there-was-no-biwab-to-support-the-men-fighting/.

Cagoco-Guiam, Rufa. 2013. *Gender and livelihoods among internally displaced persons in Mindanao, Philippines*. Brookings–LSE Project on Internal Displacement. Washington, DC: Brookings. https://www.brookings.edu/research/gender-and-livelihoods-among-internally-displaced-persons-in-mindanao-philippines/.

Calkin, Sydney. 2015. "'Tapping' women for post-crisis capitalism: Evidence from the 2012 world development report." *International Feminist Journal of Politics* 17(4): 611–629.

CBCP For Life. 2012. "March 25 marks 'Day of Unborn' in Ph, other nations." *CBCP For Life*, March 9.

CEDAW (Committee on the Elimination of Discrimination against Women). 2004. "Consideration of reports submitted by states parties under article 18 of the Convention on the Elimination of All Forms of Discrimination against Women: Combined fifth and sixth periodic reports of states parties: Philippines." CEDAW/C/PHI/5-6, August 2.

CEDAW (Committee on the Elimination of Discrimination against Women). 2006a. "Concluding comments of the Committee on the Elimination of Discrimination against Women: Philippines." CEDAW/C/PHI/CO/6, August 25.

CEDAW (Committee on the Elimination of Discrimination against Women). 2006b. "Declarations, reservations, objections and notifications of withdrawal of reservations relating to the Convention on the Elimination of All Forms of Discrimination against Women." CEDAW/SP/2006/2, April 10.

CEDAW (Committee on the Elimination of Discrimination against Women). 2015a. "Summary of the inquiry concerning the Philippines under article 8 of the Optional Protocol to the Convention on the Elimination of All Forms of Discrimination against Women." CEDAW/C/OP.8/PHL/1, April 22.

CEDAW (Committee on the Elimination of Discrimination against Women). 2015b. "Consideration of reports submitted by states parties under article 18: Combined seventh and eighth periodic reports of states parties due in 2010: Philippines." CEDAW/C/PHL/7-8, March 2.

Center for Reproductive Rights. 2016. "Hidden casualties: Sexual and reproductive health and rights and sexual violence in conflict." January. https://www.awid.org/sites/default/files/atoms/files/sexual_reproductive_rights_sexual_violence_in_conflict.pdf.

Centers for Disease Control and Prevention. 2019. "Racial and ethnic disparities continue in pregnancy-related deaths." *Press Release*, September 5. https://www.cdc.gov/media/releases/2019/p0905-racial-ethnic-disparities-pregnancy-deaths.html.

CESCR (Committee on Economic, Social and Cultural Rights). 2016. "General comment No. 22 (2016) on the right to sexual and reproductive health (article 12 of the International Covenant on Economic, Social and Cultural Rights)." E/C.12/GC/22, May 2.

Chandler, David, Erika Cudworth, and Stephen Hobden. 2018. "Anthropocene, Capitalocene and liberal cosmopolitan IR: A response to Burke et al.'s 'Planet Politics'." *Millennium* 46(2): 190–208.

Chandra, Alvin, Paul Dargusch, Karen E. McNamara, Ana Maria Caspe, and Dante Dalabajan. 2017. "A study of climate-smart farming practices and climate-resiliency field schools in Mindanao, the Philippines." *World Development* 98: 214–230.

Chant, Sylvia. 2010. "Towards a (re)conceptualisation of the 'feminisation of poverty': Reflections on gender-differentiated poverty from The Gambia, Philippines and Costa Rica." In *The international handbook of gender and poverty: Concepts, research, policy*, edited by Sylvia Chant, 111-116. Cheltenham: Edward Elgar.

Chappell, Louise. 2006. "Contesting women's rights: Charting the emergence of a transnational conservative counter-network." *Global Society* 20(4): 491-520.

Chhachhi, Amrita. 2014. "Religious fundamentalism and secular governance." In *The remaking of social contracts: Feminists in a fierce new world*, edited by Gita Sen and Marina Durano, 259–273. London: Zed Books.

Chiarella, Gregory M. 2012. "Sources of law, sources of authority: The failure of the Philippines' code of Muslim personal laws." *Pacific Rim Law and Policy Journal* 21(1): 223-254.

Chilmeran, Yasmin, and Nicola Pratt. 2019. "The geopolitics of social reproduction and depletion: The case of Iraq and Palestine." *Social Politics* 26 (3): 586–607.

Chin, Christine B. 1998. *In service and servitude: Foreign female domestic workers and the Malaysian "modernity" project*. New York: Columbia University Press.

Ching, Paola Katrina, Vikki Carr de los Reyes, Ma Nemia Sucaldito, and Enrique Tayag. 2015. "An assessment of disaster-related mortality post-Haiyan in Tacloban City." *Western Pacific Surveillance and Response Journal* 6(Suppl 1): 34-38. doi:10.5365/wpsar.2015.6.2.HYN_005.

Chinkin, Christine, and Madeleine Rees. 2019. *Commentary on Security Council Resolution 2467*. Centre for Women, Peace and Security Commentary Report. July 19. London: London School of Economics and Political Science. https://www.wilpf.org/wp-content/uploads/2019/07/19_0496_WPS_Commentary_Report_online.pdf.

Chopra, Deepta, and Caroline Sweetman. 2014. "Introduction to gender, development and care." *Gender and Development* 22(3): 409-421.

Chynoweth, Sarah K. 2015. "Advancing reproductive health on the humanitarian agenda: The 2012–2014 global review." *Conflict and Health* 9, Suppl 1(I1).

Climate Change Commission. n.d. "Programs: Gender and climate change." https://climate.gov.ph/our-programs/gender-and-climate-change.

Climate Change Commission. 2011. *National climate change action plan 2011-2028*. Manila: Climate Change Commission. https://drive.google.com/file/d/0B35e PJ5EjR1GUEotajFxVl9XRDA/view.

Cockburn, Cynthia. 2004. "The continuum of violence: A gender perspective on war and peace." In *Sites of violence: Gender and conflict zones*, edited by Jennifer Hyndman and Wenona Giles, 24–44. Berkeley: University of California Press.

Cockburn, Cynthia. 2010. "Gender relations as causal in militarization and war." *International Feminist Journal of Politics* 12(2): 139–157.

Cohn, Carol, Helen Kinsella, and Sheri Gibbings. 2004. "Women, Peace and Security Resolution 1325." *International Feminist Journal of Politics* 6(1): 130–140.

Cohn, Carol, and Claire Duncanson. 2020. "Women, Peace and Security in a changing climate." *International Feminist Journal of Politics* 22(5): 742–762.

Combahee River Collective. 1978/2014. "A Black Feminist Statement." *WSQ: Women's Studies Quarterly* 42(3–4): 271–280.

Comprehensive Agreement on the Bangsamoro. 2014. "Document. The Comprehensive Agreement on the Bangsamoro." *Official Gazette*, March 27. https://www.official gazette.gov.ph/2014/03/27/document-cab/.

Collins, Patricia Hill. 1989. "The Social Construction of Black Feminist Thought." *Signs* 14(4): 745–773.

Cook, Malcolm, and Kit Collier. 2006. "Mindanao: A gamble worth taking." Lowy Institute Paper 17. Sydney: Lowy Institute for International Policy. http://www.lowyinstitute.org/publications/mindanao-gamble-worth-taking.

Cook, Rebecca J., and Simone Cusack. 2010. *Gender stereotyping: Transnational legal perspectives*. Philadelphia: University of Pennsylvania Press.

Cook, Rebecca J., Joanna N. Erdman, and Bernard M. Dickens, eds. 2014. *Abortion law in transnational perspective: Cases and controversies*. Philadelphia: University of Pennsylvania Press.

Cooke, Bill, and Uma Kothari. 2001. *Participation: The new tyranny?* London: Zed Books.

Cooper, Melinda. 2015. "The theology of emergency: Welfare reform, US foreign aid and the faith based initiative." *Theory, Culture and Society* 32(2): 53–77.

Cornwall, Andrea. 2006. "Development's marginalisation by sexuality: Report of an IDS workshop." *Gender and Development* 14 (2): 273–289.

Corrêa, Sonia. 1994. *Population and reproductive rights: Feminist perspectives from the South*. London: Zed Books.

Corrêa, Sonia, Adrienne Germain, and Rosaline P. Petchesky. 2005. "Thinking beyond ICPD+10: Where should our movement be going?" *Reproductive Health Matters* 13(25): 109–119.

Cottingham, Jane, Eszter Kismödi, and Julia Hussein. 2019. "Sexual and reproductive health matters—what's in a name?" *Sexual and Reproductive Health Matters* 27(1): 1–3.

Crane, Barbara B., and Jennifer Dusenberry. 2004. "Power and politics in international funding for reproductive health: the US Global Gag Rule." *Reproductive Health Matters* 12(24): 128–137.

Cuomo, Chris J. 1998. *Feminism and ecological communities: An ethic of flourishing*. Hove, UK: Psychology Press.

Cupin, Bea. 2013. "Aqunio: Yolanda 'serious threat,' don't take chances." *Rappler*, 8 November. http://www.rappler.com/nation/43154-aquino-statement-yolanda.

Daguino, Dolores S., and Norma T. Gomez. 2010. "Reproductive health concerns among the internally displaced persons in Pikit, North Cotabato." *Tambara* 27(1).

David, Rina Jimenez. 2003. "Living with sin: The Catholic hierarchy and reproductive rights in the Philippines." *Conscience* 24(2): 18–21.

Davis, Angela. 1983. *Women, race and class*. New York: Vintage Books/Random House.

Davies, Sara E., Sophie Harman, Rashida Manjoo, Maria Tanyag, and Clare Wenham. 2019. "Why it must be a feminist global health agenda." *The Lancet* 393(10171): 601–603.

Davies, Sara E., Jacqui True, and Maria Tanyag. 2016. "How women's silence secures the peace: Analysing sexual and gender-based violence in a low-intensity conflict." *Gender and Development* 24(3): 459–473.

De La Rocha, Mercedes González. 2007. "The construction of the myth of survival." *Development and Change* 38(1): 45–66.

Demographic Research and Development Foundation. 2014. "Teenage pregnancy on the rise in the Philippines." February 6. http://www.drdf.org.ph/yafs4/pressrele ase/02-06-2014/06.

De Onis, Kathleen M. 2012. "'Looking both ways': Metaphor and the rhetorical alignment of intersectional climate justice and reproductive justice concerns." *Environmental Communication* 6(3): 308–327.

De Pauw. 2013. "Women's rights: From bad to worse? Assessing the evolution of incompatible reservations to the CEDAW Convention." *Merkourios-Utrecht Journal of International and European Law* 29(77): 51.

Derichs, Claudia, and Andrea Fleschenberg, eds. 2010. *Religious fundamentalisms and their gendered impacts in Asia*. Berlin: Friedrich-Ebert-Stiftung, Dept. for Asia and the Pacific.

Derichs, Claudia, and Mark R. Thompson, eds. 2013. *Dynasties and female political leaders in Asia: Gender, power and pedigree*. Berlin: Lit Verlag.

Deveaux, Monique. 1995. "Shifting paradigms: Theorizing care and justice in political theory." *Hypatia: A Journal of Feminist Philosophy* 10(2): 115–119.

Di Chiro, Giovanna. 2008. "Living environmentalisms: Coalition politics, social reproduction, and environmental justice." *Environmental Politics* 17(2): 276–298.

Di Chiro, Giovanna. 2017. "Welcome to the White (m)anthropocene? A feminist-environmentalist critique." In *Routledge Handbook of Gender and Environment*, edited by Sherilyn MacGregor, 487–505. Abingdon, UK: Routledge.

Dominguez, Silvia, and Cecilia Menjivar. 2014. "Beyond individual and visible acts of violence: A framework to examine the lives of women in low-income neighborhoods." *Women's Studies International Forum* 44: 184-195.

Doyal, Lesley. 1995. *What makes women sick: Gender and the political economy of health.* Basingstoke, UK: Palgrave Macmillan.

Dresse, Anaïs, Itay Fischhendler, Jonas Østergaard Nielsen, and Dimitrios Zikos. 2019. "Environmental peacebuilding: Towards a theoretical framework." *Cooperation and Conflict* 54(1): 99–119.

DSWD (Department of Social Welfare and Development). 2014. "Initial report on the conduct of focus group discussion on women friendly space." September 11. Tacloban: DSWD Field Office VIII.

Duncanson, Claire. 2016. *Gender and peacebuilding.* Cambridge: Polity Press.

Dwyer, Leslie, and Rufa Cagoco-Guiam. 2012. *Gender and conflict in Mindanao.* San Francisco: Asia Foundation. http://asiafoundation.org/resources/pdfs/GenderConflictinMindanao.pdf.

Economist Intelligence Unit. 2014. "The South Asia Women's Resilience Index: Examining the role of women in preparing for and recovering from disasters." Report. December. London: The Economist. https://www.gdnonline.org/resources/The%20South%20Asia%20Women%27s%20Resilience%20Index%20Dec8.pdf.

Edwards, Louise, and Mina Roces, eds. 2004. *Women's suffrage in Asia: Gender, nationalism and democracy.* London: Routledge.

Ehrenreich, Barbara, and Arlie Russell Hochschild. 2003. *Global woman: Nannies, maids, and sex workers in the new economy.* London: Metropolitan Books.

Elias, Juanita. 2004. *Fashioning inequality: The multinational company and gendered employment in a globalizing world.* Burlington, UK: Ashgate Publishing.

Elias, Juanita. 2010. "Making migrant domestic work visible: The rights based approach to migration and the 'challenges of social reproduction.'" *Review of International Political Economy* 17(5): 840–859.

Elias, Juanita. 2016. "Whose crisis? Whose recovery? Lessons learned (and not) from the Asian crisis." In *Scandalous economics: Gender and the politics of crises*, edited by Aida A. Hozic and Jacqui True, 109–125. New York: Oxford University Press.

Elias, Juanita, and Samanthi J. Gunawardana, eds. 2013. *The global political economy of the household in Asia.* Basingstoke, UK: Palgrave Macmillan.

Elias, Juanita, and Shirin Rai. 2015. "The everyday gendered political economy of violence." *Politics and Gender* 11(2): 424–429.

Elias, Juanita, and Adrienne Roberts. 2016. "Feminist global political economies of the everyday: From bananas to bingo." *Globalizations* 13(6): 787–800.

Elomaki, Anna, and Johanna Kantola. 2018. "Theorizing feminist struggles in the triangle of neoliberalism, conservatism, and nationalism." *Social Politics: International Studies in Gender, State & Society* 25(3): 337–360.

Elshtain, Jean Bethke. 1987. *Women and war.* New York: Basic Books.

Elson, Diane. 2009. "Social reproduction in the global crisis." UNRISD Conference on Social and Political Dimensions on the Global Crisis, University of Essex, November, 12–13.

Elson, Diane. 2010. "Gender and the global economic crisis in developing countries: A framework for analysis." *Gender and Development* 18(2): 201–212.

Elson, Diane. 2012. "Social reproduction in the global crisis: Rapid recovery or long-lasting depletion?" In *The global crisis and transformative social change*, edited by Peter Utting, Shahra Razavi, and Rebecca Varghese Buchholz, 63–80. Basingstoke, UK: Palgrave Macmillan.

Elson, Diane. 2013. "Economic crises from the 1980s to the 2010s: A gender analysis." *New Frontiers in Feminist Political Economy* 189: 190–212.

[206] *References*

Enloe, Cynthia. 1989/2000. *Bananas, beaches and bases: Making feminist sense of international politics*. Berkeley: University of California Press.

Enloe, Cynthia. 2000. *Maneuvers: The international politics of militarizing women's lives*. Berkeley: University of California Press.

Enloe, Cynthia. 2004. *The curious feminist: Searching for women in a new age of empire*. Berkeley: University of California Press.

Enloe, Cynthia. 2011. "The mundane matters." *International Political Sociology* 11(2): 447–450.

Enloe, Cynthia. 2013. *Seriously: Investigating crashes and crises as if women mattered*. Berkeley: University of California Press.

Estrada Claudio, Sylvia. 2010. "Sanctifying moral tyranny: Religious fundamentalisms and the political disempowerment of women." In *Religious fundamentalisms and their gendered impacts in Asia*, edited by Claudia Derichs and Andrea Fleschenberg, 13-26. Berlin: Friedrich Ebert Stiftung.

Fabros, Mercy, Aileen May C. Paguntalan, Lourdes Arches, and Maria Teresa Guia-Padilla. 1998. "From Sanas to Dapat: Negotiating entitlement in reproductive decision-making in the Philippines." In *Negotiating reproductive rights: Women's perspectives across countries and cultures*, edited by Rosalin Petchesky and Karen Judd, 217–255. London: Zed Books.

Fangen, Katrine, and Inger Skjelsbæk. 2020. "Editorial: Special issue on gender and the far right." *Politics, Religion & Ideology* 21(4): 411–415.

Federici, Silvia. 2012. *Revolution at Point Zero*. Oakland, CA: PM Press.

Federici, Silvia. 2014. *Caliban and the witch: Women, the body and primitive accumulation*, 2nd ed. New York: Autonomomedia.

Ferree, Myra Marx, and Aili Mari Tripp. 2006. *Global feminism: Transnational women's activism, organizing, and human rights*. New York: New York University Press.

Ferris, Elizabeth. 2005. "Faith-based and secular humanitarian organizations." *International Review of the Red Cross* 87(858): 311-325.

Fierke, K. M. 2012. *Political self-sacrifice: Agency, body and emotion in international relations*. Cambridge: Cambridge University Press.

Fishel, Stefanie, Anthony Burke, Audra Mitchell, Simon Dalby, and Daniel Levine. 2018. "Defending planet politics." *Millennium* 46(2): 209–219.

Folbre, Nancy. 2014. "The care economy in Africa: Subsistence production and unpaid care." *Journal of African Economies* 23(Suppl 1): i128–i156.

Fonn, Sharon, and T.K. Sundari Ravindran. 2011. "The macroeconomic environment and sexual and reproductive health: A review of trends over the last 30 years." *Reproductive Health Matters* 19(38): 11-25.

Framework Agreement on the Bangsamoro. 2012. October 15. https://peacemaker.un.org/sites/peacemaker.un.org/files/PH_121015_FrameworkAgreementBangsamoro.pdf.

Fraser, Nancy. 2005. "Mapping the feminist imagination: From redistribution to recognition to representation." *Constellations* 12(3): 295-307.

Fraser, Nancy. 2013. *Fortunes of feminism: From state-managed capitalism to neoliberal crisis*. New York: Verso.

Fraser, Nancy. 2017. "Crisis of care? On the social-reproductive contradictions of contemporary capitalism." In *Social reproduction theory: Remapping class, recentering oppression*, edited by Tithi Bhattacharya and Liselotte Vogel, 21–36. London: Pluto Press.

Gabieta, Joey A. 2015. "After 'Yolanda,' Tacloban pregnancies rise." *Inquirer*, February 14. http://newsinfo.inquirer.net/672843/after-yolanda-tacloban-pregnancies-rise.

References [207]

Gaillard, J.C., and Christopher Gomez. 2015. "Post-disaster research: Is there gold worth the rush?" *Jàmbá: Journal of Disaster Risk Studies* 7(1): 1-6.

Gezinski, Lindsay B. 2012. "The Global Gag Rule: Impacts of conservative ideology on women's health." *International Social Work* 55(6): 837–849.

Gibson-Graham, J.K. 2011. "A feminist project of belonging for the Anthropocene." *Gender, Place & Culture* 18(1): 1–21.

Gill, Stephen, and Isabella Bakker. 2011. "The global crisis and global health." In *Global health and global health ethics*, edited by Solomon Benatar and Gillian Brock, 221-238. Cambridge: Cambridge University Press.

Global Network of Women Peacebuilders. 2011. "Security Council Resolution 1325: Civil society monitoring report 2011: Philippines." New York: Global Network of Women Peacebuilders. https://gnwp.org/wp-content/uploads/Philippines_0.pdf.

Global Network of Women Peacebuilders. 2014. "Security Council Resolution 1325: Civil society monitoring report 2014: Women count." October. New York: Global Network of Women Peacebuilders. https://gnwp.org/wp-content/uploads/Civil-Society-Monitoring-Report-2014.pdf.

Global Nonviolent Action Database. 2011. "Filipino women enforce village peace through sex strike, 2011." July. Campaign. Dado, Maguindanao, Mindanao: Global Nonviolent Action Database. http://nvdatabase.swarthmore.edu/content/filipino-women-enforce-village-peace-through-sex-strike-2011.

Global Witness. 2017. *Defenders of the Earth: Global killings of land and environmental defenders in 2016*. London: Global Witness.

Goldblatt, Beth, and Shirin Rai. 2018. "Recognizing the full costs of care? Compensation for families in South Africa's silicosis class action." *Social & Legal Studies* 27(6): 671–694.

Goodenough, Patrick. 2008. "Pro-life victory as Philippines bans 'morning-after pill'." *CNSNews*, July 7. https://www.cnsnews.com/news/article/pro-life-victory-philippines-bans-morning-after-pill.

Gready, Paul, and Simon Robins. 2014. "From transitional to transformative justice: A new agenda for practice." *International Journal of Transitional Justice* 8(3): 339–361.

Griffin, Penny. 2015. "Crisis, austerity and gendered governance: A feminist perspective." *Feminist Review* 109: 49–72.

Griffin, Penny. 2016. "Gender, finance, and embodiments of crisis." In *Scandalous economics*, edited by Aida A. Hozic and Jacqui True, 179–202. New York: Oxford University Press.

Grove, Jairus. 2019. *Savage ecology: War and geopolitics at the end of the world*. Durham, NC: Duke University Press.

Guijt, Irene, and Meera Kaul Shah, eds. 1998. *The myth of community: Gender issues in participatory development*. Rugby, UK: Practical Action Publishing.

Hall, Lucy, and Laura J. Shepherd. 2013. "WPS and R2P: Theorising responsibility and protection." In *Responsibility to protect and women, peace and security: Aligning the protection agendas*, edited by Sara E. Davies, Zim Nwokora, Eli Stamnes, and Sarah Teitt, 53–80. Leiden: Brill.

Haraway, Donna Jeanne. 1988. "Situated knowledges: The science question in feminism and the privilege of partial perspective." *Feminist Studies* 14(3): 575–599.

Haraway, Donna Jeanne. 2016. *Staying with the trouble: Making kin in the Chthulucene*. Durham, NC: Duke University Press.

Harding, Sandra. 1986. *The science question in feminism*. Ithaca, NY: Cornell University Press.

Harman, Sophie. 2015. "15 years of 'war on AIDS': What impact has the global HIV/AIDS response had on the political economy of Africa?" *Review of African Political Economy* 42(145): 467–76.

Harman, Sophie. 2016. "Ebola, gender and conspicuously invisible women in global health governance." *Third World Quarterly* 37(3): 524–541.

Harris, Elise. 2015. "Pope Francis hails motherhood as the 'antidote to individualism.'" *Catholic News Agency*, January 7. http://www.catholicnewsagency.com/news/pope-francis-hails-motherhood-as-the-antidote-to-individualism-41388/.

Hartmann, Betsy. 2016. *Reproductive rights and wrongs: The global politics of population control*, 3rd ed. Haymarket Books.

HD Centre (The Centre for Humanitarian Dialogue). 2011. *Armed Violence in Mindanao: Militia and private armies*. Geneva, Switzerland: Centre for Humanitarian Dialogue. https://www.hdcentre.org/wp-content/uploads/2016/07/17MilitiainMindanaoreportfromIBSandHDCentreJuly2011-July-2011.pdf.

Hedstrom, Jenny. 2017. "The political economy of the Kachin revolutionary household." *The Pacific Review* 30(4): 581–595.

Heidari, Shirin, Monica A. Onyango, and Sarah Chynoweth. 2019. "Sexual and reproductive health and rights in humanitarian crises at ICPD25+ and beyond: Consolidating gains to ensure access to services for all." *Sexual and Reproductive Health Matters* 27(1): 343–345.

Hendrixson, Anne, Diana Ojeda, Jade S. Sasser, Sarojini Nadimpally, Ellen E. Foley, and Rajani Bhatia. 2019. "Confronting populationism: Feminist challenges to population control in an era of climate change." *Gender, Place & Culture*. DOI: 10.1080/0966369X.2019.1639634.

Herd, Pamela, and Madonna Harrington Meyer. 2002. "Care work: Invisible civic engagement." *Gender and Society* 16(5): 665–688.

Herrin, Alejandro N., and Ernesto M. Pernia. 2003. "Population, human resources, and employment." In *The Philippine economy: Development, policies, and challenges*, edited by Arsenio M. Balisacan and Hal Hill, 283–310. New York: Oxford University Press.

Hilsdon, Anne-Marie. 1995. *Madonnas and martyrs: Militarism and violence in the Philippines*. Manila: Ateneo University Press.

Hilsdon, Anne-Marie. 2009. "Invisible bodies: Gender, conflict and peace in Mindanao." *Asian Studies Review* 33(3): 349–365.

Holden, William, and Kathleen Nadeau. 2010. "Philippine liberation theology and social development in anthropological perspective." *Philippine Quarterly of Culture and Society* 38(2): 89–129.

hooks, bell. 1984. *Feminist theory: From margin to center*. Boston, MA: South End Press.

Hoskyns, Catherine, and Shirin M. Rai. 2007. "Recasting the global political economy: Counting women's unpaid work." *New Political Economy* 12(3): 297–317.

Houseman, Michael. 2013. "Make love not war: Sex and peacebuilding in Mindanao." *Insight on Conflict*, March 22. https://www.insightonconflict.org/blog/2013/03/sex-peacebuilding-mindanao/.

Hozic, Aida A., and Jacqui True, eds. 2016. *Scandalous economics: Gender and the politics of financial crises*. New York: Oxford University Press.

Htun, Mala. 2003. *Sex and the state: Abortion, divorce, and the family under Latin American dictatorships and democracies*. New York: Cambridge University Press.

References [209]

Htun, Mala, and S. Laural Weldon. 2018. *The logics of gender justice.* New York: Cambridge University Press.

Hudson, Valerie M., Donna Lee Bowen, and Perpetua Lynne Nielsen. 2015. "Clan governance and state stability: The relationship between female subordination and political order." *American Political Science Review* 109(3): 535–555.

Human Development Network. 2012-2013. *Philippine human development report 2012/2013.* Quezon City: Human Development Network.

Human Life International. 2012. "No controversy? Facts for Melinda Gates." July 12, 2012. YouTube video. https://www.youtube.com/watch?feature=player_embed ded&v=IuitL4XhDAA#.

Human Rights Watch. 2010. "They own the people: The Ampatuans, state-backed militias, and killings in the southern Philippines." Report. November 16. New York: Human Rights Watch. https://www.hrw.org/report/2010/11/16/they-own-people/ampatuans-state-backed-militias-and-killings-southern-phil ippines.

IBON Foundation. 2006. *Uncounted lives: Children, women and conflict in the Philippines.* Makati City: UNICEF and IBON Foundation.

IDMC (Internal Displacement Monitoring Centre). 2009. "Cycle of conflict and neglect: Mindanao's displacement and protection crisis." Geneva: IDMC and Norwegian Refugee Council.

IDMC (Internal Displacement Monitoring Centre). 2015a. *Disaster-related displacement risk: Measuring the risk and addressing its drivers.* Geneva: IDMC. https://www.internal-displacement.org/sites/default/files/publications/documents/20150312-global-disaster-related-displacement-risk-en.pdf.

IDMC (Internal Displacement Monitoring Centre). 2015b. "Philippines: Long-term recovery challenges remain in the wake of massive displacement." February 10. Geneva: ISMC. https://www.internal-displacement.org/sites/default/files/publications/documents/201502-ap-philippines-overview-en.pdf.

Institute of Bangsamoro Studies and the Centre for Humanitarian Dialogue. 2011. *Armed violence in Mindanao: Militia and private armies.* July. Geneva: Centre for Humanitarian Dialogue.

Inter-Agency Working Group on Reproductive Health in Crises. 2010. *Inter-agency field manual on reproductive health in humanitarian settings.* Geneva: Inter-Agency Working Group on Reproductive Health in Crises.

International Alert. 2014. "Rebellion, political violence and shadow crimes in the Bangsamoro: The Bangsamoro Conflict Monitoring System (BCMS), 2011-2013." August. London: International Alert UK. http://www.internatio nal-alert.org/resources/publications/rebellion-political-violence-and-shadow-crimes-bangsamoro.

IOM (International Organization for Migration), DSWD (Department of Social Welfare and Development), IDMC (Internal Displacement Monitoring Centre), and SAS. 2014. "The evolving picture of displacement in the wake of Typhoon Haiyan: An evidence-based overview." May. http://www.iom.int/files/live/sites/iom/files/Country/docs/The-Evolving-Picture-of-Displacement-in-the-Wake-of-Typh oon-Haiyan.pdf.

IPCC (Intergovernmental Panel on Climate Change). 2018. *Global warming of 1.5 ºC.* Geneva: Intergovernmental Panel on Climate Change. https://www.ipcc.ch/sr15/.

IUCN (International Union for Conservation of Nature). 2013. *The Environment and Gender Index (EGI): 2013 pilot.* Washington, DC: IUCN.

IUCN (International Union for Conservation of Nature). 2015. *Women's participation in global environmental decision making: An EGI supplemental report*. Washington, DC: IUCN.

Jamar, Astrid, and Christine Bell. 2018. *Transitional justice and peace negotiations with a gender lens*. Gender Briefing Series. New York: UN Women.

Jayawardena, Kumari. 1986. *Feminism and nationalism in the Third World*. London: Zed Books.

Jenkins, Katy. 2014. "Women, mining and development: An emerging research agenda." *The Extractive Industries and Society* 1(2): 329–339.

Jimenez, Laura, Kierra Johnson, and Cara Page. 2017. "Beyond the trees: Stories and strategies of environmental and reproductive justice." In *Radical reproductive justice: Foundation, theory, practice, critique*, edited by Loretta Ross, Lynn Roberts, Erika Derkas, Whitney Peoples, and Pamela Bridgewater, 361–380. New York: The Feminist Press.

Jolly, Susie. 2010. "Why the development industry should get over its obsession with bad sex and start to think about pleasure." In *Development, sexual rights and global governance*, edited by Amy Lind, 23-38. Abingdon, UK: Routledge.

Kandiyoti, Deniz. 1988. "Bargaining with patriarchy." *Gender and Society* 2(3): 274-290.

Kandiyoti, Deniz. 2015. "The triple whammy: Towards the eclipse of women's rights." *Open Democracy*, January 19. https://www.opendemocracy.net/5050/triple-whammy-towards-eclipse-of-women-rights.

Keller, Linda. 2014. "The impact of states parties' reservation to the Convention on the Elimination of All Forms of Discrimination against Women." *Michigan State Law Review*: 309–326.

Keown, Michelle. 2018. "Waves of destruction: Nuclear imperialism and anti-nuclear protest in the indigenous literatures of the Pacific." *Journal of Postcolonial Writing* 54(5): 585–600.

Klein, Naomi. 2014. *This changes everything: Capitalism vs. the climate*. New York: Simon & Schuster.

Kok, Frederik. 2015. "Philippines: Why housing rights must be prioritised to end displacement of Zamboanga's urban poor." IDMC Briefing Paper. January 15. Geneva: IDMC. https://reliefweb.int/sites/reliefweb.int/files/resources/Phil ippines%20Why%20housing%20rights%20must%20be%20prioritized.pdf.

Kothari, Uma. 2001. "Participation: the new tyranny?" In *Power, knowledge and social control in participatory development*, edited by Bill Cooke and Uma Kothari, 139–152. London: Zed Books.

Krange, Olve, Bjørn Kaltenborn, and Martin Hultman. 2019. "Cool dudes in Norway: Climate change denial among conservative Norwegian men." *Environmental Sociology* 5(1): 1–11.

Krause, Jana, Werner Krause, and Piia Bränfors. 2018. "Women's participation in peace negotiations and the durability of peace." *International Interactions* 44(6): 985–1016.

Kreft, Sönke, David Eckstein, Lukas Dorsch, and Livia Fischer. 2015. *Global climate risk index 2016: Who suffers most from extreme weather events? Weather-related loss events in 2014 and 1995 to 2014*. Bonn and Berlin: GermanWatch. https://germ anwatch.org/sites/germanwatch.org/files/publication/13503.pdf.

Kunz, Rahel. 2010. "The crisis of social reproduction in rural Mexico: Challenging the 're-privatization of social reproduction' thesis." *Review of International Political Economy* 17(5): 913-945.

Lahiri-Dutt, Kuntala. 2012. "Digging women: Towards a new agenda for feminist critiques of mining." *Gender, Place & Culture* 19(2): 193–212.

Lakshminarayanan, Rama. 2003. "Decentralisation and its implications for reproductive health: The Philippines experience." *Reproductive Health Matters* 11(21): 96–107.

Lappé, Martine, Robbin Jeffries Hein, and Hannah Landecker. 2019. "Environmental politics of reproduction." *Annual Review of Anthropology* 48: 133–150.

Lee, Romeo B. 2008. "Delivering maternal health care services in an internal conflict setting in Maguindanao, Philippines." *Reproductive Health Matters* 16(31): 65–74.

Lee, Romeo B., Lourdes P. Nacionalies, and Luis Pedroso. 2009. "The influence of local policy on contraceptive provision and use in three locales in the Philippines." *International Journal on Sexual and Reproductive Health and Rights* 17(34): 99–107.

Leyesa, Daryl. 2012. "Let peace reign in Mindanao: Support 'Kefeduwan Libun,' recognize indigenous women arbiters." Human Rights Online Philippines, March 31. https://hronlineph.com/2012/03/31/from-the-web-let-peace-reign-in-minda nao-support-kefeduwan-libun-recognize-indigenous-women-arbiters/.

Likhaan, ReproCen, and Center for Reproductive Rights. 2007/2010. *Imposing misery: The impact of Manila's contraception ban on women and families*. New York: Center for Reproductive Rights.

Lind, Amy. 2009. "Governing intimacy, struggling for sexual rights: Challenging heteronormativity in the global development industry." *Development* 52(1): 34–42.

LSE Centre for Women, Peace and Security, Women International Peace Centre and Gender Action for Peace and Security. 2021. *Defending the future: Gender, conflict and environmental peace*. https://www.lse.ac.uk/women-peace-security/assets/ documents/2021/Defending-the-Future.pdf.

Lorde, Audre. 1988. *A burst of light: Essays*. Ithaca, NY: Firebrand Books.

Lugones, María. 2010. "Toward a decolonial feminism." *Hypatia* 25(4): 742–759.

Luna, Melissa, Lorena Aguilar, Molly Gilligan, Cate Owren, Maria Prebble, and Kame Westerman. 2015. *Women in environmental decision making: Case studies in Ecuador, Liberia, and the Philippines*. Washington, DC: Global Gender Office of IUCN, in collaboration with Conservation International. https://genderandenvi ronment.org/wp-content/uploads/2015/02/CI-REPORT.pdf.

Macaraig, Ayee. 2012. "Enrile: 'Our biggest export is OFWs. That's why I'm against RH bill.'" *Rappler*, November 29. http://www.rappler.com/nation/16987-enrile-our-biggest-export-is-ofws-that-s-why-im-against-rh-bill.

Macaraig, Aye. 2013. "Anderson Cooper: An honor to report on PH." *Rappler*, November 22. https://www.rappler.com/move-ph/issues/disasters/typhoon-yolanda/ 44301-anderson-cooper-reflections-haiyan-coverage.

MacGregor, Sherilyn. 2017. *Routledge handbook of gender and environment*. Abingdon, UK: Routledge.

Magcalen-Fernandez, Ederlinda. 2006. *Conflict, state fragility and women's reproductive health: The case of Basilan, Philippines*. Davao City, Philippines: Mindanao Working Group.

Mangada, Ladylyn Lim. 2015. *Missing: Who is in charge?* Ann Arbor: WDI Publishing, University of Michigan.

Mangada, Ladylyn Lim. 2016. "Post-Haiyan adaptation and institutional barriers to women survivors in Tacloban." *Philippine Political Science Journal* 37(2): 94–110.

Manila Times. 2013. "Emily Marohombsar, MSU's first woman president, dies." May 25.

Marchand, Marianne H., and Anne Sisson Runyan. 2010. *Gender and global restructuring: Sightings, sites and resistances*. Abingdon, UK: Routledge.

Margallo, Sonia. 2005. "Addressing gender in conflict and post-conflict situations in the Philippines." Social Development Papers on Conflict Prevention and Reconstruction no. 20. Washington, DC: World Bank. http://documents.worldb ank.org/curated/en/244881468758997582/pdf/314420SDP02001public1.pdf.

Martin de Almagro, Maria, and Caitlin Ryan. 2019. "Subverting economic empowerment: Towards a postcolonial-feminist framework on gender (in)securities in post-war settings." *European Journal of International Relations* 25(4): 1059–1079.

McCoy, Alfred, ed. 2009. *An anarchy of families: State and family in the Philippines.* Madison: University of Wisconsin Press.

McCright, Aaron, and Riley Dunlap. 2011. "Cool dudes: The denial of climate change among conservative white males in the United States." *Global Environmental Change* 21(4): 1163–1172.

McCright, Aaron, and Riley Dunlap. 2015. "Bringing ideology in: The conservative white male effect on worry about environmental problems in the USA." *Journal of Risk Research* 16(2): 211–226.

McGovern, Terry, and Anand Tamang. 2020. "Exporting bad policy: An introduction to the special issue on the GGR's impact." *Sexual and Reproductive Health Matters* 28(3): 1–4.

McInnes, Colin, and Kelley Lee. 2006. "Health, security and foreign policy." *Review of International Studies* 32(1): 5–23.

McSherry, Alice, Eric Julian Manalastas, J.C. Gaillard, and Soledad Natalia M. Dalisay. 2015. "From deviant to *Bakla*, strong to stronger: Mainstreaming sexual and gender minorities into disaster risk reduction in the Philippines." *Forum for Development Studies* 42(1): 27–40.

Meger, Sara. 2016. "War as feminized labour in the global political economy of neoimperialism." *Postcolonial Studies* 19(4): 378–392.

Melgar, Junice, et al. 2018. "Assessment of country policies affecting reproductive health for adolescents in the Philippines." *Reproductive Health* 15(205): 1–13.

Merchant, Carolyn. 1981. "Earthcare: Women and the environment." *Environment: Science and Policy for Sustainable Development* 23(5): 6–40.

Merchant, Carolyn. 2017. *Science and nature: Past, present, and future.* New York: Routledge.

Mies, Maria. 1982/2012. *The lace makers of Narsapur.* Spinifex Press.

Mies, Maria. 1993/2014. "Feminist research: Science, violence and responsibility." *Ecofeminism* 36: 47.

Mies, Maria, and Vandana Shiva. 1993/2014. *Ecofeminism.* London: Zed Books.

Mertens, Charlotte, and Maree Pardy. 2017. "'Sexurity' and its effects in eastern Democratic Republic of Congo." *Third World Quarterly* 38(4): 956–979.

Mitter, Swasti. 1986. *Common fate, common bond: Women in the global economy.* Wolfeboro, NH: Pluto Press.

Mohanty, Chandra Talpade. 2003. *Feminism without borders: Decolonizing theory, practicing solidarity.* Durham, NC: Duke University Press.

Mohindra, K.S., Ronald Labonté, and Denise Spitzer. 2011. "The global financial crisis: Whither women's health?" *Critical Public Health* 21(3): 273-287.

Molyneux, Maxine. 2007. "Change and continuity in social protection in Latin America: Mothers at the service of the state?" Gender and Development Paper 1. Geneva: UNRISD.

Moore, Jason. 2017. "The Capitalocene, Part I: On the nature and origins of our ecological crisis." *The Journal of Peasant Studies* 44(3): 594–630.

References [213]

Moore, Jason. 2018. "The Capitalocene, Part II: Accumulation by appropriation and the centrality of unpaid work/energy." *The Journal of Peasant Studies* 45(2): 237–279.

Monte de Ramos, Grace. 2003. "Brave woman." In *Poets against the war*, edited by Sam Hamill, 142-143. New York: Thunder's Mouth Press/Nation Books.

Montillo-Burton, Erlinda, Moctar Matuan, Guimba Poingan, and Jay Alovera. 2014. "Responses to interkin group conflict in Northern Mindanao." In *Rido: Clan feuding and conflict management in Mindanao*, expanded ed., edited by Wilfredo M. Torres III, 118-154. Manila: Asia Foundation and Ateneo de Manila University Press.

Mora, Camilo, Daniele Spirandelli, Erk C. Franklin, Michael B. Kantar, Wendy Miles, Charlotte Z. Smith, et al. 2018. "Broad threat to humanity from cumulative climate hazards intensified by greenhouse gas emissions." *Nature Climate Change* 8(12): 1062–1071.

Mountz, Alison, and Jennifer Hyndman. 2006. "Feminist approaches to the global intimate." *Women's Studies Quarterly* 34 (1/2): 446–463.

Muehlebach, Andrea. 2013. "The Catholicization of neoliberalism: On love and welfare in Lombardy, Italy." *American Anthropologist* 115(3): 452–465.

Musawah. 2009. "Home truths: A global report on equality in the Muslim family." Selangor: SIS Forum Malaysia.

Nader, Laura. 1972. "Up the anthropologist: Perspectives gained from studying up." https://files.eric.ed.gov/fulltext/ED065375.pdf.

Nakashima, Douglas, Igor Krupnik, and Jennifer T. Rubis, eds. 2018. *Indigenous knowledge for climate change assessment and adaptation*. Cambridge: Cambridge University Press and UNESCO.

National Disaster Risk Reduction and Management Council. 2012. "National disaster risk reduction and management plan (NDRRMP) 2011-2028." https://ndrrmc. gov.ph/attachments/article/41/NDRRM_Plan_2011-2028.pdf.

New Humanitarian. 2008. "Women suffer most in Mindanao." November 28. http:// www.thenewhumanitarian.org/report/81708/philippines-women-suffer-most-mindanao-conflict.

New Humanitarian. 2010. "Early marriage puts girls at risk." January 26. http:// www.thenewhumanitarian.org/report/87873/philippines-early-marriage-puts-girls-risk.

New Humanitarian. 2012. "Lack of services fuels teen pregnancy." March 15. http:// www.thenewhumanitarian.org/report/95076/philippines-lack-services-fuels-teen-pregnancy.

Ní Aoláin, Fionnuala. 2009. "Exploring a feminist theory of harm in the context of conflicted and post-conflict societies." *Queen's Law Journal* 35(1): 219–244.

Nicolas, Imelda. 2012. "The economic crisis and overseas Filipinos' remittances: Learning to build a future back home." Paper presented at the Metropolis ISC Meeting, Mexico, March.

Nisa Ul Haqq Fi Bangsamoro. 2014. "Survey of Zamboanga IDPs." Internal Report. Geneva: UNHCR.

Nixon, Rob. 2011. *Slow violence and the environmentalism of the poor*. Boston, MA: Harvard University Press.

Norwegian Agency for Development Cooperation (Norad). 2013. *Lobbying for faith and family: A study of religious NGOs at the United Nations*. Oslo: Norad. https://www. norad.no/globalassets/import-2162015-80434-am/www.norad.no-ny/filarkiv/ vedlegg-til-publikasjoner/lobbying-for-faith-and-family.pdf.

Norris, Pippa, and Ronald Inglehart. 2019. *Cultural backlash: Trump, Brexit, and authoritarian populism*. Cambridge: Cambridge University Press.

Novales, Clementine Louise. 2014. *Haiyan gender snapshot: Leyte, Eastern Samar and Northern Cebu*. Quezon City: Oxfam.

Nunes, João. 2014. "Questioning health security: Insecurity and domination in world politics." *Review of International Studies* 40(5): 939–960.

Nunes, João. 2020. "The everyday political economy of health: community health workers and the response to the 2015 Zika outbreak in Brazil." *Review of International Political Economy* 27(1): 146–166.

OCHA (United Nations Office for the Coordination of Humanitarian Affairs). 2013. "Philippines: Typhoon Haiyan action plan." November 22. http://docs.unocha.org/sites/dms/CAP/2013_Philippines_Typhoon_Haiyan_Action_Plan.pdf.

OCHA (United Nations Office for the Coordination of Humanitarian Affairs). 2014. "Philippines: Zamboanga, a forgotten crisis in the shadow of Haiyan." January 3. http://www.unocha.org/story/philippines-zamboanga-forgotten-crisis-shadow-haiyan.

OCHA (United Nations Office for the Coordination of Humanitarian Affairs). 2015a. "Philippines: Mindanao humanitarian snapshot." March 31. http://reliefweb.int/report/philippines/philippines-mindanao-humanitarian-snapshot-31-mar-2015.

OCHA (United Nations Office for the Coordination of Humanitarian Affairs). 2015b. "Zamboanga humanitarian snapshot." Geneva: OCHA, January 30. http://reliefweb.int/report/philippines/philippines-zamboanga-humanitarian-snapshot-30-jan-2015.

OCHA (United Nations Office for the Coordination of Humanitarian Affairs). 2015c. "Philippines: Mindanao humanitarian snapshot." March 3. Geneva: OCHA. https://www.humanitarianresponse.info/en/operations/philippines/infographic/mindanao-humanitarian-snapshot-03march2015.

OCHA (United Nations Office for the Coordination of Humanitarian Affairs). 2015d. "Philippines: Autonomous Region in Muslim Mindanao (ARMM) profile." December 1. Geneva: OCHA. http://reliefweb.int/report/philippines/philippines-autonomous-region-muslim-mindanao-armm-profile-1-dec-2015.

OCHA (United Nations Office for the Coordination of Humanitarian Affairs). 2015e. "Philippines: Typhoon Haiyan—November 2013: Total funding per donor as of 17 August 2015." Financial Tracking Service. Geneva: OCHA. https://fts.unocha.org/appeals/441/summary.

OECD (Organisation for Economic Co-operation and Development). 2016. *States of fragility 2016: Understanding violence*. Paris: OECD Publishing.

Ogden, Lesley Evans. 2018. "Environmental peacebuilding." *BioScience* 68(3): 157–163.

OHCHR (Office of the High Commissioner for Human Rights). 2018. "Framework of Cooperation between the CEDAW Committee and the Special Rapporteur on Violence Against Women (SRVAW)." November 8. Geneva: OHCHR. https://www.ohchr.org/Documents/Issues/Women/SR/SRVAW_CEDAW_Framework Cooperation.pdf.

OHCHR (Office of the High Commissioner for Human Rights). 2020. "Statistical survey on individual complaints: Status of communications registered by CEDAW under the Optional Protocol." January 28. https://www.ohchr.org/en/hrbodies/cedaw/pages/cedawindex.aspx.

Ojeda, Diana, Jade S. Sasser, and Elizabeth Lunstrom. 2020. "Malthus's specter and the Anthropocene." *Gender, Place and Culture* 27(3): 316–332.

References [215]

Ong, Jonathan Corpus. 2015. "After Yolanda: A tale of 2 Taclobans." *Rappler*, March 3. https://www.rappler.com/thought-leaders/57692-tale-tacloban-post-disaster-yolanda-haiyan.

Ong, Jonathan Corpus, Jaime Manuel Flores, and Pamela Combinido. 2015. "Obliged to be grateful: How local communities experienced humanitarian actors in the Haiyan response." Plan International. May 15.

Onyango, Monica, and Shirin Heidari. 2017. "Care with dignity in humanitarian crises: Ensuring sexual and reproductive health and rights of displaced populations." *Reproductive Health Matters* 25(51): 1–6.

OPAPP (Office of the Presidential Adviser on the Peace Process). 2014. *Kababaihan at kapayapaan* [Women and peace]. Issue No. 1. Pasig City: OPAPP.

OPARR (Office of the Presidential Assistant for Rehabilitation and Recovery). 2014. *Yolanda rehabilitation and recovery efforts.* July 28. Bonifacio Global City: OPARR.

O'Reilly, Marie, Andrea Ó Súilleabháin, and Thania Paffenholz. 2015. *Reimagining peacemaking: Women's roles in peace processes.* New York: International Peace Institute. https://www.ipinst.org/2015/06/reimagining-peacemaking-womens-roles-in-peace-processes.

Ortiz, Alejandra Santillana, ed. 2016. *Linking gender, economic and ecological justice: Feminist perspectives from Latin America.* Suva: DAWN. http://dawnnet.org/sites/default/files/articles/20170117_geej_ebook_0.pdf.

O'Rourke, Catherine. 2013. *Gender politics in transitional justice.* Abingdon, UK: Routledge.

OURs (Observatory on the Universality of Rights). 2017. *Rights at risk: Observatory on the universality of rights trends report 2017.* Toronto and Mexico City: AWID and OURs. https://www.awid.org/sites/default/files/atoms/files/ours_trends_report_2017_en.pdf.

Oxfam. 2015. *Women after the storm: Gender issues in Yolanda recovery and rehabilitation.* Quezon City: Oxfam.

Oxfam. 2016. *Leaving no one behind: LGBT rights post-Haiyan.* Quezon City: Oxfam in the Philippines.

PAI. 2015. "A reproductive health index: Rights and results." Population Action International. https://pai.org/wp-content/uploads/2015/05/RHIreport.pdf.

Paredes, Oona. 2015. "Indigenous vs. native: Negotiating the place of Lumads in the Bangsamoro homeland." *Asian Ethnicity* 16(2): 166–185.

Parreñas, Rhacel Salazar. 2001. "Transgressing the nation-state: The partial citizenship and 'Imagined (Global) Community' of migrant Filipina domestic workers." *Signs: Journal of Women in Culture and Society* 26(4): 1129–1154.

Parreñas, Rhacel Salazar. 2003. "At the cost of women." *Interventions: International Journal of Postcolonial Studies* 5(1): 29–44.

Patel, Preeti, Bayard Roberts, Samantha Guy, Louise Lee-Jones, and Lesong Conteh. 2009. "Tracking official development assistance for reproductive health in conflict-affected countries." *PLoS Med* 6(6): e1000090.

Petchesky, Rosalind P. 1995. "From population control to reproductive rights: Feminist fault lines." *Reproductive Health Matters* 3(6): 152–161.

Petchesky, Rosalind P. 1997. "Power and pleasure go together—brazen proposals for a new millennium." *Reproductive Health Matters* 5(10): 27–28.

Petchesky, Rosalind P. 2000. "Rights and needs: Rethinking the connections in debates over reproductive and sexual rights." *Health and Human Rights* 4(2): 17–29.

Petchesky, Rosalind P 2003. *Global prescriptions: Gendering health and human rights.* New York: Zed Books.

Petchesky, Rosalind P. 2005. "Rights of the body and perversions of war: Sexual rights and wrongs ten years past Beijing." *International Social Science Journal* 57(184): 301-318.

Petchesky, Rosalind P. 2008. "Conflict and crisis settings: Promoting sexual and reproductive rights." *Reproductive Health Matters* 16(31): 4-9.

Petersen, Emily, et al. 2019. Racial/ethnic disparities in pregnancy-related deaths—United States, 2007–2016. *Morbidity and Mortality Weekly Report (MMWR)* 68(35): 762–765. https://www.cdc.gov/mmwr/volumes/68/wr/mm6835a3.htm?s_cid=mm6835a3_w.

Pettman, Jan Jindy. 1996. *Worlding women: A feminist international politics.* Abingdon, UK: Routledge.

Philippine Constitution 1973. Republic of the Philippines. Article XV s 10. https://www.officialgazette.gov.ph/constitutions/1973-constitution-of-the-republic-of-the-philippines-2/.

Philippine Commission on Human Rights. 2016. *"Let our voices be heard": Report of the Commission on Human Rights Philippines' National Inquiry on Reproductive Health and Rights.* Quezon City: Commission on Human Rights. https://uniteforreprorights.org/wp-content/uploads/2018/01/RH-Inquiry-Report.pdf.

Philippine Statistics Authority. 2011a. "Life expectancy at birth of women." https://psa.gov.ph/content/life-expectancy-birth-women.

Philippine Statistics Authority. 2011b. "Table 1: Total fertility rate for the three years preceding the survey, by background characteristics, Philippines: 2011." Family Health Survey. https://psa.gov.ph/sites/default/files/attachments/hsd/pressrelease/Table%201%20Total%20Fertility%20Rate%20for%20the%20Three%20Years%20Preceding%20the%20Survey%2C%20Philippines%202011.pdf.

Philippine Statistics Authority. 2014. "One in ten Filipino women age 15 to 19 is already a mother or pregnant with first child (final results from the 2013 National Demographic and Health Survey)." https://psa.gov.ph/content/one-ten-young-filipino-women-age-15-19-already-mother-or-pregnant-first-child-final-results.

Philippines Department of Health. n.d. "What are the deployment programs?" https://www.doh.gov.ph/faqs/What-are-the-deployment-programs.

Political Settlements Research Programme. 2019. *Transitional justice.* Edinburgh: University of Edinburgh. http://www.politicalsettlements.org/wp-content/uploads/2019/10/GJA_Transitional_Justice.pdf.

Politics & Gender. 2015. Critical Perspectives on Gender and Politics 11(2): 406–438.

Politics & Gender. 2017. Critical Perspectives on Gender and Politics 13(4): 710–751.

Politics & Gender. 2020. Critical Perspectives on Gender and Politics 16(3).

Pope Francis. 2015. "The family—2. The mother." General audience, Paul VI Audience Hall, January 7. https://w2.vatican.va/content/francesco/en/audiences/2015/documents/papa-francesco_20150107_udienza-generale.html.

Presidential Decree No. 79 1972. Republic of the Philippines. Presidential Decree No. 79, December 8. https://lawphil.net/statutes/presdecs/pd1972/pd_79_1972.html

Prügl, Elisabeth. 2015. "Neoliberalising feminism." *New Political Economy* 20(4): 614–631.

Prügl, Elisabeth. 2017. "Neoliberalism with a feminist face: Crafting a new hegemony at the World Bank." *Feminist Economics* 23(1): 30–53.

Prügl, Elisabeth, and Jacqui True. 2014. "Equality means business? Governing gender through transnational public–private partnerships." *Review of International Political Economy* 21(6): 1137-1169.

Pugh, Michael. 2000. "Introduction: The ownership of regeneration and peacebuilding." In *Regeneration of war-torn societies*, edited by Michael Pugh, 1–13. Basingstoke, UK: Palgrave Macmillan.

Pugh, Michael, Neil Cooper, and Mandy Turner. 2008. *Whose peace? Critical perspectives on the political economy of peacebuilding*. Palgrave.

Rai, Shirin M., Catherine Hoskyns, and Dania Thomas. 2014. "Depletion: The cost of social reproduction." *International Feminist Journal of Politics* 16(1): 86–105.

Rai, Shirin M., Jacqui True, and Maria Tanyag. 2019. "From depletion to regeneration: Addressing structural and physical violence in post-conflict economies." *Social Politics: International Studies in Gender, State & Society* 26(4): 561–585.

Razavi, Shahra. 2007. "The political and social economy of care in a development context: Conceptual issues, research questions and policy options." Gender and Development Paper 3. Geneva: United Nations Research Institute for Social Development, June.

Reproductive Health Matters. 2008. "Conflict and crisis settings." *Reproductive Health Matters*, 16(31). https://www.tandfonline.com/toc/zrhm20/16/31?nav=tocList.

Reproductive Health Matters. 2017. "Humanitarian crises: Advancing sexual and reproductive health and rights." *Reproductive Health Matters*, 25(51). https://www.tandfonline.com/toc/zrhm20/25/51?nav=tocList.

Reproductive Health Matters. 2020. "Exporting harm: Impact of the expanded Global Gag Rule on sexual and reproductive health and rights." *Reproductive Health Matters*, 28(3). https://www.tandfonline.com/toc/zrhm21/28/3?nav=tocList.

Republic of the Philippines Commission on Population (POPCOM). n.d. "About us: POPCOM history." https://popcom.gov.ph/.

Republic of the Philippines Commission on Population (POPCOM). 2019. *2019 RPRH annual report*. https://popcom.gov.ph/wp-content/uploads/2020/11/2019-RPRH-Annual-Report-Fact-Sheet.pdf.

Republic of the Philippines Department of Foreign Affairs. 2014. "Filipina peacebuilders lauded for leadership at global summit to end sexual violence in conflict." June 19. https://dfa.gov.ph/dfa-news/dfa-releasesupdate/3250-filipina-peacebuilders-lauded-for-leadership-at-global-summit-to-end-sexual-violence-in-conflict.

Rivera, Karen. 2015. "Quality care for vulnerable pregnant teens after Haiyan." UNICEF Philippines. http://www.unicef.org/philippines/reallives_24839.html#.V9Jcs_196Ul.

Roberts, Adrienne. 2015. "The political economy of 'transnational business feminism'." *International Feminist Journal of Politics* 17(2): 209–231.

Robinson, Fiona. 2010. "After liberalism in world politics? Towards an international political theory of care." *Ethics and Social Welfare* 4(2): 130–144.

Robinson, Fiona. 2011. *The ethics of care: A feminist approach to human security*. Philadelphia, PA: Temple University Press.

Robinson, Fiona. 2016. "Feminist care ethics and everyday insecurities." In *Ethical security studies: A new research agenda*, edited by Jonna Nyman and Anthony Burke, 116–130. Abingdon, UK: Routledge.

Roces, Mina. 2009. "Prostitution, women's movements and the victim narrative in the Philippines." *Women's Studies International Forum* 32(4): 270–280.

Roces, Mina. 2012. *Women's Movement and the Filipina, 1986–2008*. Honolulu: University of Hawaii Press.

Rodriguez, Fritzie. 2014. "30 years and counting: The life of a volunteer village health worker." *Rappler*, May 11. https://www.rappler.com/move-ph/57481-barangay-health-worker-story.

Rood, Steven. 2005. "Forging sustainable peace in Mindanao: The role of civil society." Policy Studies 17. Washington, DC: East-West Center Washington.

Ross, Loretta, Erika Derkas, Whitney Peoples, Lynn Roberts, and Pamela Bridgewater, eds. 2017. *Radical reproductive justice: Foundation, theory, practice, critique*. New York: The Feminist Press.

Roy, Ananya. 2010. "Millennial woman: The gender order of development." In *The international handbook of gender and poverty: Concepts, research, policy*, edited by Sylvia Chant, 548–553. Cheltenham: Edward Elgar.

Rubio-Marín, Ruth, Clara Sandoval, and Catalina Diaz. 2009. "Repairing family members: Gross human rights violations and communities of harm." In *The gender of reparations: Unsettling sexual hierarchies while redressing human rights violations*, edited by Ruth Rubio-Marín, 215–290. Cambridge: Cambridge University Press.

Ruddick, Sara. 1989. *Maternal thinking: Towards a politics of peace*. Boston, MA: Beacon Press.

Ruiz Austria, Carolina S. 2004. "The Church, the state and women's bodies in the context of religious fundamentalism in the Philippines." *Reproductive Health Matters* 12(24): 96–103.

Safri, Maliha, and Julie Graham. 2010. "The global household: Toward a feminist post-capitalist international political economy." *Signs* 36(1): 99–125.

Sarmiento, Bong S. 2012. "Euphoria sweeps MILF's Camp Darapanan as framework agreement finally signed in Malacañang." *MindaNews*, October 16. http://www.mindanews.com/peace-process/2012/10/euphoria-sweeps-milfs-camp-darapanan-as-framework-agreement-finally-signed-in-malacanang/.

Sassen, Saskia. 2000. "Women's burden: Counter-geographies of globalization and the feminization of survival." *Journal of International Affairs* 53(2): 503–524.

Sassen, Saskia. 2014. *Expulsions: Brutality and complexity in the global economy*. Cambridge, MA: The Belknap Press of Harvard University Press.

Sasser, Jade. 2014. "From darkness into light: Race, population, and environmental advocacy." *Antipode* 46(5): 1240–1257.

Sasser, Jade. 2017. "Sexual stewardship: Environment, development, and the gendered politics of population." In *Handbook on gender and environment*, edited by Sherilyn MacGregor, 345–356. Abingdon, UK: Routledge.

Sell, Susan K., and Owain D. Williams. 2020. "Health under capitalism: A global political economy of structural pathogenesis." *Review of International Political Economy* 27(1): 1–25.

Sen, Gita. 2005. "Neolibs, neocons and gender justice: Lessons from global negotiations." Occasional Paper 9. September. Geneva: United Nations Research Institute for Social Development.

Sen, Gita, and Caren Grown. 1987. *Development crises, and alternative visions: Third World women's perspectives*. New York: Monthly Review Press.

Senate of the Philippines. 2016. "Women's dignity kits now mandatory in evac centers; Recto calls for early purchase." Press Release, March 6. http://www.senate.gov.ph/press_release/2016/0306_recto1.asp.

Shannon, Geordan, Melanie Jansen, Kate Williams, Carlos Caceres, Angelica Motta, Aloyce Odhiambo, Alie Eleveld, and Jenevieve Mannell. 2019. "Gender equality in science, medicine, and global health: Where are we at and why does it matter?" *The Lancet* 393(10171): 560–569.

Shepherd, Laura J. 2011. "Sex, security and superhero(in)es: From 1325 to 1820 and beyond." *International Feminist Journal of Politics* 13(4): 504–521.

References [219]

Sherwood, Angela, Megan Bradley, Lorenza Rossi, Rufa Guiam, and Bradley Mellicker. 2015. *Resolving post-disaster displacement: Insights from the Philippines after Typhoon Haiyan (Yolanda)*. Geneva: IOM; Washington, DC: Brookings.

Sifris, Ronli. 2014. *Reproductive freedom, torture and international human rights: Challenging the masculinisation of torture*. Abingdon, UK: Routledge.

Sifris, Ronli. 2016. "The involuntary sterilisation of marginalised women: Power, discrimination, and intersectionality." *Griffith Law Review* 25(1): 45–70.

Sifris, Ronli, and Maria Tanyag. 2019. "Intersectionality, transitional justice, and the case of internally displaced Moro women in the Philippines." *Human Rights Quarterly* 41(2): 399–420.

SIPRI (Stockholm International Peace Research Institute). 2020. "Trends in world military expenditure, 2019." SIPRI Fact Sheet, April. https://sipri.org/sites/default/files/2020-04/fs_2020_04_milex_0.pdf.

SIPRI (Stockholm International Peace Research Institute). 2021. "Trends in world military expenditure, 2020." SIPRI Fact Sheet, April. https://www.sipri.org/sites/default/files/2021-04/fs_2104_milex_0.pdf.

SisterSong: Women of Color Reproductive Justice Collective. 2012. *What is RJ*. http://www.sistersong.net.

Sjoberg, Laura, and Caron E. Gentry. 2007. *Mothers, monsters, whores: Women's violence in global politics*. London: Zed Books.

Sjoberg, Laura, and Caron E. Gentry. 2015. *Beyond mothers, monsters, whores: Thinking about women's violence in global politics*. London: Zed Books.

Sjoberg, Laura, Heidi Hudson, and Cynthia Weber. 2015. "Gender and crisis in global politics: Introduction." *International Feminist Journal of Politics* 17(4): 529–535.

Smith, Karen. 2011. "Sex strike brings peace to Filipino village." *CNN*, September 19. http://edition.cnn.com/2011/WORLD/asiapcf/09/19/philippines.sex.strike/index.html.

Smyth, Ines, and Caroline Sweetman. 2015. "Introduction: Gender and resilience." *Gender and Development* 23(3): 405–414.

Social Weather Stations. 2013. *The 2013 SWS annual survey review*. January 24. Makati City: Asian Institute of Management, Konrad Adenauer Stiftung, and SWS.

Social Weather Stations. 2015. "SWS launches publication, 'Filipino public opinion on the Bangsamoro Basic Law (BBL) and the Mamasapano incident.'" SWS Media Release, August 24.

Solamo-Antonio, Isabelita. 2015. "The Philippine *Shari'a* courts and the code of Muslim personal laws." In *The sociology of* Shari'a: *Case studies from around the world*, edited by Adam Possamai, James T. Richardson, and Bryan S. Turner, 83–101. Cham: Springer.

Spitzer, Denise L., and Nicola Piper. 2014. "Retrenched and returned: Filipino migrant workers during times of crisis." *Sociology* 48(5): 1007–1023.

Stevens, Jacqueline. 1999. *Reproducing the state*. Princeton, NJ: Princeton University Press.

Su, Yvonne, and Ladylyn Lim Mangada. 2016. "Bayanihan after Typhoon Haiyan: Are we romanticising an indigenous coping strategy?" Humanitarian Practice Network, August 10. http://odihpn.org/resources/bayanihan-after-typhoon-haiyan-are-we-romanticising-an-indigenous-coping-strategy/.

Su, Yvonne, Ladylyn Mangada, and Jessa Turalba. 2018. "Happy-washing: How a 'happiness campaign' hurts disaster survivors." *New Mandala*, April 27. https://www.newmandala.org/happy-washing-happiness-campaign-hurts-disaster-survivors/.

Su, Yvonne, and Maria Tanyag. 2019. "Globalising myths of survival: Post-disaster households after Typhoon Haiyan." *Gender, Place and Culture: A Journal of Feminist Geography*, online, June 11: 1-23. DOI: 10.1080/0966369X.2019.1635997.

Sweetman, Caroline. 2017. "Introduction: Gender, development and fundamentalisms." *Gender and Development* 25(1): 1-14.

Tanabe, Mihoko, Kristen Schaus, Sonia Rastogi, Sandra K. Krause, and Preeti Patel. 2015. "Tracking humanitarian funding for reproductive health: A systematic analysis of health and protection proposals from 2002-2013." *Conflict and Health* 9(Suppl 1): S2.

Tan, Michael Lim. 2004. "Fetal discourses and the politics of the womb." *Reproductive Health Matters* 12(24): 157–166.

Tanyag, Maria. 2015. "Unravelling the intersections of power: The case of sexual and reproductive freedom in the Philippines." *Women's Studies International Forum* 53: 63-72.

Teaiwa, Teresia. 1994. "Bikinis and other s/pacific n/oceans." *The Contemporary Pacific* 6(1): 87–109.

Teehankee, Julio. 2007. "And the clans play on." Philippine Center for Investigative Journalism, March 7. http://pcij.org/stories/and-the-clans-play-on/.

Tickner, J. Ann. 1992. *Gender in international relations: Feminist perspectives on achieving global security*. New York: Columbia University Press.

Tickner, J. Ann. 1993. "An ecofeminist perspective on international political economy." *International Political Science Review* 14(1): 59–69.

Tickner, J. Ann. 2015. "Revisiting IR in a time of crisis." *International Feminist Journal of Politics* 17(4): 536–553.

Torres, Wilfredo M. III, ed. 2014. *Rido: Clan feuding and conflict management in Mindanao*, expanded ed. Manila: Asia Foundation and Ateneo de Manila University Press.

Towns, Ann E. 2010. *Women and states: Norms and hierarchies in international society*. Cambridge: Cambridge University Press.

Towns, Anne E. 2014. "Carrying the load of civilisation: The status of women and challenged hierarchies." *Millennium* 42(3): 595–613.

Transitional Justice and Reconciliation Commission. 2016. *Report of the Transitional Justice and Reconciliation Commission*. Makati City: TJRC. https://www.men schenrechte-philippinen.de/tl_files/aktionsbuendnis/dokumente/weiterfu ehrende%20Dokumentensammlung/Transitional_Justice_and_Reconciliat ion_Commission_-_Report_2016.pdf.

Trojanowska, K. Barbara. 2019. ""Courage is very important for those who wage peace": Conversation with Jasmin Nario-Galace, peace educator, on the implementation of the UN's Women, Peace and Security agenda in conflict-ridden Philippines." *International Feminist Journal of Politics* 21(2): 317–325.

Tronto, Joan C. 1994. *Moral boundaries: A political argument for an ethic of care*. Abingdon, UK: Routledge.

True, Jacqui. 2012. *The political economy of violence against women*. New York: Oxford University Press.

True, Jacqui. 2013. "Women, peace and security in post-conflict and peacebuilding contexts." Expert Analysis, March 14. Oslo: Norwegian Peacebuilding Resource Centre. http://www.peacebuilding.no/Themes/Inclusivity-and-gender/Publicati ons/Women-peace-and-security-in-post-conflict-and-peacebuilding-contexts.

True, Jacqui, and Yolanda Riveros-Morales. 2019. "Towards inclusive peace: Analysing gender-sensitive peace agreements 2000–2016." *International Political Science Review* 40(1): 23–40.

True, Jacqui, and Maria Tanyag. 2019. "Gender-responsive alternatives on climate change from a feminist standpoint." In *Climate Hazards and Gender Ramifications*, edited by Helle Rydstrom and Catarina Kinnvall, 29–47. Abingdon: Routledge.

Tuaño-Amador, Maria Almasara, Veronica Bayangos, Marie Edelweiss Romarate, and Carl Francis Maliwat. 2022. *Remittances from overseas Filipinos in the time of COVID-19: Spillovers and policy imperatives*. BSP Discussion Paper Series No. 10. BSP Research Academy. https://www.bsp.gov.ph/Pages/MediaAndResearch/PublicationsAndReports/Discussion%20Papers/DP202201.pdf.

UK Parliament. 2020. "NHS staff from overseas: Statistics." June 4. https://commons library.parliament.uk/research-briefings/cbp-7783/.

UN Committee on Economic, Social and Cultural Rights. 2016. "General comment No. 22 (2016) on the right to sexual and reproductive health (article 12 of the International Covenant on Economic, Social and Cultural Rights)." E/C.12/GC/22, May 2.

UN Security Council. 2004. "The rule of law and transitional justice in conflict and post-conflict societies: Report of the Secretary-General." S/2004/616, August 23.

UN Security Council. 2019a. "Resolution 2467 (2019)." S/RES.2467, April 23.

UN Security Council. 2019b. "8514th meeting." S/PV.8514, April 23.

UNESCO (United Nations Educational, Scientific and Cultural Organization). n.d. "Darangen epic of the Maranao people of Lake Lanao." Intangible Cultural Heritage. http://www.unesco.org/culture/ich/en/RL/darangen-epic-of-the-maranao-people-of-lake-lanao-00159.

UNESCO (United Nations Educational, Scientific and Cultural Organization). 1972. Convention Concerning the Protection of the World Cultural and Natural Heritage. Adopted by the General Conference at its seventeenth session, Paris, November 16. https://whc.unesco.org/archive/convention-en.pdf.

UNFPA (United Nations Population Fund). 1994/2014. *Programme of action*. 20th anniversary edition. Adopted at the International Conference on Population and Development, Cairo, September 5-13. https://www.unfpa.org/sites/default/files/pub-pdf/programme_of_action_Web%20ENGLISH.pdf.

UNFPA (United Nations Population Fund). 2013. "Contraceptives and condoms for family planning and STI/HIV prevention." http://www.unfpa.org/publications/contraceptives-and-condoms-family-planning-and-stihiv-prevention.

UNFPA (United Nations Population Fund). 2015. *Shelter from the storm: A transformative agenda for women and girls in a crisis-prone world: State of world population 2015*. New York: UNFPA.

UNFPA (United Nations Population Fund). 2019. "Humanitarian action 2019 overview." https://www.unfpa.org/humanitarian-action-2019-overview.

UNFPA (United Nations Population Fund). 2021. *State of world population*. New York: UNFPA.

UN General Assembly (UNGA). 1948. *Universal declaration of human rights*.

UN General Assembly (UNGA). 1966. *International Covenant on Civil and Political Rights*.

UN General Assembly (UNGA). 1975. "Resolutions adopted on the reports of the Third Committee." https://www.un.org/en/ga/search/view_doc.asp?symbol=A/RES/3520%20(XXX).

UN General Assembly (UNGA). 1979. *Convention on the Elimination of All Forms of Discrimination against Women*.

UN General Assembly (UNGA). 1998. "Statements on reservations to the Convention on the Elimination of All Forms of Discrimination against Women adopted by the Committee on the Elimination of Discrimination against Women." Excerpt from A/53/38/Rev.1, May 14.

UN General Assembly (UNGA). 2010a. "Report of the special rapporteur on violence against women, its causes and consequences, Rashid Manjoo." A/HRC/14/22, April 23.

UN General Assembly (UNGA). 2010b. "Resolution adopted by the Human Rights Council." A/HRC/RES/15/23, October 8.

UN General Assembly (UNGA). 2010c. "Women's participation in peacebuilding: Report of the Secretary General." A/65/354–S/2010/466, September 7.

UN General Assembly (UNGA). 2011. "Report of the Special Rapporteur on violence against women, its causes and consequences, Rashida Manjoo." A/HRC/17/26, May 2.

UN General Assembly (UNGA). 2013. "Report of the Special Rapporteur on the right of everyone to the enjoyment of the highest attainable standard of physical and mental health." A/68/297, August 9.

UN General Assembly (UNGA). 2016a. "One humanity: Shared responsibility: Report of the Secretary General for the World Humanitarian Summit." A/70/709, February 2.

UN General Assembly (UNGA). 2016b. "Analytical study on the relationship between climate change and the human right of everyone to the enjoyment of the highest attainable standard of physical and mental health: Report of the Office of the United Nations High Commissioner for Human Rights." A/HRC/32/23, May 6.

UN General Assembly (UNGA). 2016c. "Report of the Special Rapporteur on the human rights of internally displaced persons on his mission to Philippines." A/HRC/32/35/Add.3, April 5.

UNHCR (United Nations High Commissioner for Refugees) and Mindanao Protection Cluster. 2015. "Displacement dashboard: Mindanao, Philippines forced displacement annual report, 2015." Manila and Cotabato: UNHCR. https://relief web.int/sites/reliefweb.int/files/resources/2015_mindanao_displacement_das hboard_annual_report_lr.pdf.

UNHCR Philippines. 2016. "3 years since Zamboanga clashes: A chance to dream again." August 2. https://www.unhcr.org/ph/10211-3-years-since-zamboanga-clashes-chance-dream.html.

UN Treaty Collection. 1969. "1. Vienna Convention on the Law of Treaties." *Treaty Series* 1155: 331. https://treaties.un.org/doc/Publication/MTDSG/Volume%20 II/Chapter%20XXIII/XXIII-1.en.pdf.

UN Treaty Collection. 1979. "8. Convention on the Elimination of All Forms of Discrimination against Women." *Treaty Series* 1249: 13. https://treaties.un.org/ doc/Publication/MTDSG/Volume%20I/Chapter%20IV/IV-8.en.pdf.

UN Treaty Collection. 1999. "8. b) Optional Protocol on the Convention on the Elimination of All Forms of Discrimination against Women." *Treaty Series* 2131: 83. https://treaties.un.org/doc/Publication/MTDSG/Volume%20I/Chap ter%20IV/IV-8-b.en.pdf.

UN Women. 2009a. "Convention on the Elimination of All Forms of Discrimination against Women: History of the Optional Protocol." https://www.un.org/wom enwatch/daw/cedaw/protocol/history.htm.

UN Women. 2009b. "Convention on the Elimination of All Forms of Discrimination against Women: Why an Optional Protocol?" https://www.un.org/womenwa tch/daw/cedaw/protocol/why.htm.

UN Women. 2011. "Progress of the world's women 2011-2012: In pursuit of justice." https://www.unwomen.org/-/media/headquarters/attachments/secti ons/library/publications/2011/progressoftheworldswomen-2011-en.pdf?la= en&vs=2835.

UN Women. 2014. *The global economic crisis and gender equality.* New York: UN.

UN Women. 2015. *Preventing conflict, transforming justice, securing the peace: A global study on the implementation of United Nations Security Council Resolution 1325.* New York: UN Women.

UN Women. 2020. "World Conferences on Women." https://www.unwomen. org/en/how-we-work/intergovernmental-support/world-conferences-on-women#nairobi.

Uppsala Conflict Data Program. 2017. *UCDP conflict encyclopedia.* Uppsala: Department of Peace and Conflict Research, Uppsala University. www.ucdp.uu.se.

Urdal, Henrik, and Chi Primus Che. 2013. "War and gender inequalities in health: The impact of armed conflict on fertility and maternal mortality." *International Interactions* 39(4): 489-510.

US Department of State. 1975. *Implications of worldwide population growth for US security and overseas interests: NSSM 200.* Washington, DC: The White House. https://static.history.state.gov/frus/frus1969-76ve14p1/pdf/d121.pdf.

Vaittinen, Tiina, and Catia C. Confortini (eds). 2019. *Gender, global health, and violence: Feminist perspectives on peace and disease.* Lanham: Rowman & Littlefield International.

Valerio, Kristine Aquino. 2014. "Storm of violence, surge of struggle: Women in the aftermath of Typhoon Haiyan (Yolanda)." *Asian Journal of Women's Studies* 20(1): 148-163.

Vargas, Anthony. 2014. "ARMM is most peaceful Philippine region—PNP." *Manila Times*, January 25.

Vatican Radio. 2016. "Card. Tagle: 'Humanitarian summit to promote trust in religious organisations.'" May 20. http://en.radiovaticana.va/news/2016/05/20/card_ tagle_%E2%80%98humanitarian_summit_to_promote_trust/1231204.

Weldon, S. Laurel. 2006. "The structure of intersectionality: A comparative politics of gender." *Politics and Gender* 2(2): 235-248.

WHO (World Health Organization). n.d. "Density of physicians (total number per 1000 population, latest available year)." http://www.who.int/gho/health_wo rkforce/physicians_density_text/en/.

WHO (World Health Organization). 2012. "Spending on health: A global overview." Fact sheet no. 319, April 17. http://www.who.int/mediacentre/factsheets/ fs319/en/.

WHO (World Health Organization). 2013. "Typhoon Yolanda (Haiyan), Philippines." Situation Report No. 2, November 17. http://www.who.int/hac/crises/phl/sitr eps/philippines_sitrep_17november2013.pdf?ua=1.

WHO (World Health Organization). 2014a. "Trends in maternal mortality: 1990 to 2013: Executive summary." WHO/RHR/14.13. Geneva: WHO.

WHO (World Health Organization). 2014b. "Typhoon Haiyan (Yolanda): One year on." Fact Sheet: Maternal and Child Health. Manila: WHO Philippines.

WHO (World Health Organization). 2015. "State of inequality: Reproductive, maternal, newborn and child health." WHO/HIS/HIS/2015.2. Geneva: WHO.

WHO (World Health Organization). 2016. "Global strategic directions for strengthening nursing and midwifery 2016–2020." Report. Geneva: WHO. https://

www.who.int/hrh/nursing_midwifery/global-strategic-midwifery2016-2020.
pdf?ua=1.

WHO (World Health Organization). 2017. "Density of physicians (total number per 1000 population, latest available year)." https://www.who.int/data/gho/data/themes/topics/health-workforce.

WHO (World Health Organization). 2018. "Emergency contraception." February 2. http://www.who.int/mediacentre/factsheets/fs244/en/.

WHO (World Health Organization). 2018. "Adolescents: Health risks and solutions." December 13. http://www.who.int/mediacentre/factsheets/fs345/en/.

WHO (World Health Organization). 2020. "State of the World's Nursing 2020: Investing in education, jobs and leadership." Report. Geneva: WHO. https://www.who.int/publications/i/item/9789240003279.

WHO, UNICEF, UNFPA, World Bank Group, and United Nations Population Division Maternal Mortality Estimation Inter-Agency Group. 2015. *Maternal mortality in 1990–2015: Philippines*. Geneva: WHO. http://www.who.int/gho/maternal_health/countries/phl.pdf.

WHO, UNICEF, UNFPA, World Bank and UN Population Division. 2019. "Trends in maternal mortality 2000 to 2017." https://apps.who.int/iris/bitstream/handle/10665/327596/WHO-RHR-19.23-eng.pdf?sequence=13&isAllowed=y.

Wibben, Annick T.R., ed. 2016. *Researching war: Feminist methods, ethics and politics*. New York: Routledge.

Wilcox, Lauren. 2015. *Bodies of violence: Theorizing embodied subjects in international relations*. New York: Oxford University Press.

Wilson, Kim, and Roxanne Krystalli. 2017. "The financial journey of refugees: Evidence from Greece, Jordan, and Turkey." Henry J. Leir Institute for Human Security, Occasional Paper Series 2, Number 1. http://fic.tufts.edu/assets/Financial-Journeys-of-Refugees.pdf.

WE Act 1325 (Women Engaged in Action on 1325). 2016. *Women, peace and security in the autonomous region in Muslim Mindanao (a civil society report)*. Quezon City: WE Act 1325.

Women Deliver. 2021. *The link between climate change and sexual and reproductive health and rights: An evidence review*. https://womendeliver.org/wp-content/uploads/2021/02/Climate-Change-Report-1.pdf.

Women's International League for Peace and Freedom (WILPF). 2019. "Madeleine Rees on UN Security Council Resolution 2467." https://www.wilpf.org/madeleine-rees-on-un-security-council-resolution-2467/.

World Humanitarian Summit and Agenda for Humanity, eds. 2016. *Religious engagement: The contributions of faith communities to our shared humanity: Special session summary*. Istanbul: World Humanitarian Summit. https://reliefweb.int/sites/reliefweb.int/files/resources/Religious%20Engagement.pdf.

Yamin, Alicia Ely. 2017. *Power, suffering, and the struggle for dignity: Human rights frameworks for health and why they matter*. Philadelphia: University of Pennsylvania Press.

Yeates, Nicola. 2009. *Globalizing care economies and migrant workers: Explorations in global care chains*. Basingstoke, UK: Palgrave Macmillan.

Yuval-Davis, Nira. 1997. *Gender and nation*. London: Sage.

Yuval-Davis, Nira, and Floya Anthias, eds. 1989. *Woman, nation, state*. Basingstoke, UK: Palgrave Macmillan.

INDEX

For the benefit of digital users, indexed terms that span two pages (e.g., 52–53) may, on occasion, appear on only one of those pages.

activism, 3–4, 9–10, 13–14, 17–18, 89–90, 93, 99–101, 120–21, 126–27, 129, 130–31, 132, 133–34, 140–41, 142, 146, 147–49, 150–51, 152–53, 155–56, 157, 165, 172–73, 181, 182–83, 184, 185, 186–87, 188

adolescent pregnancy, 55, 103–4
    teenage pregnancy, 55

aid, 5, 12, 32, 33, 38, 49–50, 61, 65–66, 68, 75–76, 81–82, 85, 86, 97–98, 110–11, 114, 115–16, 133, 135–37, 140, 146–47, 148, 162–63

Anthropocene, 151, 159–62, 164, 166, 177, 182

anti-feminist backlash, 13, 14, 119–21, 129, 146, 147, 181, 182, 187

Aquino, Benigno "Noynoy" III, 32, 78–79, 91, 92

armed conflict, 2, 4–7, 9, 10, 11–12, 16, 21–22, 23–25, 28–29, 31, 33–34, 35–36, 39–40, 41, 42–43, 45, 46–47, 48, 49–51, 52–53, 54, 56, 57, 58–60, 61–62, 63–64, 66–67, 73–74, 75–79, 84, 90–93, 99, 101, 102, 103, 105–7, 133, 136, 141, 145, 158–59, 160, 167, 171, 182–85

    conflict prevention, 7–8, 64, 68, 75, 99, 148–49, 180–81

    conflict strings, 42–44, 53, 105–6

    post-conflict, 20–21, 28, 75, 85–86, 93–95, 104, 148, 152, 154–55, 166–67, 168–71, 172–75, 176–77, 186–87

Asian financial crisis, 36–38

Association for Women's Rights in Development (AWID), 130, 133–34, 137–38

austerity, 21, 26, 29–30, 36–37, 65–66, 182–83

bakla, 80, 81

Bangsamoro, 12–13, 31, 42–43, 90–95, 101–3, 104–5, 109–10, 116–17

    Autonomous Region in Muslim Mindanao (ARMM), 70

    Bangsamoro Basic Law, 91, 93–95

    Comprehensive Agreement on the Bangsamoro (CAB), 90–91, 93–95, 102–3

Bangsamoro Islamic Women Auxiliary Brigade (BIWAB), 47–48, 93–95, 104–5

barangay, 12, 31, 67, 68, 69–70, 72, 84, 97–98, 99–100, 108, 136–37

Barangay Health Workers (BHWs), 70–72, 73, 74, 77

Basic Ecclesial Communities (BECs), 136–37, 142, 144

basic needs, 140–42

bayanihan, 78–82

Beijing, 3, 127–30, 131–32, 148–49
    Declaration and Platform, 126–27

Bill and Melinda Gates Foundation, 141, 163

black birding, 153–54

Black feminism, 152–53, 179

Cairo, 3, 126–30, 131–32, 148–49

capital, 37–38, 65–66, 79–80
capital accumulation, 18–19
capitalism, 7, 18–19, 32, 33–34, 38,
63, 131–32, 152–53, 156, 159, 161
Care, 7–9, 11–12, 14, 15, 22, 41–42, 47,
58, 62–67, 136–37, 144, 151–52
care chains, 113–14
care debt spiral, 16, 29–33
care diamond, 24
care economies, 19–21, 29, 62,
152, 167–69
care ethics, 19–20, 157–60, 176
See also social reproduction
Catholic Church, 13, 32, 69, 137, 138,
142–43, 144
Christianity, 140–41
civil society, 90–91, 92, 93–95, 98,
100, 136–37
climate change, 2, 14, 22, 28–29, 46,
66, 89–90, 96, 97–98, 115, 170,
171–72, 173–74, 175–77, 180–81,
183, 186–87
Code of Muslim Personal Laws (CMPL),
102, 103, 104, 108–9, 123
colonialism, 89–90, 152–53, 155–
56, 187–88
postcolonialism, 176
community
communities of care, 75–78
communities of harm, 79–80
myths, 63–64, 65–66, 79–80
continuum of violence, 17–18, 24–
25, 172–73
contraception, 3–4, 57, 109, 139,
143, 164–65
emergency contraceptive (EC) pill,
134–35, 138
Convention on the Elimination of All
Forms of Discrimination against
Women (CEDAW), 3, 89–90, 102,
119, 120, 121, 147
Optional Protocol, 119, 124, 125
reservations, 121–25, 126, 127
Coronel-Ferrer, Miriam, 92, 101–
2, 116–17
Corrêa, Sonia, 120–21, 128, 129, 147
crisis
crisis as junctures or situations, 18,
87–88, 99, 148
crisis competition, 45–46

crisis of basic reproduction or
reproduction failures, 18–19
crisis of culture, 126 (*see also under
culture*)
crisis of social reproduction or social
reproduction crises, 13–14, 16–22,
31–32, 39, 41, 46, 56, 182
crisis narratives, 17, 79, 88
crisis responses, 63–64, 65–66, 81–82
systemic crises, 19, 22, 41–42, 151
culture, 106, 108, 112
crisis of culture, 126
culture of Life, 32
cultures of disaster, 79

decentralization, 68–69
Deles, Teresita Quintos, 92
development
human development, 11, 111
international development, 52, 56–
57, 58, 61–62, 65–66, 81, 103,
115, 162–63
official development assistance (ODA),
5, 37, 93–95, 141
Development Alternatives for Women in
the New Era (DAWN), 18–19, 126,
129, 156
Depletion through Social Reproduction,
22, 23, 56, 62, 67, 87, 93, 112–13
neoliberal logic, 8, 11, 13–14, 15–16,
22–34, 73, 88, 120, 148, 168–
69, 175–76
dignity kits *also known as hygiene kits*, 82,
83, 99–100, 158–59
disasters, 78, 98–99
post-disaster, 12–13, 79–80, 111, 112,
113–14, 115
risk reduction, 89–90, 96, 97–
98, 99–100
See also climate change
doctors to the barrios program, 31, 71
domestic violence, 39–40, 52, 59
Doyal, Lesley, 6

Eastern Visayas, 9, 55, 70, 76, 110–
11, 113–14
ecofeminism, 150–51, 152–53, 157–
58, 176
ecological feminism, 157–58
ecological security, 13–14

[228] *Index*

Elson, Diane, 24–25, 65–66

faith-based, 10–11, 13, 115–16, 135–38, 139, 142, 144, 148–49, 181
family planning, 3, 21–22, 35, 69, 70, 134, 163–64, 180
Federici, Silvia, 24, 188
female altruism, 7–8, 12, 15, 26–27, 28–30, 31–32, 34, 52–56, 66–67, 77–78, 81, 85, 109–10, 180, 183
feminization of responsibility and obligation, 7–8, 164–65
feminization of survival, 15, 16, 26–29, 30, 33–34, 39, 183
Fraser, Nancy, 18–19, 131–32, 175–76, 181

gendered division of labor. *See* care; social reproduction
global financial crisis (GFC), 7, 26–27, 33, 36–37, 41–42
Economic crisis, 22, 63–64
Global Gag Rule, 146–47
globalization, 26, 36, 39, 41–42, 126, 160–61, 175
Global South, 19, 39, 128, 135–36, 141–42, 146–47, 157, 165–66, 168–69, 172–73, 185, 186
Grown, Caren, 18, 156

harms, definitions, 15–17, 21–22, 23, 145
HIV/AIDS, 2, 5–6, 55, 67, 109
household, 35–42
female-headed households, 49–51
global households, 36–39
transnational families, 37, 49–50
humanitarianism, 50–51, 56–57, 65–66, 75–76, 80, 81–82, 83, 97–98, 103–4, 115, 136, 141
human rights, 3–6, 119, 128–29, 140–45, 163
Right to health, 4
human security, 19–20, 41–42
hygiene kits. *See* dignity kits
hypervisibility, 8, 15, 26–28, 162
See also superheroines

identity, 12–13, 40, 87, 91, 106–7, 122, 170–71

Inter-agency Field Manual for Reproductive Health in Humanitarian Settings, 4–5
Inter-agency Working Group on Reproductive Health in Crises, 4–5
Intergovernmental Panel on Climate Change (IPCC), 160
internal displacement, 2, 9, 10–11, 16–17, 42–46, 50, 54, 56, 58, 59–60, 103, 114, 158–59
IDPs, 43–44, 50–51, 53, 54, 57, 58, 76–77, 78–79
Internal Displacement Monitoring Centre, 9–10, 91–92, 96–97
International Conference on Population and Development (ICPD), 3, 140–41
Programme of Action, 3, 126–27
International Monetary Fund (IMF), 132, 134
intersectionality, 11
intimacy, 57–58
Islam, 93, 103, 122–23, 127, 131, 140–41

justice
justice systems, 30, 68–69, 83, 85, 102, 108–9
regenerative justice, 13–14, 173–77
reproductive justice, 151, 165–66, 176, 185
See also transitional justice

Kissinger, Henry, 162–63

lesbian, gay, bisexual, and transgender (LGBT), 80, 81–82, 128–29, 130–32, 139, 140, 148–49
liberation theology, 142, 144
love, 15, 19, 56, 57–58, 144–45, 158–59, 179, 184–85, 187
Lumad, 31, 93, 106, 169

Magna Carta of Public Health Workers, 71
Magna Carta of Women, 98
maratabat, 106–8, 109
Marohombsar, Emily, 92
marriage, 80, 107, 108–9, 114, 121–22, 123–24, 126, 143, 178
early marriage, 58, 102, 103–4

Index [229]

masculinities, 19–21, 26–27, 28–29, 39–40, 58, 104–5, 106–7, 109, 110, 146–47
hypermasculinity, 39, 145–47
maternalism, 27, 40
maternal mortality, 1–2, 54–55, 57, 179, 182–83
maternal deaths, 1–2, 7, 31
matrix of domination, 155–56
matrix of oppressions, 152–53
Mies, Maria, 155–56
migration, 26, 31–32, 42, 82, 113–14, 180–81
militarism, 16, 17–18, 19–20, 23–24, 32, 39–40, 41, 46, 128–29, 133, 152–53, 154–55, 156, 172
militarised security, 20–21, 173–74
Mindanao, 9, 42, 44–45, 46–47, 53, 70, 71–72, 80, 84, 92, 105
See also Bangsamoro
Minimum Initial Service Package (MISP) for Sexual and Reproductive Health, 4–5, 99
Moro, 47–48, 50, 53, 54, 76, 80, 102, 103, 106, 108–9
Moro Islamic Liberation Front (MILF), 90–91, 93–95, 101, 102–3, 104, 105–6, 110
Moro National Liberation Front (MNLF), 91, 105–6

nation
exceptionalism, 89–90, 100–1
nation-building, 87–88, 105–6, 110–11
national action plan, 95, 96
National Disaster Risk Reduction and Management Act of 2010, 97
Nisa Ul Haqq Fi Bangsamoro, 9, 44, 59, 103

Office of the Presidential Adviser on the Peace Process (OPAPP), 93
order, 7, 8, 11, 12–13, 15–16, 17, 22, 28, 33–34, 48, 63, 88, 89–90, 100–1, 110, 116, 132–33, 144, 156–57, 162, 167, 168–69, 180, 185–87, 188
Organization of the Islamic Conference, 127

overseas Filipino workers (OFWs), 32, 37–38, 114
Oxfam, 81, 82, 84, 87–88

participation, 77–78, 89, 93–95, 96, 104
tyranny of participation, 64–65
patriarchy, 11, 49–50, 59, 63, 87–88, 101–10, 127–28, 130
patriarchal bargains, 12–13, 14, 89, 104, 105, 110, 111–12, 115–17
peace
invisible or slow peace, 170–73
peacebuilding, 76, 77, 92, 109–10
peace process, 7–8, 14, 28, 90–91, 92, 93–95, 99, 102–3, 104–5, 109–10, 116–17, 167, 177, 180–81, 183
Petchesky, Rosalind, 32, 128–29, 131–32, 140–42, 147–48
Philippine Commission on Human Rights, 57, 69, 74, 115, 138
Philippine Commission on Women, 98
Philippine National Police, 4, 83, 84, 107, 108
pleasure, 2, 3–4, 13–14, 121, 128, 131–32, 143, 177, 178, 179, 184–85, 186–87
population control, 134, 141–42, 153–54, 162–63, 173–74
privatization, 134, 148, 162–63, 182–83
pro-life, 13, 32, 69–70, 120, 125, 134–36, 138, 139, 140–41, 143, 148, 178–79, 181

Rai, Shirin, 151–52
regeneration, 13–14, 150–77
religious fundamentalisms, 13, 121, 126, 129–45
Catholic fundamentalism, 13, 69, 120, 141–42, 181
Christian Right, 120, 127, 128–29, 130, 135–36, 146–47
remittances, 26, 32, 37, 113–14
resilience, 12, 38, 66–67, 78, 79, 97–98, 111–12, 115–16
Responsible Parenthood and Reproductive Health Act of 2012, 31–32, 99
RH or RPRH Law, 69, 99–100, 139, 143, 178

[230] *Index*

rido, 42–43, 51, 58–59, 80, 105–9, 110

Santiago, Irene, 92
Sassen, Saskia, 26–27
scalar analysis, 8–9, 15, 63, 117, 121, 126–27, 157
self-care, 14, 53, 60, 156, 158–59, 179
self-determination, 3–4, 91, 101–10, 119, 155–56, 166, 180–81, 188
self-reliance, 65–66, 67, 86, 111–12, 115–16, 134–35
  self-sufficiency, 67, 68
self-sacrifice, 8, 12, 15, 27, 29–30, 34, 46–47, 50, 52–53, 56, 107–8, 109–10, 144, 180, 183
Sen, Gita, 18, 156
sex strikes, 58–59
sexual and gender-based violence (SGBV), 2, 9, 43–44, 51, 53, 59, 60, 80, 81–83, 84, 85, 98–99, 106, 107–9
sexually transmitted diseases (STDs), 2, 3, 21–22, 55, 109
Sharia law, 102–3, 116–17, 122–23
social reproduction, definition, 11, 16–22, 41–42, 61–62, 74, 75
  social reproductive labor, definition, 8, 25–26, 27, 35, 46–52, 61–62, 80
  See also care
superheroines, 7–8, 28–29
super typhoon Haiyan, 9, 44–45, 48, 54–55, 64–65, 73, 75–76, 78, 81, 82, 83, 84, 96, 100–1, 110–11, 112, 114, 115, 138
sustainable development goals (SDGs), 3–4, 66–67, 133

Tacloban, 10, 45, 48, 54–55, 72–73, 110–11, 112, 114, 115, 138
Third World, 19, 26–27, 142, 151, 152–53, 156, 162–63, 176, 186
  See also Global South
Tickner, J. Ann, 153

traditional birth attendants, 1–2, 76
transitional justice, 91–92, 167, 174–75
Transitional Justice and Reconciliation Commission, 91
Trump, Donald, 119–20, 145–47

ulama, 93
United Nations Committee on Economic, Social and Cultural Rights, 5
United Nations High Commissioner for Refugees (UNHCR), 78–79, 82
UN Population Fund (UNFPA), 3–4, 51, 82
UN Security Council Resolution 2106, 119
UN Security Council Resolution 2122, 4–5, 119
UN Security Council Resolution 2467, 118, 119–20

Vatican, The, 120, 127, 131
violence
  political violence, 105–7
  slow violence, 172
  violence against women, 83, 84, 101
  (*see also* SGBV)
volunteerism, 21, 31, 61, 62, 65–66, 70–71, 74, 111, 137, 144

wages for housework, 24
Women Friendly Spaces, 82–85, 100–1
Women Living Under Muslim Laws, 148–49
Women, Peace and Security (WPS) agenda, 4–5, 28–29, 75, 77, 90–96, 118, 119–20, 121, 147–49
World Bank, 132, 162–63
World Health Organization, 70

Yuval-Davis, Nira, 146–47

Zamboanga, 44, 45, 46, 50–51, 54, 78–79